THE SERVICE INNOVATION HANDBOOK

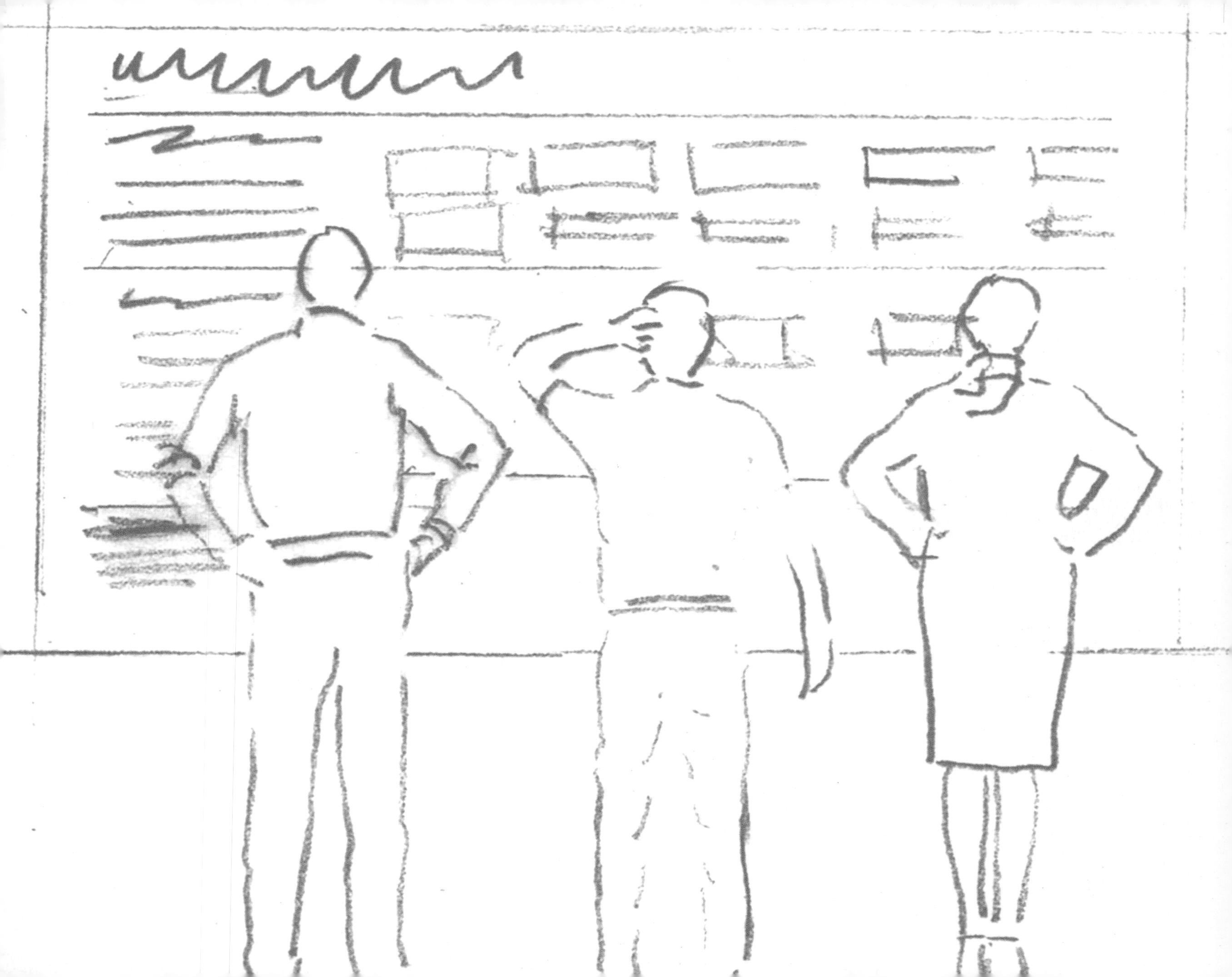

– *Action-oriented creative
thinking toolkit for service
organizations*

The Service
Innovation
Handbook

TEMPLATES · CASES · CAPABILITIES

BIS PUBLISHERS

Lucy Kimbell

Published in 2014 by

BIS Publishers, Building Het Sieraad, Postjeweg 1,
1057 DT Amsterdam, NETHERLANDS

bispublishers.nl
T +31 (0)20 515 02 30
bis@bispublishers.nl

ISBN 978-90-6369-353-4

Designed, typeset, illustrated, and made into pages by
Andrew Boag (andrew@boag.org.uk)

Copy-edited by Warren Davis
(wozzadavis@hotmail.com)

Foreword

Everything about a business (or other organization) is designed. How it appears to potential customers, the way it selects and motivates its employees and partners, the routes its drivers use to get from place to place, its vision and strategy…all of it…is designed. Sadly, the approach commonly taken to implementing a new policy, practice, system or other designed aspect of most companies is to simply copy someone else's design. When a formal approach is undertaken to select which alternative to copy, we refer to it as an exercise in best practices.

This quest for best practices limits us, though, to the currently best. Moreover, given the history of an organization, its unique alignment of assets and capabilities, and the particular ecosystems in which it operates, we are unlikely to find an ideal match anyway. This is particularly the case in modern service contexts, where the offerings are so often emerging.

Many senior executives seem to appreciate the need for something more, even if only intuitively. In a 2010 interview-based study that IBM conducted with over 1500 CEOs in 60 countries and 33 industries, 60% identified creativity as one of the three most important leadership qualities given the complex environments that companies are facing.

But what exactly will that something more be? It is a good bet, I think, that a piece of it will come as service providers see customers less as markets to be researched and more as partners in the co-design of new ecosystems in which their organization can flourish. And that is the space into which Lucy Kimbell's book presses us full force.

Designing is about specifics. Unlike science or even art, which both deal mainly in abstraction, design brings the focus of our attention to the concrete. So design is especially important in a world in which an organization's context, resources, needs and objectives are unique and changing. Design offers attitudes, methods, and ideas that we need in order to act on the concretes that define our current opportunities.

Books about design generally separate the why and the how of design. The paradox is that learning a *how* unconnected to its *why* is very like the search for best practices I described above. You end up imitating a practice (a design technique, method, framework) that has relevance elsewhere without a deep appreciation for how it fits the actual conditions you face. Lucy Kimbell has wisely chosen to weave the hows and the whys of her designing together, so that you are able to draw on techniques with an understanding of where each works, why it was developed as it was, and how the conditions for which it was created affect its use. In doing so she invites you to make design your own

FRED COLLOPY

Professor of Design and Innovation,
Weatherhead School of Management,
Case Western Reserve University

Contents

Acknowledgements

This book integrates teaching, research and consulting over the past decade or so, in which I have been influenced by many people. I thank the friends and colleagues who have helped, challenged, inspired and supported me including Anna Best, Suky Best, Simon Blyth, Jamie Brassett, Monika Büscher, Rachel Cooper, Chris Downs, Duncan Fairfax, Lorraine Gamman, Felicity Gillespie, David Gossip, Dee Halligan, Janet Harbord, Guy Julier, Kat Jungnickel, Sylvia Lambe, Rona Lee, Anna Lucas, Cat Macaulay, Noortje Marres, Derek Miller, the late Wally Olins, Teresa Parker, Nina Pope, Landé Pratt, Alison Prendiville, Ben Reason, Helena Reckitt, Lisa Rudnick, Daniela Sangiorgi, Shazia Sardar, Ofra Shelef, Chris Smith, Cameron Tonkinwise, Laurene Vaughan and Nina Wakeford.

At Saïd Business School I have benefited from the support of many colleagues since I started there as the Clark Fellow in Design Leadership in 2005, especially Kate Blackmon, Eamonn Molloy, Steve New, Rafael Ramírez and Marc Ventresca, as well as the MBA students taking my classes who I get to experiment with. At the University of Brighton I've been stimulated by working with Leah Armstrong, Anne Boddington, Jocelyn Bailey and Guy Julier on the Mapping Social Design Research and Practice project for the Arts and Humanities Research Council. At Central Saint Martins, designing the prospective MBA in dialogue with Jonathan Barratt, Amanda Bright, Jamie Brassett, Richard Reynolds, Dani Salvadori, Dominic Stone and Jeremy Till resulted in productive insights for this book. Collaborating with Rafael Ramírez, Cynthia Selin and Yasser Bhatti to organize the Oxford Futures Forum 2014 provided some timely examples I've used.

I also acknowledge the role of my ad hoc editorial team of Kate Blackmon, Tim Dingle, Monika Hestad, Graham Hill, Cat Macaulay, my researcher Joe Julier and especially Tom Penney. I thank the people Joe and I interviewed and talked to: Joel Bailey, Simon Blyth, Leon Cruikshank, Daniel Freeman, Futuregov, Graham Hill, Phillip Joe, Matt Jones, Oliver King, Gordon Lee, David Lipkin, Christian Madsbjerg, Laura Pandelle, Jack Schulze, Lars Thuesen, Vinay Venkatraman and Laura Winge. Any mistakes I've made in discussing their work are mine. Thank you to my publisher Rudolf van Wezel who gave me the opportunity to create this particular book. Andrew Boag brought the ideas to life with his wonderful information and graphic design. Warren Davis improved my use of language and kept me amused with his challenges when I slipped into journalese.

Virginia Woolf reminded us in *A Room of One's Own* how hard it is to find time and space to write. I thank my extended family, Moya, Deirdre and Marua, who gave me time, space and reasons to write.

This book is dedicated to my parents, Peter and Deirdre.

London, August 2014

1 *Getting ready*

snapshot

– *This book provides people design-ing innovative services with con-cepts to think with, cases to learn from, and methods and templates to work with.*

– *We all have habits for how we start new things — the opportuni-ties for innovation are shaped by how and why we begin.*

– *Innovation involves creating both new concepts and new com-petencies and knowledge, and working inside and outside of organizations.*

YOU'RE ABOUT TO START A NEW PROJECT. How do you go about this? Perhaps, after fighting off numerous distractions, you sit down at last with your preferred kind of drink (mine is green tea), make space at your table by shuffling papers out of the way, open your notebook at a clean page, and reach for just the right pen. Perhaps your preparation starts earlier, by going for a walk, or with a session at the gym. Or maybe it is triggered by an online event such as a status update, or anger at a news item or tweet. But then you put down the smartphone to think things through. Perhaps you allow yourself to pick up an object you are drawn to, something with a tactile quality that invites handling. You discover there is no particular purpose to this handling, but the sensuousness of your interactions with the object opens up something in your mind that you can't yet grasp. Maybe you have a space arranged as you want it where you live or work, which enables you to take a different approach to launching a new project. Or maybe you find what you need in a coffee shop where you can be anonymous in the crowd. Perhaps you can't start a project on your own, but need to be with others from the outset, so you convene a meeting to explore a way forward together.

We make our own rituals in the ways we stage the beginning of things. We find ways to step out of the regular way of doing things, which acknowledges that to start something new requires moving into a different kind of state, one that is dreamy, disordered, passionate, at odds with the focused, analytical, systematic state of being that is required to perform as a successful professional. There must be enough of the familiar – this kind of light, these people, this coffee – and enough of the unfamiliar to cause some disruption. These musings and wanderings, the trying to start and the really getting going, are the territory of this book.

1 Getting ready

Doing things differently

For people intending to design innovative services, this book opens up a set of possibilities for acting and thinking differently. It draws on recent books, blog posts and academic research about design, innovation, customer experience and agile approaches to creating new products, software and ventures. Forebears include John Kao, author of *Jamming*,[1] and people arguing for "design thinking" such as Roger Martin and innovation consultancy IDEO, to be discussed shortly. Even these few examples show the diversity of responses to the idea that business-as-usual is not adequate to situations facing nearly all organisations and communities grappling with issues such as climate change, scarce resources, and inequality, or with more local or organization-specific concerns such as improving customer experiences, involving employees or citizens in decision-making or making positive change happen. The need for different, creative responses is well-understood. But how creativity is to be engaged with and made use of is not. In this context, what this book does that is distinctive is five things.

First, it focuses on services, understood as configurations of resources that are bundled together into innovation ecosystems through which the various actors involved aim to achieve something but which also result in unexpected consequences. Much of the other recent literature focuses on web ventures or software, or is based on a logic of "adding value" to products to differentiate them. The next chapter takes this on, making an argument that service innovation requires reconfiguring these bundles of resources and looking at the key economic and social concepts that are embedded in the idea of service.

Second, it focuses on the beginning stages of designing innovative services. The early exploratory phase is most uncertain. There may be insights coming from research findings or observations about people's behaviours, but no clear ideas about what to do. There may be hunches and concepts for new initiatives that are disconnected from people's lived experiences. By focusing on the early stages of something new, this book helps managers and designers make good use of their time, budgets and talents and build collective visions, strategies and plans.

Third, it draws on sociological and anthropological traditions that see the world as social *and* material *and* technological, and on our experiences of living and working as embodied in day-to-day practices. It recognizes that structure is a product of and a constraint on action. Doing things differently requires working within existing structures that shape agency in particular ways, at the same time as trying to change structures and enable different kinds of agency.

Fourthly, it combines ideas which are now well-established in many organizations, such as customer experience, with others that exist at the margins. The result is that the pages of this book combine recognized researchers and managers from the worlds of management and design, alongside designers, artists and comedians you are unlikely to have heard of.

Finally, many of the ideas have evolved through teaching an MBA class in design thinking and service design at a top business school for eight years and delivering workshops for people designing new services and ventures. As a result, the methods and templates have been iterated many times in response to how managers and entrepreneurs have used them to collaborate and begin to think and act differently.

Between thinking and doing

Most other books on innovation and design aimed at managers fall into one of three types. The first type offers concepts grounded in a single perspective or organization's experiences, illustrated with case studies that demonstrate these ideas in practice, but without the broader, critical lenses that academic research offers. The second type is academic volumes, which give overviews of concepts and theories but do not do much to help readers apply them in their own organizations. The third type is practical guides that suggest activities and support readers to try them out, without explaining the underlying theories that shape the approach. This book aims to combine aspects of these approaches, allowing you to read and use this book in different ways depending on your interests, purposes and what else is on your bookshelf or digital device.

It offers:

- *Ways of approaching service innovation.* Combining several academic traditions including services management, customer experience management, innovation studies, ethnography and design, this book mashes up concepts that are not usually brought together. The chapters are dense, so reading and digesting them will make you work. But they provide powerful concepts to help you think in new ways about responding to challenges organizations face, what you think service innovation is concerned with and how to go about it.

- *Cases.* Each chapter provides two descriptions of what different kinds of organization have done that relate to different aspects of designing innovative services. These 16 cases illustrate the challenges involved in designing innovative services, including things that did not quite work or

had unexpected results. Some of them have been made public elsewhere, while others are based on original research. They range from commercial, large-scale firms to complex public sector organizations to start-ups.

- *Practical activities.* Spread out through the book are 14 methods and three recipes you can use to explore these approaches and make them useful in your own context. Each method has a template you can adapt to make it relevant to your own purposes and contexts.

This book aims to make academic research accessible to readers whose primary domain is taking action. So the language will shift between the cultures of business (using terms such as customers, operations, goals and outcomes), design and the arts (experiences, inspiration and sensuousness) and sociology and anthropology (practices, actors and hybrids). As a result, it's not a handbook in the sense of a step-by-step "how to" guide. It's more of a multi-layered "how to think" guide. It's something to keep ready to hand to trigger practical experiments in developing a different approach to designing innovative services to address organizational and community challenges. It aims to inspire you to close the book and get on with trying things out.

Giving things shape and form, to change the future

To launch this discussion on designing innovative services, I briefly review an approach that gained currency over the past decade. Often called design thinking or strategic design, the basic idea is that organizations and ventures have something to learn from the ways that (expert) designers approach their work. This approach has been summarized by writers

Tim Brown from the innovation consultancy IDEO, management educator Roger Martin and others.[2] Design thinking initiatives have been set up in a wide range of organizations including many not usually associated with design, from the United Nations and the UK Cabinet Office, to consultancies such as Deloitte and Accenture, as well as firms such as Proctor and Gamble and SAP. These developments, and the academic research that is in dialogue with them, have been part of the inspiration for this book.

One of the key tensions that emerges is between a view of design that it is primarily concerned with idea generation, visualization and prototyping, and an alternative idea that design is about making change happen. The former is associated with writers such as architect Christopher Alexander, who said that the work of designers is to give form to things[3]. The latter view is most closely associated with economist and management writer Herbert Simon, who wrote, "Everyone designs who devises courses of action aimed at changing existing situations into preferred ones."[4] These contrasting theories of what design is concerned with matter, because for all the talk of design thinking, many managers remain confused about what design is and how it is relevant to their challenges.

The version of design that emphasizes concept generation and visualization requires craft skills in material and digital making. It is the domain of designers who are adept in working with materials to realize their ideas, who are recognized and valued for having competences in doing a particular kind of work. But it begs the question as to who sets the questions, defines the contexts or provides the resources in which such idea generating, visualizing and making takes place.

In contrast, the version of design that sees it as concerned with changing things tends to abstraction. It says little about material practices, and instead emphasizes being able to explore a problem and structure a way to generate solutions to it. Simon's version of design sounds a lot like other kinds of expertise. Indeed, he described managing and practicing medicine as a kind of designing, since they are fields that are also concerned with making change happen. This then begs the question as to what, if anything, is distinctive about designing if it is so broadly defined.

As a way to avoid these tensions, in this book I will draw on a different theory to discuss designing innovative services to address contemporary challenges. What follows in the next section opens up a view of design-led innovation that avoids these contrasting positions. It proposes seeing innovation as generating both concepts and knowledge, resulting in changes to future situations.

Acting towards service innovation

C-K theory is a way of describing innovation that aims to clarify the processes by which new concepts (C) are created, expanding the universe of possibilities, that can then be developed alongside generating new knowledge (K) and competencies, resulting in

concept space

initial concept

conjunction

knowledge space

isjunction

Existing knowledge

Added knowledge
from concept
exploration

Added knowledge
from further
exploration

nal
oncept   Becomes
           new
           knowledge

valuable propositions that organizations can harness as opportunities.[5] Over two decades, researchers Armand Hatchuel, Pascal Le Masson, Benoît Weil and colleagues at Ecole des Mines in Paris have developed a research programme that aims to describe and test this approach.[6] They often work with big firms that want to understand how to develop their capabilities and where to invest resources to innovate more effectively.

Hatchuel and colleagues make a distinction between *knowledge*, which they see as things that can be known or found out, and *concepts*, which are ideas untethered from formal knowledge, which do not have the status of being true or false. Concepts just *are*. What C-K theory does is help explain the generation of new concepts within innovation processes. It resolves a problem in academic literatures which tend to focus on what successful firms do, and which often see design as problem-solving, but which are not able to explain the mysterious bit involving the expansion of possibilities that happens when new concepts are generated[7].

A brief example of a firm that demonstrated three decades of repeated successful innovation brings this to life. Though less glamorous than, say, Apple, the French firm Tefal in the small household electrical goods sector provides a useful case that shows how innovation involves developing new products alongside new knowledge and competencies. A careful study of Tefal showed how it developed product lineages with uncertain identities[8]. That is to say, as it

began developing new lines such as non-stick frying pans or raclette appliances, the firm's work included not just technical activities and competency-building (K) to design new products, but also cultural work to establish what the new concepts (C) meant for households. For example, having developed competencies to launch a domestic waffle maker in the 1970s, Tefal discovered in how people used it a new cultural concept of *informal meals*, which it then responded to as an opportunity for other successful products. This account of long-term, profitable innovation at Tefal sees it as the co-generation of lineages of products that are based on new concepts and identities that gradually stabilize, and new knowledge and competencies.

As a way of understanding innovation, C-K theory recognizes the diverse actors involved in a process of generating new concepts and knowledge, and the outcomes that result in the resulting configuration being seen as innovative. However, much of its emphasis is on what happens *inside* organizations, rather than what happens outside. To address this it is worth turning to fields that highlight the roles of actors *outside* organizations and their involvement in innovation[9]. The first field is known as design ethnography, in which social and cultural research of the sort undertaken by anthropologists and sociologists generates knowledge about people in their day-to-day lives and the meanings that products and services have within people's experiences and practices. The second field, participatory design, emerged within software development. This field recognizes the creativity

1 Getting ready

people exhibit when they generate workarounds in response to constraints or opportunities, and involves them in co-designing new products and services, not just studying them or consulting them.

Bringing these together in Figure 1, the x axis makes the distinction between *concepts* and *knowledge*. The top of the y axis is labelled *inside organizations*, and the bottom is labelled *inside users' worlds*, distinguishing between two major sites of activity and attention. Together, these axes help identify distinct kinds of action within innovation processes. The framework provides an analytical tool to help people designing innovative services work out what capabilities they have or need to develop, as teams navigate between these kinds of action.

In the top right corner is the traditional home of corporate innovation – *R&D or lab research* which exists inside the organization or its network of partners, and which is focused on the production of new knowledge. This might take the form of technical knowledge, such as new kinds of materials, software or hardware, or procedural knowledge, such as business processes. The concept of open innovation developed by Henry Chesbrough[10] argues that organizations need to go beyond their boundaries to find new ideas and routes to market. This has resulted in changes to the way some big firms operate and has seen the development of intermediary firms such as 100% Open, which specializes in mediating between organizations and externals. But despite the spread of open innovation, in many organizations there remain complex

financial, legal and organizational commitments to and investments in traditional R&D.

In the top left corner, the mode of action takes place inside organizations and their networks, but is focused on the generation of concepts, not knowledge. This is labelled *studio inquiries*, since it is associated with the serendipitous, messy and exploratory activities evident in art and design. Here, what is valued is novelty and originality, and the disruption of existing ways of doing things, in contrast to the careful building on others' research that are part of the lab/R&D mode of action. Creativity matters here, in the sense of generating new concepts, but so too do exploratory inquiries that give them shape and form and explore

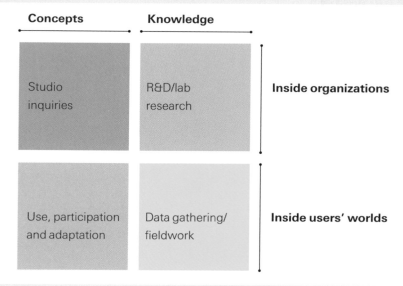

Figure 1 Modes of action for designing innovative services

what they might mean at an early stage. This mode of action can take the form of an in-house design innovation team, such as at manufacturer Philips, at the Australian federal government's social innovation organization TACSI, or through engaging external consultancies with capabilities in design research. Creativity in the context of service innovation is discussed further in Chapter 5.

The bottom right corner is focused on the production of knowledge and is sited inside users' worlds and in their consumption practices, labelled *data-gathering and fieldwork*. There are two main ways this mode of action takes place in contemporary organizations. The first is qualitative fieldwork that aims to generate insights about customer or user behaviour, often gathered from being "in the field" with people in their homes, public spaces, workplaces or online. The second is the domain sometimes called big data, which is the result of organizational capacities to capture, store and analyze large quantities of data. These two capabilities rest on very different worldviews about what counts as valid, reliable and useful knowledge, although there are efforts to find ways of bridging these divides, discussed further in Chapter 4. In both cases, one of the challenges is to make sure that the knowledge about what goes on in users' worlds, however it is produced, becomes a resource for organizational activities.

Finally, the bottom left corner is also sited in users' worlds and is concerned with the generation of novel concepts, not knowledge, in consumption practices.

Labelled *use, participation and adaptation*, this is the territory that is least available to organizations as a resource. It exists outside of their territory, so it's hard to access, and is less amenable to knowledge production through fieldwork or customer data capture. This is where users create their hacks and workarounds. It's how they get things done despite organizations and services, rather than because of them. Discussed further in Chapter 6, this is a mode of action associated with improvisation and adaptation, that results in pulling things together in new ways. However, any new concepts that emerge may not be recognisable to the people involved, or shareable.

These four quadrants describe four modes of action that organizations can take as part of their efforts towards designing innovative services. By combining C-K theory with traditions of design ethnography, big data and participatory design, the framework helps managers locate where their organizational capabilities are stronger and where they are weaker. However, as with all such 2x2 frameworks there is a danger of imposing simplicity on the complexities of what goes on in organizations of different kinds and in people's everyday lives. Instead of seeing these as discrete boxes, what is important here is to recognise how these modes of action connect during projects aiming to drive service innovation. So it is useful to identify some of the ways that teams designing innovative services move between these modes of action.

1 Getting ready

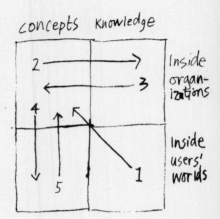

Move 1: Fieldwork to studio inquiries

This is a well-established activity, which involves using specialist researchers using ethnography or digital customer data to analyze what goes on in people's day-to-day or work lives. A typical output is presentations about customer insights, frameworks or models of behaviour or experience, which can then be used by service teams working in the studio inquiry action mode to generate ideas from those insights. An example in this book is how researchers at Lego developed an analysis of how and why children play, leading to new concepts to underpin business opportunities (Case 7).

Move 2: Studio inquiries to lab research/R&D

Part of the competencies associated with studio inquiries is creating early-stage mock-ups, scenarios or exploratory prototyping that helps a project team and wider stakeholders see what a concept might be like as experienced by and through the interaction with users or customers. After exploratory research, which opens up understanding, a different kind of prototyping is required. This is a kind of research that aims to answer questions through hypothesis-based prototyping, to shape the next iterations of the service concept. An example is how consultancy Engine helped Mercedes-Benz prototype future service experiences that then led to a one-year pilot (Case 12).

Move 3: Lab research/R&D to studio inquiries

This is what happens when people with skills in studio inquiries, typically designers, are given opportunities to engage and play with emerging research at an early stage before it is developed into a product or service. Through their studio inquiries, designers, film-makers and artists find ways to explore and bring into view the possibilities and implications of new research. An example is how the Google Creative Lab got involved in exploring and creating scenarios for Google Glass (Case 9).

Thus far, thus familiar. But this is where things get more interesting. Innovation is centrally concerned with creating new patterns of behaviour – not out of nowhere, but rather identifying early signals about cultural changes and people's workarounds in day-to-day life. This requires attending to the mode of action located in the bottom left-hand corner, labelled use, participation and adaptation.

Move 4: Studio enquiries to use, participation and adaptation

The field of participatory design developed methods that involve designers creating or co-creating mock-ups of touchpoints or doing role play about future service encounters for users to participate in. Sometimes called design games, these interactions open up possibilities for people to collaborate in creating and making sense of new service concepts. An example is the Danish government innovation unit MindLab's game that involved teachers in generating concepts that combined existing ways that teachers plan lessons with the Ministry of Education's new framework (Case 11).

Move 5: Use, participation and adaptation to studio inquiries

This is what happens when designers are able to access and become inspired by users' workarounds and hacks, but without full-on fieldwork. When a service encounter results in a failure from the point of view of any of the actors involved, resulting in improvised responses that see people achieving what they want to, as best they can, with the resources available, this can challenge or augment the underlying service concept. At an early stage of exploring people's worlds and daily lives, giving people unfamiliar objects to engage and interact with and analyzing what happens can result in inspiration for new product or service concepts. An example is consultancy Actant's use of cultural probes for a manufacturer to explore and generate concepts associated with families at home in the evening (Case 8).

This introduction to the modes of action framework for service innovation helps identify capabilities that managers and entrepreneurs can resource. What the framework does is connect the distinction between generating concepts and generating knowledge that are both essential to innovation (from C-K theory), with developments in innovation practices that draw on social and cultural knowledge, insights about people's behaviours, and design research. The distinctions it makes between four modes of action – lab/R&D, studio inquiries, data-gathering/fieldwork, and use, participation and adaptation – helps managers clarify where their organizations and project teams have capabilities and how they can be bridged more effectively.

The modes of action for service innovation are not necessarily reducible to phases of an innovation process. Indeed, this book avoids prescribing any definitive process since it is covering many different organizational types and industries. But nonetheless the linear experience of time is a main way that managers, customers and users experience organizations and projects. The next section clarifies why focusing on the beginning phases of an innovation process is particularly important.

Beginning things

The approach taken in this book is to highlight the beginning of things – when ideas are hazy, evidence is minimal, commitments are vague and there are always other things that seem more pressing or easier to grapple with. The term "fuzzy front end" introduced by Anil Khurana and Stephen Rosenthal highlighted the characteristics of the very early stage of projects, which managers say they find tricky[11]. Figure 2 shows the influence on project success, the cost of changes and the amount of information available during an innovation process.

At the fuzzy front end of an innovation project, there is little information available and the cost of changes is low. This stage has an enormous impact on the future direction of the project as things are very undefined. If concept exploration and early prototyping reveal insurmountable problems, the team can pivot

1 Getting ready

and go in a quite different direction. However, once feasibility and marketing studies have taken place, and investment has been made in people and other resources to further develop concepts and gather information, then the cost of changes is higher. As a result, later phases have less influence on a project direction as they are basically iterating a direction of travel. In contrast, during the fuzzy front end, entirely new directions can be taken.

In recognition of the importance of the beginning of things, this book will concentrate on this key phase of an innovation process. It will explore the interplays between generating concepts and knowledge generation, and what happens inside organizations and within users' worlds in the early stages of a project when resources are yet to be committed, solutions are hunches without much supporting data, and their possible implications not yet understood.

But this emphasis on the beginning of things is not simply about the time that elapses during the first weeks or months of a project. It's also an orientation to taking action in the world, recognizing the rapidity of change in an interconnected world and how this prompts teams and organizations to refresh themselves through iterative cycles of research and action. An orientation to the beginning of things stimulates awareness that inviting in or identifying new participants and different concepts within an innovation process results in an opportunity to look at things anew.

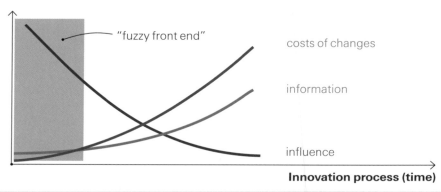

Figure 2 Influence, the cost of changes and information available during an innovation (from Herstatt and Verworn 2001)[12].

As a result, this book does not offer detail on operational knowledge you need once things have got going. It won't help you create the detail of a business model, a service specification, or a project plan to launch a new service. But it will help you do the early work you need to do *before* being able to produce any of these. It helps readers get to grips with launching a project when it is not yet a project, dealing with matters such as how to understand the nature of the issue you think you want to respond to, or building a team when there is not yet a team.

What lies ahead

This chapter started by prompting you to reflect on how you start a project – how you get yourself into a state of mind to allow you and your collaborators to be creative. It then outlined a way of thinking about innovation that links the generation of novel concepts, with the production of knowledge and competencies, and combined this with perspectives linking organizations and users' worlds. The rest of this book aims to make the approaches and methods associated with these modes of action accessible to managers and entrepreneurs at the early stage of designing innovative services.

Chapter 2 mashes up concepts from three academic traditions – strategy, services marketing, and science and technology studies – to describe the current environment facing organizations. It then combines these into five capabilities for service innovation: launch clumsy solutions and learn; recombine capacities into new hybrids; understand value as created in practice; increase the variance/bring in new actors; and move between concepts and knowledge, and inside and outside organizations. Method 2 shows how you can visualize the drivers of change you and your colleagues believe to be shaping the future environment. Method 3 helps you map the ecology of actors you see as part of an existing or future innovation ecosystem.

Chapter 3 summarizes different ways of thinking about experience, which is key to understanding value-in-use in service innovation. Some ways of thinking have their origins in behavioural approaches, which focus on what individuals do, say, think and know *in* a context, seen from outside. Some originate in socio-cultural approaches, which see behaviours and experiences as co-constituted through social processes, seen from inside people's worlds. The former are more closely linked to improvement, whereas socio-cultural approaches support service innovation.

The practice perspective, which sees the social world as constituted by dynamically combining stories, skills and stuff, offers a way into understanding the actors involved in an innovation ecosystem. Method 4 shows how to map a user journey, which can be used to analyze interactions with organizations or services. Method 5 helps you bring into view a user, customer or other person connected to an innovation ecosystem by describing his or her "storyworld" in which habits and activities come to have meaning.

Chapter 4 looks at research and analysis in the context of service innovation. It reviews three important developments – big data, qualitative ethnographic data and open data. It shows how these different approaches can be combined so that organizations can better understand the worlds of people they want to involve in service innovation. Method 6 shows how to create a draft segmentation of users or customers by focusing on insights about what things mean. Method 7 provides a way to map opportunity spaces by connecting drivers of change with insights about changes in people's behaviours and capacities. Method 8 prompts a team to articulate the issue they think they are addressing, alongside the proposition that aims to tackle it.

Chapter 5 focuses on what is distinctive about creativity when designing innovative services. It offers examples of different kinds of practice including design fiction, stand-up comedy, video scenarios and artists using data. It identifies four habits related to service innovation: moving between excess and simplicity, making the familiar strange and the unfamiliar familiar, zooming in and out, and connecting and disconnecting, that describe how novel configurations of actors and new kinds of value-in-use come into being. Method 9 shows how to guide and capture the sketching of touchpoints in an innovation ecosystem. Method 10 offers a structure to guide telling stories about users that communicate a change introduced through a new service and its technological and organizational implications.

Chapter 6 discusses how to do early-stage, exploratory prototyping at the initial stage of designing innovative services. It shows how design games, role play and blueprinting generate and give shape and form to future concepts that recombine existing habits and ways of doing things with new resources. Method 11 helps get the most from prototyping by forging links between insights, concepts and what prototyping needs to explore further. Method 12 explains how to use service blueprinting to help a team see how the experiences of user segments are linked to organizational resources and infrastructures backstage.

Chapter 7 helps readers grapple with the paradox facing all projects, that in order to secure resources and sponsors, a team will need to be able to demonstrate impact, even while the results of their proposed activities are unknown and will lead to unintended consequences. Understanding how to design for outcomes, identify accountabilities, and set up ways to gather and learn from data, is something to consider early on. Method 13 shows how to sketch a first draft of an outcomes framework. Method 14 suggests how to articulate design principles for a service innovation team to use to shape its work.

Chapter 8 concludes by reviewing how organizations can develop capabilities at the early stage of designing innovative services. When resources are yet to be committed, it is still possible to begin to practice the habits associated with innovation capabilities. Concepts such as agile collaboration, creating boundary objects and increasing an organization's absorptive capacities help organizations start doing things differently. Finally, a set of recipes for designing innovative services helps readers pull together concepts and methods from the whole book to adapt to support their own initiatives.

Things you'll need as you get ready

Before moving on, there are a few items you will need to have to hand as you go through the cycles of action and research that are embedded in this book and strengthen the innovative capabilities in your team or organization. First, everyone will need a sketchbook. It's important that you have at least two kinds – a small one for carrying around with you to jot down notes or ideas as you go about what you are doing and to flick through when you are sitting still for a few moments. You also need a larger one to pull out when you need to start developing and sharing ideas with other people.

Then you and the team need a studio wall and a habit of fiddling with what is on it. You may not ever have a studio, but to help you develop and practice your innovation capabilities, you and your team need to have a space that anyone feels empowered and legitimized to contribute to. This could take the form of putting up printed items such as postcards, application forms, advertisements cut out from magazines, or marketing material that relates to what you are working on. These are the ephemera that in some small way bring into view the jumbled nature of everyday life. The studio wall should never be a final display ("here are our great ideas") but rather a working space and invitation to contribute ("here is where we have got to so far").

A third key component you need to help you build the capabilities championed in this book is a culture of regular mini-reviews. In art and design school studio culture these are called critiques. It is important that they are embedded in openness to giving and receiving feedback. Even better if you can build a culture of mutual peer review, so that you construct frequent but possibly quite short reviews with colleagues working on other projects that benefit everyone. Most project or organizational structures involve formal processes of review. However, the culture of regular mini-reviews should work alongside these, starting on day one of a project. For example, you can ask members of your team to present what they are working on to members of another team or project, and then swap over. Such reviews should be *short* (no longer than 10 minutes for each party involved), *sharp* (make your feedback pointed and specific, rather than offering generalizations that aim to avoid ruffling feathers), and *shared* (both parties take turns so no one feels they are giving more than they get).

These three things – your personal sketchbooks, your team's studio wall, and your culture of mini-reviews – are described here to give you a practical focus at the end of this chapter, before the hard work really starts. But before moving on to exploring the wider context of service innovation, let us start with you. Method 1 invites you to spend time on self-reflection to help you clarify what drives and inspires you. If you are aiming at innovation as an *outcome*, what are you aiming to achieve and why? What commitments and beliefs shape your understanding of the issue you want to address? To who or what do you hold yourself accountable and over what timeframes? How do you think and feel about change as you embark on an innovation *process* by doing things differently? What capacities, resources and weak and strong ties do you have available? Why does any of what you are doing matter?

1 Getting ready

Case 1 Turning data about phone usage into a resource at 3

Like other telecommunications companies (or telcos), 3 operates in a saturated market in which customer churn remains a concern, impacting on growth and profits. Frequent introductions of new handsets and new services present consumers with opportunities, but many are left confused by the wide range of technologies, functions and service plans available. In Sweden and Denmark, 3 addressed this by making its billing more transparent – to reduce the burden on call centres and to increase customer satisfaction. To do this, 3 engaged service design consultancy Fjord[13]. 3 took a service design approach to differentiate itself from other telcos and to increase customer satisfaction and loyalty through engagement. The project that resulted was not simply an example of using design to improve the transparency of interactions between customers and an organization. It can also be seen as an example of service innovation, since it turned data about customers' usage into a resource that reconfigured the service ecosystem resulting in new kinds of value-in-use for customers and for the telco.

The first stage of the project was to explore the issues in more depth from both the business and customers' perspectives. This involved analyzing the telco's billing processes and 200 subscription models, customer satisfaction data, and doing qualitative fieldwork. Daniel Freeman, Fjord's lead designer on the project, explains:

"Speaking to the different bits of the business was important, including the marketing and loyalty teams and the product owners. But what was more valuable was listening in on calls to the call centre and speaking with customer service teams, as well as doing 'guerilla research' in 3's retail stores." [14]

Analyzing this research led to insights about the pain points for customers, such as not understanding their phone bills, the packages they were signed up to or their own usage. Freeman says this suggested an initial quick win, which the Fjord team resisted:

"While we saw the enormous spike in calls when bills are sent – in Sweden and Denmark, it's at the same time of the month for all subscribers – we had to resist the urge to focus on redesigning the actual bill. Instead, we came to the conclusion that we would be better off reinventing what a bill was, and create a living bill using live data that the user could track throughout the month."

Using methods such as personas at the beginning of the project helped the design team focus on people's practical concerns, such as helping people set up automatic payments for their bills, reminding people what their actual phone numbers were and the model numbers of their phones. The service design team used an iterative approach to explore ways to redesign the bill and the services it was embedded within. For example, the team documented hunches and insights and used them to generate design concepts and assess competing

Mobile operator 3's app showing customer usage data

suggestions and priorities by referring back to the insights. They also used "sprints" – intense, day-long, collaborative design workshops – to focus the entire project team on a single challenge at a time. During the sprints, they used concept-generation methods and sketching to generate solutions to particular aspects of the live bill concept. To engage internal stakeholders, Fjord created a visualization of the service experience, relating the proposed new service to its business and design drivers. They also created an early mock-up of the proposed live bill user interface on a phone that communicated the solution to senior executives.

The result was a smartphone app service called My 3, launched in 2013. This presented users with an overview of their billing and usage using live data, and allowed them to look in more detail at data about their own usage over the previous six months for voice, messaging and data, compared with average 3 usage. This was overlaid with recommendations about how to get the most out of the service, with suggestions about how to change the service plan. The app was highly visual, using simple devices such as "donuts" to depict usage and allowances related to voice, messaging and data. The app also allowed 3 to push personalized messages to customers based on their own usage data – for example, suggesting that users could top up their monthly data allowance if they were running low. As well as focusing on usage from the point of view of how someone engaged with 3's services, the app presented users with a dynamic phonebook showing the numbers they called most frequently.

In terms of impact, half of the users of the app said they called the customer service team less because of it. Introducing the app also led to a shift in how 3's customers self-served, with 60% of customer self-service carried out via the mobile app rather than the web. Data showed that 70% of people who downloaded the app used it more than once a month, and 40% used it more than once a week. While these metrics established that the mobile app was taken up and used by customers, more inter-esting is how the development of the app created a new service ecosystem for 3 and its customers. By identifying customers' data as an untapped resource, the project team brought customers into relation with their own usage habits by displaying the data through carefully designed info-graphics on customers' devices. Instead of being hidden and inaccessible, the usage data became a resource for customers and for the company. Hence, although the explicit driver for the project was to increase transparency about the telco and its billing and ser-vice plans, what the emerging service ecosystem also enabled was transparency about people's own usage practices.

1 Getting ready

Case 2 Staging a different conversation about digital services at Microsoft

Microsoft might appear an unlikely firm to be associated with designing innovative services. But a design hothouse team in one of Microsoft's consulting groups developed capabilities to help the firm's corporate and public sector clients make better use of their digital assets – their own, context-specific databases and the Microsoft tools and platforms they invest in. A project for a large police force illustrates how the team's early work led to the client taking a new approach to designing its services.

First, a brief detour is required to explain how this specialist team fits with the rest of Microsoft. Phillip Joe, user experience architect with Microsoft Consulting Services, explains:

> "Historically, Microsoft has been a very product-focused organization, complemented by Microsoft Research's technological expertise. Teams design products such as Windows or Xbox in Redmond, and then the rest of the world is basically a sales organization, with some specialist technology consultancy. What we are now doing differently is helping clients who, for example, buy thousands of Office licences by providing services to integrate this technology with their other software and platforms." [15]

The hothouse team helps those clients who start off thinking they need to buy software to go down a different path, towards designing innovative services.

The approach starts with research (understanding the client's business goals, existing technologies,

and user needs and contexts), followed by envisioning (suggesting and visualizing new concepts for software applications or services), followed by design (making these concepts come to life). Joe says customers increasingly ask that Microsoft bring all the different parts of the firm together, to help them address their challenges. This includes Microsoft's communications platforms such as Skype, SharePoint and Yammer, search engine Bing and Nokia's mobile phone business, as well as the familiar desktop software. The hothouse team plays a key role in working out how to help clients craft solutions that deliver user experiences based on technological solutions that increase organizational effectiveness. Methods such as ethnographic research, rapid visualization and service blueprinting are used alongside Microsoft's established technical consulting methods.

For the project with the police force, Microsoft began by digesting the organization's challenges: reducing crime, improving public confidence in the police, and reducing costs. The hothouse team's approach was to address these challenges by understanding existing technology investments and capabilities, combining these with other resources, and customizing them to help the client build new digital policing services. This meant considering what databases and software the police force already had available, and what other public,

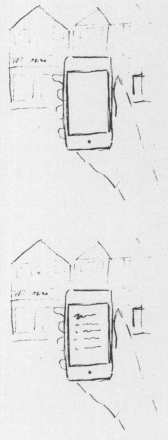

commercial or social media resources they could be combined with, to enable the organization to make sense of its data and act on it. A snapshot of the early stages of the project illustrates the approach.

In the first workshop with the client, the Microsoft team presented its understanding of the drivers of change shaping the environment in which the organization was operating, including technological developments. They also shared sketches of service concepts they thought might help the organization achieve its goals, based on a very partial understanding at that stage of the organization.

One sketch Microsoft created showed a person's hand holding up a smartphone, against an urban background. This was inspired by Nokia's City Lens, an augmented reality application that gives dynamic information about users' surroundings overlaid on a phone's camera display. The sketch showed some of the data that could be shown on the smartphone, both data from the police's databases as well as social media and municipality data feeds. Even though the details were far from worked out, let alone costed, the sketch helped the client see the potential to combine things in new ways in relation to officers' day-to-day work realities and to current consumer technology. Says Joe:

"The benefit was that the assistant commissioners did not have to translate an Excel chart or flow diagram in order to see what our suggestions would mean for police officers on the street. They could understand straight away what the officers' experience would be like. And since we are Microsoft, they knew we could build it."

The idea of using mock-ups to suggest future user experiences is well-established in retail, telco and other consumer organizations, which often have research teams focusing on customer experience. But in many hierarchical large organizations, especially those with statutory obligations, operating with high levels of security, and under huge pressure to cut costs, thinking about users' experiences of software might seem like a luxury. The hothouse team helps such clients shift towards thinking about value-in-use: how software is embedded into work practices and citizens' behaviours, rather than just being something that organizations buy and install on devices.

It is often hard for user experience researchers to gain access to interview or shadow personnel in high security contexts. As part of the pre-sales engagement, two members of the Microsoft team were able to visit a detention centre, taking videos of officers explaining what went on there. As well as learning more about the contexts in which police software systems are used, the hothouse team used this visit as an opportunity to get officers' comments on wireframe sketches of possible future software screens. Findings from the research visit,

Case 2 (continued) Staging a different conversation about digital services at Microsoft

including responses to the sketches, were then presented at a second workshop.

Subsequent ethnographic research uncovered opportunities and key issues for officers and citizens, alongside technological analyses of existing systems and potential. Together, the research, envisioning and design activities helped the client's team shift towards understanding how their decision to invest in software could impact directly on frontline employees' work and on citizen confidence in the police.

These early interactions with the potential client resulted in two deliverables. The first was a highly visual printed brochure presenting a vision of what digital policing might look like, mapped against the organization's goals, with a detailed proposal for how Microsoft would take the research, envisioning and design work forward. Some of the early concepts for new services included algorithmic analyses of the police's own data to identify trends, sentiment tracking using internal data and social media, and taking data available to the police and making it available to citizens. The suggested approach included agile work processes involving mixed teams of technologists, user experience designers, and management specialists to develop the new concepts and undertake research in parallel. The brochure also included scenarios showing

how police offers and citizens would interact with software – for example, through smartphones or desktop computers – in their own contexts, linking user activities with technological resources and data to deliver business goals.

The other deliverable – a contract – formalized this into a consultancy engagement. Having staged a different kind of conversation with a potential client during the earliest phases of the engagement, Microsoft was successful in winning the work. This case illustrates activities that can reframe an organization's understanding about what it is trying to achieve. By linking organizational goals to technological research and new concepts for services, and connecting what happens inside the organization to wider socio-cultural contexts, the hothouse team shifted the conversation from buying software to designing innovative services.

Method 1: Self-reflection

Time involved	Using the method, 30+ minutes
Associated capabilities	Launch clumsy solutions and learn Increase the variance/bring in new actors
Methods to use before or after this one	Method 2 Visualizing drivers of change Method 9 Sketching

What you'll need

A large piece of paper

Coloured marker pens

key question

'What matters to you and why?'

Purpose

Using this method brings into the open what shapes you as an individual and the capacities, values and accountabilities you bring to a project.

Outcomes

You will gain insights into your own values and capacities and how these come into play in projects through the way you approach learning and change. You will clarify the sets of accountabilities and networks you are embedded in.

How to do it

Carry this out on your own. Copy a larger version of the template onto a large sheet of paper. Pick any of the boxes and begin to add detail inside it. Make a mark to show where you stand between the two ends of each axis. Work your way round the template in any order.

Issues and challenges. Think about the issues that you are currently working on. If they have recently come to your attention, why now? If you have been working on the same issues for some time, what keeps you working on them?

My accountabilities. Looking at your personal, professional and community activities, to who or what do you make yourself accountable? What does this look like in practice?

Tip

Use this at the beginning of a project, *and* at the end.

My vision and values. What futures do you want to help bring into being? How are your visions for the future shaped by your values and political commitments or by the values and commitments of people you are working with, among or for? Are you vision and values mostly shared with others? To what extent are they driven by your personal experiences?

My beliefs about change. How do you think and feel about future possibilities and challenges? How do you experience change?

Weak ties. Thinking about your weaker connections with other people and organizations in personal, professional and community contexts, what makes them meaningful to you?

Strong ties. Considering your strong ties with other people and organizations in your personal, professional and community contexts, what makes them strong?

My capacities and resources. Reflect on your current skills, knowledge, understanding, emotional resources, social capital and financial resources in personal, professional and community contexts.

My approach when starting off. How able and willing are you to try new ways of doing things? How often do you involve different approaches and people in a new project?

My intention. What are you trying to achieve and why does it matter to you?

Reflection. Consider if you always approach new things the same way. How have your ways of working and learning shaped previous projects? Do your habits lead you to acting in particular ways? What matters to the people with whom you have strong and weak ties and to whom you hold yourself accountable?

About the methods and worked examples

Throughout the book I'll show how the methods can be used in relation to one project, to help readers see how they can be adapted. Although the worked examples are semi-fictional, they draw on several projects I have been involved in.

The starting point for the worked examples is to find ways to address the loneliness faced by many older people. According to Age UK, half of all people in the UK aged 75 and over live alone, and 1 in 10 people aged 65 or over say they are always or often feel lonely – that's more than a million people. There are several social enterprises in the UK addressing aspects of ageing and older people's care. These include Circles, a membership organization for people over 50, which helps with social activity, practical jobs around the home, learning, and health and wellbeing; GoodGym, which enables runners to support local communities by doing physical tasks; and Spice, a time-banking platform. The project described in the worked examples shares some of the thinking and values behind these ventures.

1 Getting ready

continued...

Self-reflection

Use this to help you locate what inspires and drives you towards action

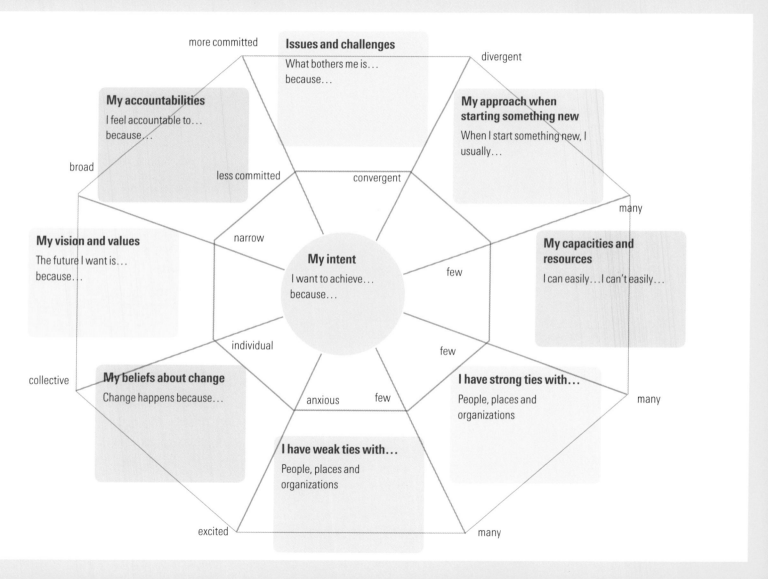

Example

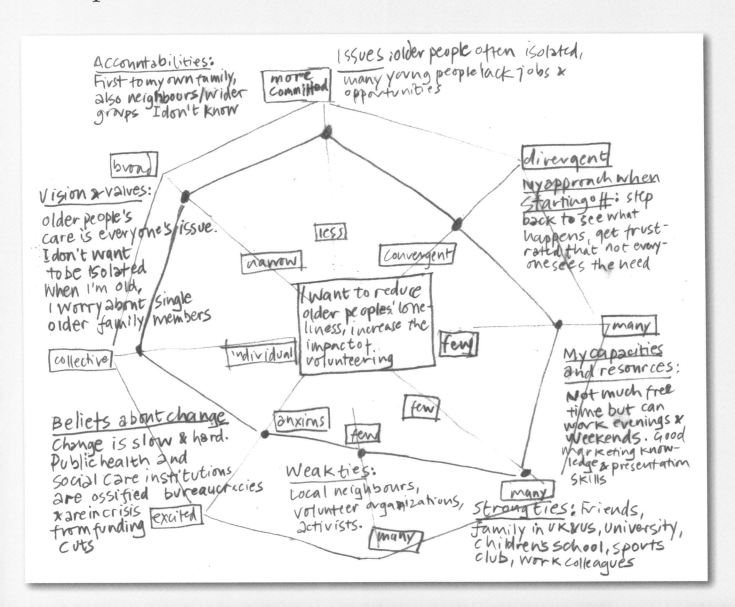

Accountabilities:
First to my own family, also neighbours/wider groups 'I don't know

Issues: older people often isolated, many young people lack jobs & opportunities

more committed

divergent

My approach when starting off: step back to see what happens, get frustrated that not everyone sees the need

broad

Vision & values:
older people's care is everyone's issue. I don't want to be isolated when I'm old, I worry about single older family members

less

narrow

convergent

I want to reduce older people's loneliness, increase the impact of volunteering

few

individual

many

collective

My capacities and resources:
Not much free time but can work evenings & weekends. Good marketing knowledge & presentation skills

Beliefs about change
Change is slow & hard. Public health and social care institutions are ossified bureaucracies & are in crisis from funding cuts

anxious

few

few

excited

Weak ties:
Local neighbours, volunteer organizations, activists.

many

many

Strong ties: Friends, family in UK & US, University, children's school, sports club, work colleagues

2 *Contexts, strategies, value creation*

snapshot

– *Services are more than customer service added on to products. The basic concept of service is the co-creation of value by actors combining and exchanging resources within value constellations.*

– *Service rests on the idea of value-in-use over time, not value-in-exchange in a transaction.*

– *Service innovation involves recombining capacities and actors into new innovation ecosystems.*

– *Five service innovation capabilities help organizations respond to turbulent environments through strategic wayfinding.*

YOU WANT A NEW MOBILE PHONE, BUT YOU ARE frustrated with the fast cycles of replacing phones offered by the mobile telecommunications operators, with whom you need to have a contract to access voice, messaging and data services. You are also concerned about the environmental and social impacts of the materials and manufacturing processes associated with mobile technologies. Fairphone[16] sells you a smartphone manufactured in factories with fair wages and safe working conditions, using "conflict-free" minerals from the Democratic Republic of Congo that is designed with its use, reuse and recycling in mind. Having bought your Fairphone, you can select a SIM-only contract with a mobile operator. But you remain connected to Fairphone, its online community of customers, its networks of suppliers and the contexts it operates within, because you share their values and commitments to doing things differently.

A division of a bank wants to improve the way market intelligence and customer contacts are shared between different parts of the organization to enable cross-selling. The IT team starts to scope a knowledge management system with the aim of employees sharing their specialist, hard-won knowledge. An early stumbling block is that some staff see this knowledge and these relationships as their own, rather than the bank's. The IT team realizes the proposed knowledge management system will fail because it ignores employee behaviour and culture. It starts to think afresh about how the bank can leverage employees' knowledge by experimenting with gaming and co-design, using the bank's competitive culture as a resource, rather than a constraint.

Faced with continuing budget cuts alongside high demand for its services, a municipality decides to experiment with new ways to support older people living in the area, whom it has a statutory responsibility to support. The team partners with Casserole Club[17], a social venture that matches people living in an area with older nearby residents. A volunteer cooks an extra portion of home-cooked food and takes it round to an older person's home, and commits to doing this on a regular basis. The services team at the municipality try to work out how nurturing weak social ties through volunteer services such as this can help them support older people to live better for longer.

What these examples share is an orientation to creating economic and social value by combining resources in new ways. First identified by Schumpeter over a century ago, recombining resources into new configurations is the fundamental activity associated with innovation. Although in popular and academic thinking on innovation there is a strong emphasis on developing new technologies, what is more significant is how innovation, as process and outcome, exists through the bundling and unbundling of resources and capacities, resulting in new ways of doing things that become – for a time – the norm.

This chapter does two things. Firstly, it opens up ways of thinking about the environment in which organizations operate and their possible strategic responses.

2 Contexts, strategies, value creation

These lenses include acknowledging a turbulent, dynamic operating context in which strategic way-finding on the ground, rather than the traditional bird's eye view of strategy, supports agile responses. It prompts attending to the multiple and varied inter-connections between people and resources lashed-up into configurations we call organizations and services. A shift towards seeing value as co-created through participation in innovation ecosystems prompts new ways of thinking about designing innovative service offerings. This shift focuses attention on how services are as much social and cultural as concerned with business. The chapter then combines these concep-tual lenses into five capabilities that orient organiza-tions towards service innovation. Together they frame the concepts and methods – discussed in the rest of the book – that organizations use to develop and transform resources to prepare themselves for future uncertainties.

Two case studies show how these lenses help explain how some organizations innovate. One describes how a small team of entrepreneurs identified emerging behaviours and capacities that they linked via digital networks into a new platform for value co-creation, Airbnb. The second shares the approach taken by a multi-partner team designing services in support of the democratic voting process in New York City, which allowed candidates and voters to combine resources in new ways.

The two methods that follow provide an opportunity to integrate concepts discussed here into early stage service innovation projects. Method 2 helps teams bring into view the things they think are part of the future operating environment. Method 3 shows how to identify actors and capacities in the environment, and how to think about ways to combine them into new innovation ecosystems.

The new post-normal

There are many ways to describe the operating envi-ronment facing managers and entrepreneurs. The media, blogs, think tanks, consultancies, academia and political institutions all offer different ways to describe what is happening. Every 24-hour news cycle brings stories of political failings and new hope, finan-cial scandals and renewed probity, economic growth here but budget cuts there, severe weather events and depleted resources, medical breakthroughs alongside worrying increases in chronic disease, passion and shared joy here in contrast to misery and despair else-where. Despite the diversity of ways of making sense of all of this, there are shared themes that characterize the environment in which organizations operate and in which people live as:

- Dynamic;
- Turbulent;
- Involving many actors and elements that interact with one another; and
- Non-linear, so that a minor change can have dis-proportionate effects[18].

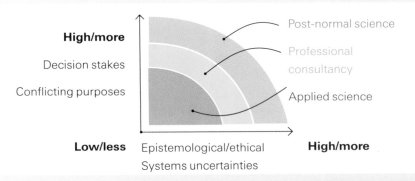

High/more

Decision stakes

Conflicting purposes

Post-normal science

Professional consultancy

Applied science

Low/less Epistemological/ethical
Systems uncertainties   **High/more**

Figure 3 Post-normal science (adapted from Funtowicz and Ravetz 1993)

In a context of rapid and complex change, uncertainty and ambiguity are high, so existing knowledge is of relatively little value. Concepts, theories, methods and tools derived from the past are not necessarily helpful for the future, given the many diverse unknowns and the turbulence of the environment. Such contexts require different ways of thinking and acting. To get to grips with this, Silvio Funtowicz and Jerry Ravetz distinguish between post-normal and normal science[19]. They argue that conventional problem-solving strategies rest on *normal* science, in which human values are not acknowledged, high degrees of certainty are required, and quality assurance is managed relatively informally by peer review. In contrast, Funtowicz and Ravetz suggest that when there are high levels of uncertainty around ethics and epistemology (what counts as valid and reliable knowledge), and when decision stakes reveal conflicting purposes among stakeholders, the methodologies of normal science are ineffective. This is what they call *post-normal* science.

In such contexts it is difficult for managers and others such as policy-makers to make decisions, since the knowledge that shapes them is open to challenge from other disciplines and from diverse stakeholders (see Figure 3). Continuing claims by some politicians and business people that climate change is not a result of human activity, despite overwhelming academic agreement that it is, is one example. In such contexts, decision-making processes should acknowledge uncertainty and include in dialogue those with a stake in the issue. And yet engaging in dialogue at scale is extremely difficult.

The implication for managers designing innovative services is to recognise that in a post-normal organizational environment, facts are uncertain, knowledge is uncomfortable and solutions need to be what environmental researcher Steve Rayner calls "clumsy"[20]. Clumsy solutions are not the result of selecting between well-defined alternatives based on knowledge, the certainty and quality of which have been assured. Instead, clumsy solutions recognize the lack of certainty and knowledge about what might happen and what could work. Clumsy solutions recognize that stakeholder engagement can only ever be partial and unfinished. Even with the best intentions, taking action leads to unintended negative and positive consequences, and involves excluding some people and organizations that could be considered central to an issue.

2 Contexts, strategies, value creation

Moving strategically, not thinking in the abstract

This context of irreducible uncertainty, turbulence and contestation raises questions for the role of strategy, the conventional starting point for organizational change and action. The perspective taken in this book is to draw on research into strategy that emphasizes improvisation and emergence in doing, rather than a top-down view of strategic planning that is formalized before action takes place.

In their book *Strategy Safari*[21], Henry Mintzberg and colleagues offer a tour of the main ways of thinking about strategy, and their strengths and weaknesses. Organizing their book into ten main schools of strategy, they outline some of the areas of agreement, which include these[22]:

- Strategy concerns both the organization and the wider environment. It is concerned with what goes on inside organizations and what happens outside, and with the boundaries and intersections between the two. It's complex, non-repetitive and in flux.

- Strategy affects the overall performance and welfare of the organization.

- Strategies are not purely deliberate. Sometimes strategies emerge and even if there are intentional strategies, the ways things turn out in practice may result in important differences from what was intended.

- Firms have different levels of strategy – for example, corporate strategy asks "what business shall we be in?", whereas business strategy asks "how shall we compete in each business?"

- Doing the work of strategy combines both analytical and creative work, but it is typically seen as conceptual work done by leaders of organizations.

- Strategic management is a process that organizations follow, as well as the content of the decisions and actions.

Despite the diversity of schools of thought on strategy, Mintzberg and colleagues argue that there remains a bias evident in many contemporary commercial and public sector organizations and among management consultancies. This version of strategic management sees it as an activity that proceeds through discrete phases of formulation, implementation, and control, carried out in linear steps. Here, being strategic is a quality associated with individuals, usually those at board level, rather than being something that is seen as a dynamic collective capability within an organization. It is associated with explicit intentions, often formalized in presentations and other documents, which often ignores that successful strategies that were not intended can emerge.

In contrast, researchers Robert Chia and Robin Holt[23] propose a view of strategy not as something explicitly stated upfront, but as something that takes shape organically but still purposefully, that is infused into the everyday actions of individuals and organizations. They distinguish between the act of navigation associated with the dominant view of strategy ("We managers will lead the organization through a sea of external complexity"), and a process of *wayfinding*. Using the term wayfinding opens up the idea of "progressing tentatively and incrementally reaching out from one's situated circumstance, using oneself, not some independent external point, as the basis of reference. For the wayfinder, the territory is boundless and bottomless, using self-referential devices to express experience there and then as he or she moves through the landscape. Wayfinding precedes navigation"[24]. By using this metaphor, Chia and Holt move strategy towards being an active and exploratory process of information gathering and use, that extends beyond the mental activities of one person, top management team or single organization.

Understood like this, strategic action can be consistent, even if not based on goals that were specified in advance. As Chia and Holt put it,

> "attending to and dealing with the problems, obstacles and concerns confronted in the here and now may actually serve to clarify and shape the initially vague and inarticulate aspirations behind such coping actions with sufficient consistency that, in retrospect, they may appear to constitute a recognizable 'strategy'."[25]

One example is Grameen Bank, Bangladesh's micro-credit lending institution founded in 1983 by Muhammad Yunus, who was jointly awarded the Nobel Peace Prize in 2006. Chia and Holt describe Yunus' growing awareness of the failures of the theories he and his colleagues, as academic economists, promoted, evident in the day-to-day needs of the poor who have limited access to capital, because they have no capital. He co-founded Grameen Bank, a financial institution that contradicts the dominant logic of banking practice. Grameen starts with the situation of the would-be borrower, and her immediate needs for finance, and lends to her without collateral. It assumes that the borrowers will make repayments, especially if their activities and the implications of not paying back loans are tied to the communities they are part of.

With more than eight million members by early 2014, most of them women[26], Grameen Bank has grown to become an important actor in the lives of its borrowers and their families and communities, and also a player in regional and international discussions about poverty reduction. Chia and Holt say that Yunus did not deliberately set out to create a successful bank. But they see the rapid growth of micro-credit banking within, and then beyond, Bangladesh, as resulting from the cumulative constructive actions of Yunus and colleagues, which remained focused over decades on finding ways to increase the capacities of poor people with limited access to financial credit.

Drawing this perspective on strategy together with the earlier discussion of uncertainty and major global challenges, it is clear that Chia and Holt's vision of strategic management is more appropriate to the dynamic, turbulent environment that contemporary organizations find themselves in, than the procedural top-down version which is strategy-in-advance. A top-down perspective imagines it is possible to create a map of the environment. Instead, being open to wayfinding within the environment, through

2 Contexts, strategies, value creation

improvisation and responses to new situations, and forging relations with different actors and seeing what unfolds, will lead to consistency of purpose that, in retrospect, can be identified as an emergent and yet valid strategy.

Everything is hybrid

Having sketched out the uncertain contexts in which organizations are operating, it is now time to draw on another lens from academic research. This helps managers conceptualize the wider environment and the organizations, technologies, institutions and people that are active within it. I'll call these constituents *actors*, because this term emphasizes that they have roles to perform, and capacities to enable them to take part in constituting a service or venture (see Table 1). A common way of thinking about the various elements in an environment is to see them as inputs to a system that then does things to them, resulting in outputs. This is based on a mechanical model of what organizations do. However, another way of looking at the constitutive elements described above is to see them as having agency because of where and how they are connected to other actors.

To illustrate this, I will use the example of an everyday industrial object, the electric toaster, to see how this analysis can be applied. Think about a toaster you have used. Perhaps you will start off by thinking of the materials it is made from, its colour, size and shape and who manufactured it. Maybe you will think about where it sits, who uses it and how they go about this.

Perhaps you'll have memories of what you have eaten that was prepared with the help of the toaster and what it tasted and smelled like. Now start thinking about other things that are required for the toaster to have any significance or value. As things like toasters become part of ordinary life, they become somewhat invisible to us and we tend not to notice them, nor the systems of consumption, and technological, economic and political networks they are part of. The aim here is to get away from thinking about the discrete boundaries of the toaster-object, and explore its mutual dependency on many different kinds of expertise and system, and its connections with many other actors.

Designer Thomas Thwaites' toaster project[27] reveals some of these interconnections. Over nine months he gave himself the task of trying to go through the steps involved to manufacture a toaster, using pre-modern industrial methods. Instead of the hundreds of materials involved in producing a cheap toaster, Thwaites used just five: copper for the pins of the electrical plug, the cord and the internal wires; iron for the steel grill; plastic for the casing, plug and wire insulation; nickel for the heating elements; and mica, a mineral like slate around which the heating element is wound. He mined iron and smelted some ore, first in a microwave oven and then in a leaf burner. He created an electrical circuit with a heating element. He made some plastic. After many months of work, and having spent rather more than the £3.99 he could buy a toaster for at UK discount retailer Argos, Thwaites had produced what he called "a kind of half-baked, hand-made pastiche of a consumer appliance"[28].

Term	Meaning
Actor	The constituent elements that make up organizations, teams, projects and services including people, material and digital objects, technologies, resources such as data, knowledge or financial capital.
Hybrid	A configuration of actors that comes into existence through interacting with one another. A service innovation ecosystem is a hybrid that can be viewed through business, social impact or environmental lenses.

Table 1 Terms used in this book

Thwaites' magnificent failure of a toaster, now in the collection of the Victoria and Albert Museum in London, reminds us quite how technically and operationally complicated even everyday objects in the Global North are. But sociologist Harvey Molotch's[29] analysis goes even further. He shows how corporations, retailers, advertisers, and others – and not just designers – influence what a thing can be and how it is made. Together, he says, these actors create "lash-ups" with one another, resulting in and reinforcing lifestyles and needs that otherwise would not exist in those forms.

Looking at the toaster by identifying the various resources and capacities required for it to have any meaning or value at all, these can be identified as:

- Technological systems: the socket in the wall into which the toaster plugs; the electrical supply at the right level of current and voltage for the toaster element to brown but not burn the toast and to give the user feedback about whether it's on or not, or hot or not; relationships with other devices such as smoke alarms that go off when they smell burning toast.

- Socio-cultural practices: habits and preferences about what to eat for breakfast or at other times of day; the ability to bake bread from particular kinds of wheat in such a way that it slices and toasts well and is suitably absorbent – for example – for butter, jam, marmalade, peanut butter or, if you are Dutch, those chocolate sprinkles.

- Economic systems: the agricultural production processes; manufacturing infrastructures and processes; supply chains and retailing and marketing systems that result in toasters being designed, manufactured, on sale and delivered to people's homes; and fresh bread being available for toasting.

In short, the toaster is far from being a stand-alone item. It needs bread, electrical power, sockets at kitchen worktop height, and expectations and preferences about what breakfast should include and taste like. It's not just a complicated bit of modernity that an intelligent person like Thwaites, with time on his hands, will fail to reproduce with the resources he has available. The toaster has little value without being wrapped into these other networks and practices – what Molotch calls lash-ups.

In this book, I'll call the configurations of actors that are lashed up together *hybrids*. A hybrid is a bundle

2 Contexts, strategies, value creation

of actors, which might be people, physical and digital objects, and resources such as data, knowledge or financial or social capital. This term helps make clear that in this analysis, there are no such things as stand-alone objects. Every object is connected to, and relies on, other kinds of device, or capacity, or locatedness within an environment or network, in order to have its capacities. Understanding how some hybrids are successfully held together as business offerings is useful when aiming to create new configurations when designing a new service offering.

Taking the example of IKEA, discussed by Richard Normann and Rafael Ramírez in their book *Designing Interactive Strategy*[30], clarifies what this means in practical terms for organizations. Normann and Ramírez point to how IKEA's business model is based on customers having resources that they bring into play in the exchanges they have with the furniture manufacturer. In contrast to the previously dominant model in which a customer buys a ready-to-use piece of furniture, IKEA involves customers in the transport and assembly of the furniture. Firstly, the value for customers is realized in the collaborative exchange of resources in the value constellation that IKEA invites them to be part of. IKEA configures the resources of suppliers of materials that are the components of pieces of furniture, and invites consumers to be active participants in a value constellation in which producers and consumers are connected in new ways. Secondly, the customers who are part of the IKEA value constellation are different kinds of customers – not in the sense of being different people in terms of age,

gender, or cultural or socio-economic background. They are different customers in the sense that in the IKEA hybrid, they are constituted as customers-with-capacities, able to transport and assemble furniture.

Imagine someone who has just moved home. She might go to shops and look online for furniture as she settles into her new home. On one occasion she might order and pay for a chest of drawers online, and have it delivered. All she has to do is to arrange for someone to be there to accept delivery and decide where the piece goes. In the same month, she goes to IKEA, but here she becomes a customer-with-capacities. She pushes the huge trolley round the store, picks up some flatpack furniture, takes it to her (borrowed) car, drives it home and then spends several hours assembling the object with help from friends. In these two configurations, the exact same person is constituted differently. In the first case, she's a conventional customer with needs and requirements. In the second, she is a customer-with-capacities; the value constellation does not work unless she is able to configure her resources (her and her friend's expertise, a car, her skill in navigating through the store, the tools and skills to assemble the furniture) to be the kind of customer IKEA needs her to be.

What this approach offers is a way to see that actors within a hybrid, which might be people, organizations, or digital or material things, have capacities, not just needs or requirements. Rather than seeing needs or product characteristics as pre-existing, this perspective recognizes that configuring resources in particular ways results in particular kinds of capacities

or qualities. This, then, highlights how bringing value constellations into being is an important part of the strategic work of responding to turbulent operating environments. The next section adds depth to this with a focus on understanding how economic and social value are co-created through combining resources and capacities in new ways.

Innovation ecosystems

There are many variants of the idea of value constellations within academic research on innovation, strategy and marketing. Other terms include value networks, value nets, strategic networks and business networks[31]. In this book I will adopt the term *innovation ecosystems*, which emphasizes how innovation (as outcome) results from the interconnections between actors of many different types, playing different roles and with mutual interdependencies involved in activities over time (innovation as process).

Turning now to how innovation systems are distinct in the case of services, one version of this approach comes from marketing researchers Steve Vargo and Bob Lusch[32]. Briefly stated, service-dominant logic is a way of thinking about the organization of resources to create value that is distinguished from what they call goods-dominant logic. To illustrate the distinction, I'll take the example of a fridge. In goods-dominant logic, value creation comes from identifying features that consumers want in fridges, manufacturing fridges with these characteristics, and then selling them to consumers via retailers. The key moment here is the transaction when someone pays

for the fridge and takes legal ownership of it. Under that logic, "service" or often "customer service", is what happens after purchase when, for example, the fridge breaks down and an engineer visits the home to repair it.

In contrast, in service-dominant logic, people want access to cooling but that does not necessarily mean they want to own a fridge. It's hard to imagine what cooling services might look like from the perspective of mature markets such as North America or Europe where nearly every home has a fridge. But it's possible to identify alternative approaches in economies where informal models of access have emerged. For example, researchers from manufacturer Electrolux found that owners of fridges in poor communities in the Global South rented out space inside them to community members[33]. This involved the creation of a different kind of innovation ecology around the fridge, which was not based on a singular transaction or ownership.

This lens on understanding value co-creation focuses on the exchange of resources between actors in an innovation ecology for mutual benefit, defined by the actors themselves. It requires a focus on what unfolds in practice as people have access to resources over time, instead of emphasizing the moment of an economic transaction such as a purchase/sale. Here are some of the major themes:

- **From value-in-exchange to value-in-use.**
  Early contributors to the field of economics discussed value-in-use, which was later obscured by value-in-exchange. In contrast, the

service-dominant logic approach sees the fundamental basis of economic activity as the exchange of service for service. What matters here is the value that is co-created through someone using or engaging with resources or organizational artefacts in their day-to-day interactions with them.

- **Value is realized through co-creation.** The service-dominant logic approach highlights the role played by people in collectively generating value in the exchange of service. Instead of the production/consumption dyad in which value is consumed, service-dominant logic sees customers, end users, and other stakeholders as involved in co-creating value. Customer value-creating processes are dynamic, interactive and non-linear.

- **Actors have capacities.** Service-dominant logic starts with the assumption that actors, both organizations and people, (can be configured to) have resources and capacities. This corresponds to a similar view in the field of social innovation and community development. Known as the asset-based model[34] of community development, the starting point is that people have resources, including the capacity to act together to address issues, not just needs that outside actors such as firms will help them meet.

- **The actors involved determine what the nature of the value is.** This approach starts with the experience and understanding of the actors (people and organizations) involved in an innovation ecosystem. Value is determined from their perspective, not by one dominant actor. The field of customer experience highlights the preferences, attitudes and motivations of people who are typically seen as "consumers" with "needs". In contrast, consumption studies recognize the diversity of people and concepts that mediate how an individual experiences their interactions with a product or service.

- **Service requires access to resources, not ownership.** The growth of collaborative consumption has resulted in new business models which give people access to resources they want for a period of time. Ventures such as RelayRides (access to someone's car when you want to rent one) make explicit the innovation ecology around assets. Although they typically involve financial transactions between two people ("I'll pay you $50 to borrow your car for a day"), these ventures restore sociality to value co-creation. Instead of an individual trusting a manufacturer's brand (and related institutions such as regulators or banks), the service perspective foregrounds weak social ties between people.

- **Innovative services involve new platforms, combinations of assets and alliances.** With multiple actors involved in innovation ecosystems, there are different kinds of participants, taking on specific roles, and existing within mutual interdependencies within service configurations. The boundaries of service ecosystems are not given or pre-defined, but result from the processes of negotiation and participation between and among actors.

These factors have several implications for organizations aiming to create new innovation ecosystems. Firstly, service innovation is centrally concerned with something that organizations cannot directly control, and rarely have much knowledge of or insight into – customers' or users' behaviours and experiences, shaped by their socio-cultural practices in the form of routines, habits and unacknowledged ways of behaving. For many organisations, "using" happens in all sorts of places beyond their boundaries, where they have limited opportunities to engage with users, and about which they typically do not have effective ways of understanding what happens as value is co-created in use. Even in the context of digital services, in which users engage with an organization through digital channels, and from which organizations can easily capture data about user activity, understanding how value is constituted in use through users' behaviours remains a methodological challenge.

Secondly, temporality becomes a key new variable for people designing innovative service ecosystems to get to grips with. Instead of focusing on transactions such as the moment of purchase, or closely related time slices such as when a customer decides to make a purchase, the service-dominant logic perspective has an expanded view of time. The marketing concept of customer lifetime value begins to move towards this. But in practice, in many organizations this is a quantitative and financial analysis about the value of the customer to the firm, not an analysis of the user or customer's experience over time based on how value unfolds in practice in the context of use.

A third implication is a move from seeing users and customers as having "needs" or "requirements", in the language of much product and service development, to seeing them as having resources and capacities. The challenge for people designing innovative services is then to find ways to co-design innovation ecosystems that combine organizational and user capacities in creating value dynamically for all parties.

The service innovation imperative

Combining these ideas opens up a different way of thinking about the challenges for managers in fast-changing, complex environments. For people designing innovative services facing questions similar to the ones outlined at the beginning of this chapter, the implications are:

- Recognizing that the uncertainty of the wider environment leads to a move from normal science, in which previous knowledge from the past is assumed to work in the future, and facts are not contested, towards post-normal science, in which purposes are conflicted, stakes are high and facts and knowledge are not considered to be reliable.

- Moving from a view of strategy as abstracted and top-down with a bird's eye view, towards seeing it as guiding improvisational activity based on wayfinding on the ground.

- Shifting from a view in which value is added to objects and then extracted through ownership, towards an orientation in which value is understood as created and realized in use by combining resources within an innovation ecology involving different kinds of actors.

- Transitioning from a focus on value-in-exchange, towards recognising the complex day-to-day worlds and social practices shaping how customers and users live and work, in which many other people, technologies, behaviours, and capacities can shape experiences, impact and value-in-use.
- A shift from customers and users having needs, to their having capacities that can be enrolled in an innovation ecosystem.
- A move away from consumption and use based on models of ownership, to opportunities to access, use and develop capacities and resources.

Figure 4 summarizes these shifts and defines the capabilities that organizations need to develop to respond to them. Here, a capability is understood as a collective capacity to act, at the level of organizations, not just associated with individuals but the result of shared policies, processes, cultures, and behaviours. The term capability includes knowledge, skills, know-how, activities and functional competencies that are repeated – the ways things are done, what is known, and the ability of the organization to use its knowledge and skills to respond to its environment through routines.

Thinking of these as *dynamic capabilities* emphasizes that organizational resources are not fixed, but could change and develop as the operating environment changes and organizations learn and develop and

respond to opportunities[35]. A dynamic capability is not simply the sum of an organization's resources, but the capacity of the organization to purposefully create, extend or modify its resource base. As bundles of resources, capabilities should not be thought of as "things" that an organization "has". Instead, dynamic capabilities are generative ways of knowing and doing that are performed, are repeatable, become routinized and habitual and can change.

Launch clumsy solutions and learn. If the environment is fast-changing and uncertainty is irreducible, then organizations that have a capability for learning as they go are more likely to be able to adapt. Strategic action through wayfinding on the ground involves iterative efforts to try things out and learn from doing things that managers know in advance will not quite succeed, and that will have positive and negative unintended consequences. Managerial resource becomes less focused on achieving on getting things (nearly) right first time. Instead, organizational capacities distribute learning from repeatedly trying things out, gathering data to analyze what happened, reframing opportunities, and then reconfiguring resources. Learning from clumsy solutions requires building processes with fast feedback loops, gathering and interpreting data, and using interpretations to shape decision-making.

Recombine capacities into new innovation ecologies. If organizations are bundles of resources configured into offerings, involving the active participation of a range of actors, then value creation is distributed and

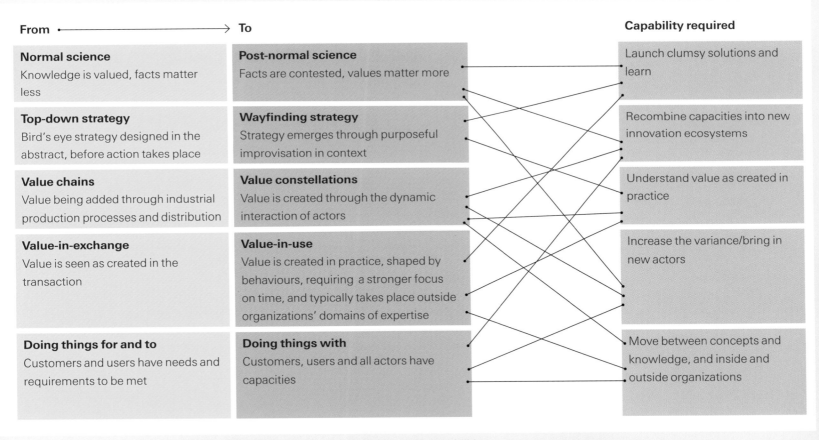

From →	To	Capability required
Normal science Knowledge is valued, facts matter less	**Post-normal science** Facts are contested, values matter more	Launch clumsy solutions and learn
Top-down strategy Bird's eye strategy designed in the abstract, before action takes place	**Wayfinding strategy** Strategy emerges through purposeful improvisation in context	Recombine capacities into new innovation ecosystems
Value chains Value being added through industrial production processes and distribution	**Value constellations** Value is created through the dynamic interaction of actors	Understand value as created in practice
Value-in-exchange Value is seen as created in the transaction	**Value-in-use** Value is created in practice, shaped by behaviours, requiring a stronger focus on time, and typically takes place outside organizations' domains of expertise	Increase the variance/bring in new actors
Doing things for and to Customers and users have needs and requirements to be met	**Doing things with** Customers, users and all actors have capacities	Move between concepts and knowledge, and inside and outside organizations

Figure 4 Key shifts shaping service innovation capabilities

cannot be solely controlled or even guided by one actor. Value creation can be thought of as recombining capacities into new value constellations, by bringing actors together into new ways and giving them access to resources, without requiring exchanging money for ownership. It involves doing things with actors, not just for them. Value creation recognizes that the capacities that actors are deemed to have do not necessarily pre-exist, but are enabled and brought into being by their roles in a value constellation. This organizational capability involves creating lash-ups, practising bricolage, and bundling and unbundling actors. Through such recombining, resources are connected and made available to people in new ways, and new capacities are brought into being.

2 Contexts, strategies, value creation

Understand value as created in practice. If value emerges in use, then this capability is about understanding how things unfold on the ground in context as organizations and people engage with other actors and capacities they are connected and have access to. This organizational capability involves developing an orientation to how things unfold over time, to experiences instead of transactions, and to events instead of objects. It supports strategic wayfinding as interpretations of new data prompt responsive adaptation and changes in direction on the ground. It requires learning from how actors experience and understand value within their own contexts, rather than relying on a dominant model of value. This capability is sensitive to diversity and difference, to what happens at the margins rather than normalization.

Increase the variance/bring in new actors. If the wider environment is turbulent and dynamic, then issues and opportunities arise as new and unfamiliar actors and capacities emerge in relation to existing innovation ecosystems. If innovation has always been about looking at the margins, then this capability requires an orientation to identifying new and unfamiliar actors and capacities, and engaging actively with them. This capability prompts organizations to look beyond their boundaries and existing customers, partners, competitors and users, and explore re-configuring innovation ecosystems by forming connections with unfamiliar actors.

Move between concepts and knowledge and inside and outside organizations. If there is a shift to doing things with users, customers, employees and other stakeholders, not just for them, then organizations need better ways to move repeatedly between inside and outside their boundaries. If value is created through the active participation of actors within an innovation ecosystem and unfolds through use over time, then organizations must orient themselves towards supporting and enabling different kinds of value co-creation at different times and places.

Some of these service innovation capabilities may look familiar. Competencies such as scenario planning, agile product development, user experience design and ethnographic fieldwork are part of this orientation. But the analysis offered here is distinctive because it clarifies the strategic value of wayfinding. The approach presented here emphasizes the iterative learning cycles that such activities need to take place within, through which new concepts and new knowledge and competencies are generated to develop and sustain innovation ecosystems. It helps connect discrete activities and initiatives to learning and change, as organizations find their way through, and improvise in relation to, rapidly changing environments.

The rest of this book provides practical ways for people designing innovative services to explore and develop these capabilities at the early stage of a project. The chapters that follow introduce approaches and methods associated with these capabilities, and describe cases of successful and less successful service innovations. By learning from trying the methods out, readers can begin to develop their own versions of these capabilities, dynamically adapted to their own contexts of use.

Case 3 Turning sofabeds into resources and rethinking travel experiences at Airbnb

Service providers give people or organizations temporary access to resources they do not own, through mechanisms such as leasing, hiring, or borrowing. A fast-growing area of service innovation involves creating platforms that connect people who have a resource, such as a spare bedroom in a popular city, a car or a drill, with people who want temporary access to it. Sometimes called the sharing economy, this development has been termed "collaborative consumption" by authors Rachel Botsman and Roo Rogers[36]. Along with earlier developments such as product-service systems, the hope is that sharing services will change consumption habits, resulting in less materials waste from unwanted or under-used products. It is too early to tell if sharing-based services will become significant in terms of contributing substantially to conventional measures of economic production, or through becoming the regular way of doing things for many people, let alone impacting positively on climate change. But they illustrate ways to combine resources into new innovation ecosystems, resulting in different kinds of value for the actors involved and emergent behaviours.

One example of a service based on these principles that has grown fast is Airbnb. By mid 2014, it was offering visitors to its website somewhere to stay in more than 600,000 properties in 35,000 cities in 192 countries, from people's spare rooms to entire homes, including more than 600 castles[37]. The online marketplace had served more than 11 million people by early 2014.[38] Airbnb's revenues come from taking a percentage of the transaction from the host, and a larger percentage from the person travelling.

The origins of this business date back to 2008, when designers Brian Chesky and Joe Gebbia created a website offering people who wanted cheap accommodation in San Francisco airbeds on the floor of their apartment in exchange for a fee[39]. Chesky and Gebbia were pleased to make $1,000. But the insight underpinning what became their successful venture came from their surprise at who stayed with them, and at how quickly the strangers they had let into their home did not feel like strangers any more[40]. Having done this several times, the two founders then collaborated with a third co-founder, Nathan Blecharczyk, to experiment on a larger scale and co-founded Airbnb. They targeted events where lots of people wanted to visit the city, when hotels were fully-booked or affordable accommodation was limited.

What's distinctive about contemporary sharing services is that they foregrounded the things that other service businesses would consider a risk to be avoided or very carefully managed – social relations and high variability of provision. In the case of Airbnb, this means travellers see their travel

2 Contexts, strategies, value creation

Case 3 (continued) Turning sofabeds into resources and rethinking travel experiences at Airbnb

experience not just as having access to a room or apartment and expectations of particular levels of quality, but also access to someone's life. Gebbia explains by describing his own visit to Japan:

> "As Westerners, it's really easy to feel out of place in Japanese culture. So I booked with Airbnb and I stayed with a local in Japan named Ryu. He's a 26-year-old aspiring tech entrepreneur, so we had a lot in common. By staying with Ryu, I basically was brought into the fabric of the city: his friends became my friends, his favourite noodle shop became my favourite noodle shop, his favourite sake place became my favourite sake place. We explored the neighbourhoods of Tokyo together, and on New Year's Eve he took me to his local temple, where I got to participate in an ancient tradition that they do. I was afforded this incredibly local experience because of Ryu, and if I had not had connection through an Airbnb host I probably would have only skimmed the surface of Japanese culture."[41]

This is a story about a service enabling access to someone's particular lived experiences in an unknown place. It also surfaces the authenticity and particularity of the travel experiences afforded by services like Airbnb, in contrast to the carefully-managed consistency and lack of variability in hotel chains.

The venture that became Airbnb began by connecting the difficulty that travellers face finding affordable accommodation, and the untapped resources that some people have, such as spare rooms. But the insights into the importance of the relations between visitors and hosts shifted Airbnb's focus to redefining hospitality[42]. New services explored that are part of this emerging focus include cleaning apartments and preparing them for visitors, and helping visitors get the most from their visit by providing tours, home-cooked meals and other add-ons.

Other peer-to-peer ventures that operate similarly include a lift in someone's car, borrowing a car for a fee, parking in someone's front garden, getting short-term use of an expensive product such as camping equipment, food processors or electronic goods owned by someone near you, and hiring clothes. Other ventures help connect people who want help with something with people who can perform services. For example, the start-up TaskRabbit helps you find someone willing to run errands for a fee, such as picking up and delivering things, or helping with tasks such as typing up notes. On the one hand, such businesses foreground the social connections that are part of an experience and that add sociality to financial transactions. On the other hand, such ventures turn social relations – helping someone with whom you have weak social ties, or no ties at all but who you are near – in to a marketplace.

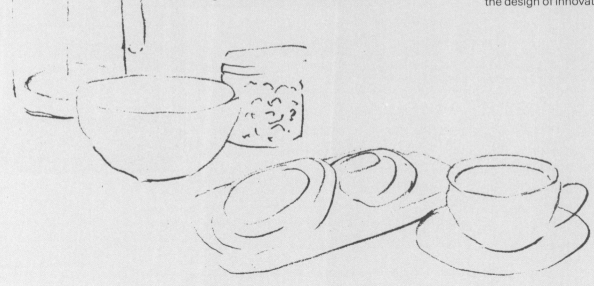

It is unclear how sharing services and the emergent behaviours they rest on might have a greater impact, given growing interest from large corporations and from regulators. Although proponents of collaborative consumption emphasized how it brings regular people with untapped resources into a marketplace, there are also opportunities and challenges for companies operating in adjacent spaces. For example, General Motors and Toyota have explored how to engage with car-sharing services, which disrupt the model of manufacturing that puts the emphasis on owning cars. There are also challenges to early-stage ventures based on sharing resources which often operate in a regulatory grey zone. For example, regulators are concerned about how to tax income earned from sharing services, how to ensure safety for service users and how to protect parties in sharing services from fraud and liability.

Typically started by entrepreneurs rather than corporations, sharing platforms increase the variance of the actors involved in a marketplace, bringing in new resources and different people into an innovation ecosystem. Triggered by insights into how people experience things and find workarounds by reconfiguring resources, they create new kinds of value-in-use that emphasize sociality and trust in the design of innovative services.

2 Contexts, strategies, value creation

Case 4 Agile organizing for democracy by reconfiguring resources through NYCVotes

NYCVotes is a project built around a mobile website launched in 2013, that aims to lower the barriers to meaningful democratic participation in local elections. The project aimed to make the political process accessible and convenient for voters and candidates in a country that ranks 138th in the world for voter turn-out[43]. The project came together through a coalition of public and private organizations committed to supporting democracy by promoting voter registration, participation and civic engagement in New York City elections, through digital technology. However, the project was not simply about using digital technology to reach potential or actual voters or to make things easier for election candidates. As an example of service innovation, it reconfigured some of the resources in the political ecosystem.

David Lipkin at design consultancy Method, one of the organizations involved, explains the drivers behind the project: "A number of people were hoping to improve dismal voter turn-out in what is not a functional democracy, recognizing that solutions were not likely to come from government on its own, but from working with government."[44] The other organizations involved were the New York City Campaign Finance Board (CFB), the Voter Assistance Advisory Committee (VAAC), and software developers Pivotal Labs and AppOrchard.

A little background is required to explain these organizations[45]. The CFB is an independent, non-partisan city agency. Its role is to counteract the influence of big money in the political process by encouraging candidates for New York City office to raise small contributions from residents, which it then matches. The goal of VAAC is to increase civic engagement in all local elections, by encouraging more New Yorkers to register and vote. But the ways these organizations' processes work, and the touchpoints they offer voters and candidates and their helpers, in effect, make it hard for people to engage in the basic tasks of voting and standing for office, which shapes participation.

There were two main aspects to the NYCVotes mobile digital platform. First, it enabled candidates and campaign staffers to collect and process credit card contributions on smartphones. Instead of handling bank cheques and manually entering data into the CFB's complex reporting software, candidates could use the app to export the data and upload it directly into the CFB's system, simplifying compliance with legal requirements. There were also tools for candidates to solicit, process and then track the financing they receive from individuals, typically in amounts such as $25-$100.

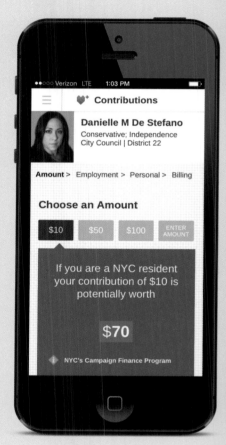

The NYCVotes app that enables people to make contributions to New York City election candidates

Lipkin explains the impact of this, especially on candidates without a party machine behind them:

> "At the national level, the ability to raise money is key. At local levels it's not as important. But lots of the candidates have grassroots teams, not professional organizations, behind them and they don't have lots of staff. So the app supports them practically and levels the playing field a little."

The second release of the software provided voters the ability to see who was on the ballot in their district, to view the candidates' official voter guide profiles, and to connect easily with social networks, enabling them to interact with candidates.

To design the app, Method's designers did what Lipkin calls "guerilla research" and fieldwork with friends and family, trying to understand the complex nature of the existing platforms and what the rules require electoral candidates to do when standing for office. Then the wider project team used agile work sessions to design the mobile application. As an example, Lipkin states: "We had a software developer in the room, the CFB, a user interaction specialist, and a visual designer, who together produced wireframes of the best case process in one afternoon."

Along with US-based organizations like Turbo-Vote[46], which provides a low or no-cost service to help people register for voting, the NYCVotes project intervenes into what is traditionally considered a public, not commercial, sphere. "What we are seeing is more organizations set up to do this," says Lipkin, "combining commercial skills, a public mind set and an entrepreneurial, agile way of working that recognizes that government does not work that way."

Working over six months to get the app live, the coalition had to build software that integrated with municipal government legacy systems designed for different functions. Not only did building the technology require specialist skills, but the coalition's working processes too required careful negotiation. Lipkin explains: "Government's ways of working hampers agile innovation. They sign up for 24-hour turnarounds and sign-offs, but when it comes down to it they don't really understand what it means." So designing and developing the mobile app required both technological innovation – connecting the new platform with legacy systems – and complex interactions with civic institutions and stakeholders.

In terms of impact, the team behind NYCVotes saw it as a multi-year process that will result in the mobile app being adopted within other voting districts. The expectation was that through gathering a user base and demonstrating success, this would put pressure on politicians to change some of the laws. "We'd like to have digital voter registration and digital voting," says Lipkin, "but election laws prohibit this as every voter registration form has

2 Contexts, strategies, value creation

Case 4 (continued) Agile organizing for democracy by reconfiguring resources through NYCVotes

to have an ink signature, even though that is easily forged." By convincing the New York City authorities to make the project open source, the team ensured that its work can be a resource for other US voting districts.

This is an example of an informal temporary organization coming together to address a shared concern. Using agile software development methods, and driven by insights about user behaviours, the resulting innovation ecosystem increased the fundraising and supporter engagement capacities of those standing for public office. The app's connection to municipal infrastructures and compliance with US legislation about reporting fundraising made it particularly useful to candidates without professional organizations behind them. Further, through helping link voters with information about how to register, and providing information about candidates and voting locations, the mobile app drew voters into the democratic process. The NYCVotes mobile app is the visible part of an emerging innovation ecosystem that connects actors in the voting and fundraising process in new ways, and brings different resources and actors into a contested political landscape.

Method 2: *Visualizing drivers of change*

Time involved	Preparation, 10 minutes + optional extras
	Using the method, 90 minutes
Associated capabilities	Recombine capacities into new innovation ecosystems
	Increase the variance/bring in new actors
Methods to use before or after this one	Method 4 Mapping the user experience
	Method 10 Telling stories

What you'll need

Masking tape, Post-it notes, Blu-Tack, marker pens

A flipchart

A facilitator to guide the teams

A documenter to photograph the results

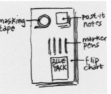

key question

'What do you and your team think the future looks like?'

Purpose

Using this method helps a team identify the drivers of change it thinks are shaping the issue it plans to address. It helps a group articulate reasons why a service innovation initiative might be necessary, and provides detail on what team members think are the key prompts for change.

Outcomes

A shared view of the drivers of change shaping the context for your issue, service or organization. Co-creating the drivers of change grid helps a team see things from different perspectives and supports sense-making and creativity. It also highlights important areas of consensus and disagreement and reveals lack of knowledge.

Preparation

Ahead of time, invite an academic, artist or futurist – or all three – to join the workshop to provoke or inspire you. Alternatively, a couple of days before the workshop, circulate links to videos, articles or blog posts discussing future developments from a range of fields, not just your organization's core areas.

Add a visual dimension to this method by printing out in advance images such as photographs, screengrabs, drawings, and icons that you associate with future developments. Cut them up to be approximately A5 size.

Tip

While facilitating, push participants towards extremes. Encourage them to speculate, imagine and be ridiculous.

2 Contexts, strategies, value creation

continued...

On the day, mark out a large grid using masking tape along a wall or a window, approximately two metres wide. Put your time horizons running across the top (x axis) – for example, three columns labelled three-five, 10 or 20 years (or choose timeframes that work for you). Along the left hand side (y axis), vertically list various aspects of change. Familiar ones to use are: political, economic, socio-cultural, technological, legal, environmental. But you can add others specific to your field, such as chronic disease, immigration, or demographic changes.

How to do it

Capture ideas. Distribute Post-it notes to participants (ideally 10–15 people). Ask them to write on them examples of future issues, opportunities, events, products, services, organizations or people they associate with any of the categories in the framework, over any of the timeframes. They do not have to create Post-it notes about every topic. They can focus on just one time horizon. They should each aim to create about 20 Post-it notes. If you are able to provide images, have these displayed on a wall or table for people to look through. People should start from their own perspectives, knowledge of a place or community, organizational function, community or profession, rather than trying to cover everything, and they can draw on things they have read, seen or discussed.

Share and tell. Ask people to share their future drivers with the group. They should get up in turn, and add their Post-it notes (and images, if you are using them) to the grid on the wall, explaining what the driver is and what it will do to the context or environment. You will find that there is some repetition. Participants do not have to agree with one another.

Reflect. Consider as a group what this picture of the future looks like. Are there any surprises? What might it mean for the organizations, projects and communities you are part of, and their users, staff, partners, customers, funders and investors? How do participants think things will change over the time horizons on the grid? Are there important tensions or disagreements?

Synthesize. Pick a horizon that makes sense to the group (for example, in one year's or in five years' time), pull out about 5–10 key uncertainties, extracted from the grid and the discussion, that participants feel they need to be attentive to. Capture these on a flipchart. Discuss how to find out more about these areas so that these uncertainties become something the team engages with.

Visualizing drivers of change

Use or adapt this to share perspectives about futures over several time horizons

	3–5 years	5–10 years	>10 years
Political			
Environmental			
Socio-cultural			
Technological			
Legal/regulatory			
Economic			
Other factor			

2 Contexts, strategies, value creation

Example

Drivers of change shaping/being shaped by ageing in the UK

	1–3 years	3–5 years	10–20 years
Socio-cultural	Older people increasingly visible as carers themselves, higher consumer expectations of care	Life long learning, more cross-generational initiatives, older people as a resource	Families very dispersed, older people living alone, the UK state will not provide.
Demographic/ health	growing awareness of ageing as an issue – more data & analysis	old beggars on streets in UK, caring crisis more visible, dementia & chronic diseases increasing	older people much higher % of population, living longer with chronic disease & dementia
Political (UK)	Austerity, public sector cuts, open policy making but lack of political will to provide quality care	Some experimental public-private sector caring delivery models take off at scale	older people as activists and entrepreneurs, multiple models embraced to reduce public spending
Economic	UK patchy growth, food banks, regional health disparities	Raised retirement age? Fracking increases tax income, older people working longer	wealth inequalities increased
Environmental	Extreme weather events – drier/wetter/hotter/colder in UK – risks to people in their homes or in care	more extreme weather events including global travel related high food and energy prices hit older people	Global refugees from climate change, resources diverted from supporting the older poor
Legal/ Regulatory	More scrutiny about quality of care, with public ratings but also scandals & abuse	New legislation re caring responsibilities focussed on individuals or local authorities, but real debate avoided	Less focus on individuals and more on collective/ shared caring provision
Technology	Silver surfers v digitally excluded, more mobile broadband, more attention paid to inclusive design	systematic use of electronic patient records and time-banking credits, in-home monitoring services based on internet of things	Remote caring services & Healthcare for the wealthy/emergency care

Method 3: Mapping innovation ecosystems

Time involved	Preparation, 120 minutes
	Using the method, 90 minutes
Associated capabilities	Recombine capacities into new innovation ecosystems
	Increase the variance/bring in new actors
Methods to use before or after this one	Method 4 Mapping the user experience
	Method 5 Creating a persona/storyworld

What you'll need

One table per group

Large sheets of paper, Post-it notes, Blu-Tack, marker pens

One set of cards per group (see preparation)

A facilitator to guide the teams

A documenter to photograph the results

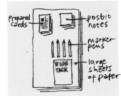

'What are the actors involved in an innovation ecosystem, what are their roles and how do they connect?'

Purpose

This method stimulates participants to shift towards identifying the diverse actors involved in an innovation ecosystem, such as people, things and technologies, organizations, the roles they play and how they connect. It involves creating a visual map of the actors involved. One way of using the method is for participants to analyze the current ecosystem (the as-is). Another is to assemble actors and capacities together into a new ecosystem (the to-be).

Outcomes

Creating a collective visual map results in a shared understanding of the complex world of people, things and organizations involved in co-creating value. It opens up understanding of connections and interdependencies between actors and the contingencies shaping how they connect. Instead of focusing exclusively on people and organizations, it highlights the sometimes mundane material and digital things within an ecosystem, thus offering an on-the-ground view of a value constellation that is oriented to value-in-use. Using this method allows teams to explore what could happen in the future, by adding in new actors to a value constellation, or by combining actors and capacities in new ways.

Tip

Preparing a visual deck of cards allows participants to draw on different parts of their brains, increasing the diversity of ideas generated in the process.

2 Contexts, strategies, value creation

continued...

Preparation

You'll get most out of this method if you customize it to your specific context by preparing a deck of cards in advance. You don't need graphic design skills, just an enquiring mind, access to the web, a printer, paper or card, sticky tape and scissors. Involve several people in making at least 30-50 cards to increase the diversity of ideas.

First, create a list of different actors with some connection to your issue. The aim is to harvest a diversity of digital and material things, people, organizations, technologies, capacities and places as part of the lives of the people and contexts you are thinking about working with, or already work with. Use the checklist on the template, but modify or add to any of the actors, to keep it relevant to your context. Make one card for each actor. Each actor needs a description, and some needs and capacities. If possible, get colour images that capture or allude to these actors. Be specific. For example, if you want to include a major supermarket chain as an actor, name it.

Print out the cards approximately eight to an A4 page. Prepare enough sets of cards for small groups to use in the workshop. Make sure they also have blank cards to create other actors if they need to.

How to do it –
Version 1: Describing the as-is

Explore the shared issue. Introduce the issue or opportunity you want to analyze. For example, this might be a question relating to a goal such as "How can we encourage customers to self-serve using the web?" Or it could be an issue such as "How can we support young people with limited social capital to improve their employability?" If you have created persona storyworlds (Method 5) or mapped user journeys (Method 4), have these available for people to explore and share.

Identify the actors. If you have not made a card deck in advance, the first job is to make one. Invite people to create cards based on the template, to describe actors they think are part of the issue or service. Each actor needs a description, and some needs and capacities. The template suggests some of the people, technologies, organizations, digital and material things, and needs and capacities that might be involved in, or connected to, the issue or opportunity. Each group should make about 30-50 actor cards.

If you have made a card deck, make sure everyone has access to it, along with some blank cards. Ask participants to look through the cards and review whether or not they make sense, by asking if – together – these actors are a reasonable approximation of the various people, organizations, technologies and capacities involved in an issue.

Identify the central actors. Ask participants to draw a set of concentric circles on a large piece of paper. Now, ask the groups to choose actors to be located at the centre of the circles. These could be one or more cards representing a segment of customers or users, but people could also choose a resource such as a database or building. Be clear who or what this is and why it has been chosen.

Arrange the actors. Then ask groups to select and loosely arrange the cards on the circles in relation to the central person or thing. The more important an actor is to how value is co-created, the closer it should be to the centre. Aim to place a minimum of 20 actors onto the map. People may not agree how closely related things are or what their roles are – which is useful discussion.

Identify the flows. Ask participants to use marker pens to draw flows of money, data, or brand associations between the actors.

Identify the roles. Now ask participants to use marker pens to identify actors that play key roles in holding the value constellation together. Use the template for some suggestions.

Share and tell. Finally, ask participants to present their maps to the wider group. Discuss what makes a strong ecosystem (e.g. formal or informal partnerships, socio-cultural factors, proximity) and which actors might be important but hidden from view because they are considered mundane (e.g. databases).

Reflect. Discuss how stable the ecosystem is and what might disrupt or change it. Which actors are on the margins? Is it important or inevitable that they are there, or should they be closer to the centre?

Synthesize. Finally, summarize observations about the key roles and resources of the ecosystem as it is right now. Note these down on a flipchart.

Version 2: Reconfiguring the hybrid to-be

Ask "what if?" This variant starts by asking people to focus on what an ecosystem could look like in the future over a particular horizon (e.g. next year or in five years). Begin with a blank piece of paper marked with concentric circles. Pick some actor cards to be in the centre, and invite people to arrange the other cards in relation to these central actors. Again, draw the flows of money, data and brand associations between actors. Identify key roles that actors play in holding the ecosystem together.

Ask questions that focus on imagining what could happen to the people or organizations involved – e.g. "What if X happened?" Imagine adding a new digital or material object, organization, group of people, or technology into the ecosystem. How would the addition of something new disrupt the ecosystem? How would other actors respond to accommodate the change? Invite participants to move the cards around to result in different combinations. Do you need to add new actors or change their roles? How could the flows of money, data and brand associations change?

Reflect. Compare the future configuration to today's ecosystem. What would need to happen for the new ecosystem to exist?

2 Contexts, strategies, value creation

Mapping innovation ecosystems

Use this to describe key actors that co-create value together

Card format

Actor name
Description
Capacities
Needs

Descriptions

People

Adult
Child
Family member
Friend
Neighbour
Employee
Volunteer
Manager
Expert
By-stander
Person with special needs
(others you can think of)

Things and technologies

Smartphone
Tablet computer
PC
Database
Software application
Sensor
Website
Mobile app
Application form
Poster
Retail outlet
Call centre
Web chat
Email
Package
(others you can think of)

Organizations

Large consumer organization
B2B organization
Non-profit organization
Community group
Small business
Entrepreneur
Venture
Municipality/local authority
Technology provider

Utility
Central government
Regulator
University
Intermediary
Public institution
Financial institution
Investor
(others you can think of)

Roles actors play

User
Customer
Beneficiary
Connector
Solution creator
Resource provider
Infrastructure provider
Hub
Influencer
(others you can think of)

Needs and capacities

Knowing
Doing
Having
Relating
Earning
Connecting
Nurturing
Sharing
Learning
Sustaining
Assembling
Creating
Resourcing
Providing
(others you can think of)

Example

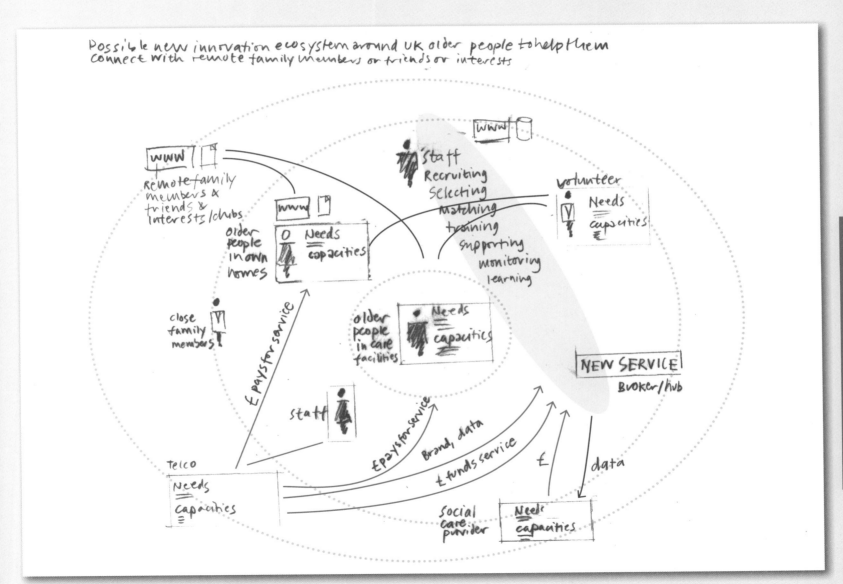

Possible new innovation ecosystem around UK older people to help them connect with remote family members or friends or interests

www
remote family members & friends & interests/clubs

www
older people in own homes

O Needs / capacities

Staff
Recruiting
Selecting
Matching
training
Supporting
monitoring
learning

www

volunteer
Needs / capacities

close family members

£ pays for service

older people in care facilities
Needs / capacities

NEW SERVICE
Broker/hub

staff

Telco
Needs / capacities

£ pays for service

Brand, data
£ funds service

£   data

social care provider
Needs / capacities

3 Behaving and experiencing

snapshot

– For users, customers and others such as employees, the value of services is the integration of their interactions with and experiences of organizations over time.

– The behaviour lens on people's activities focuses on what goes on in people's minds and how this drives what they say, know, feel and do.

– The socio-cultural or practice lens sees people's habits and routines as resulting from dynamic mixtures of collective meanings (stories), bodily and mental activities (skills), and materials and infra-structures (stuff).

– Service innovation involves changing practices, resulting in different experiences for users and customers, in which they behave differently.

A FEW MONTHS AFTER THE 9/11 ATTACKS ON the World Trade Center in 2001, although there was continuing uncertainty about the prospects for the air travel industry, Virgin Atlantic Airways decided to invest substantially in redesigning its business class service[47]. Its team of architects, product designers, and interior and graphic designers, then under head of design Joe Ferry, came up with a number of new concepts. One was the first fully-flat bed in business class, part of a new "Upper Class" suite with an onboard bar and personal media system.

Over the next few years, further investment followed. The vision driving this was for an integrated experience, from the moment the passenger left for the airport (by Virgin limo) until she reached her destination. As Ferry put it, "Everything the passenger touches has had design input from the team".[48] The £105 million Upper Class Cabin project was unveiled in 2003 and rolled out to the airline's fleet[49]. This included access to Virgin's lounge for Upper Class passengers, which opened at London Heathrow in 2006, later followed at other airports. The Virgin Clubhouse offered not just somewhere to relax or work. It was a space in which to participate in Virgin's travel experience before even getting on the plane, including cocktails from a 15-metre-long bar, spa treatments, a brasserie and a games room. The design of the clubhouse experience aimed to make the airport somewhere you wanted to go, not just a place you had to be, to get somewhere else. Later, there was a new wing at London's Heathrow Airport dedicated to Virgin Atlantic's business class passengers, with its own drop-off point and route through passport control.

For the Virgin design team, innovation in travel services centred on redefining people's experiences of travel, and not on technological innovation. Many organizations now try to bring customer experiences to market, not products or services. But often the concept of experience they are using seems hard to pin down. In the many books, articles, blogs and discussions about customer experience over the past decade, there is a lot of confusion about the differences between experience, interaction, behaviour and related terms such as empathy.

This matters to people developing innovative services. If service innovation is seen as configuring ecosystems involving multiple actors, through which value is co-created involving the active participation of users and other participants, then what exactly is being designed? The concept of customer experience presents a potential candidate. But service innovation requires attending to all the relevant actors involved, not just focusing on customers and their experiences as they engage with organizational touchpoints and employees.

This chapter first explores several fields concerned with designing and managing experiences. It then goes more deeply into two underlying approaches to understanding and designing experiences. The behavioural approach highlights individuals and what goes on in their minds, while the socio-cultural approach aims to understand activities from inside people's lives, and links individual experiences to wider social and cultural patterns. The latter is explored in more depth to highlight opportunities for innovation. The argument is that when unexpected things happen, this reveals unspoken assumptions about what the world could or should be like and what the world is made up of. Put another way, recombining actors in new ways is part of service innovation, which requires identifying the constituent actors in an innovation ecosystem and how they connect. The concept of practice, from the social sciences, provides a powerful way to conceptualize what the world is made up of. It links people's behaviours with the materials and technologies they engage with, underlying infrastructures, and the meanings associated with them. So designing an innovative ecosystem can be seen as requiring modifying or creating new practices. The chapter concludes by reviewing how these concepts open up the service innovation capabilities identified in Chapter 2.

Two cases then describe the difficulties of changing experiences and behaviours. The first comes from a healthcare provider, Kaiser Permanente, which describes the challenges of changing the experiences of staff members and patients to improve the effectiveness of communication and result in better patient outcomes. The second case shares the Danish Prison and Probation Service's experience of using a positive deviance approach to change staff and inmate behaviours.

Two methods then follow. At the beginning of a new project, resources may not be available to engage specialists in understanding customer experience. So what these methods do is support a team to create a snapshot of their current thinking about what shapes users' behaviours and the meanings this has for them, situated within broader social practices. Method 5 shows how to go about mapping someone's experience of interactions with an organization or service over time. Method 6 illustrates how to bring an individual user or customer profile into view by describing his or her world.

A world of interactions

Think about a recent trip you have taken on a plane. Remember what airport you flew from, how you got there and what you did straight away on arrival there. What happened during check in or the bag-drop process? If this was a trip you regularly make, did you find yourself doing things almost without thinking as you moved through the airport? If this was an unfamiliar airport or trip, what kinds of resources and skills did you need in order to be a customer-with-capacities within this ecosystem? What went smoothly? What frustrated you?

Experiencing an airport and flight is not just a single experience. Memories of previous visits to airports and previous flights shape expectations of what will happen. This includes interactions with many different kinds of organization, from government-controlled functions such as customs and passport control, to airlines and airport service providers, and food and retail outlets. Understanding the experience of flying can start earlier, when the passenger is at home preparing for their journey. Take a moment to think about your preparations before you took the flight.

I've used this exercise of analyzing a recent flight many times when teaching my MBA class. With such an international group, many students resist the idea that analyzing their individual experiences of flying will be productive, as they know these will most likely be quite different from their classmates'. I ask them to interview each other about a specific recent flight, and capture the experience using a template similar to the one at the end of this chapter. Going through the activity of interviewing someone else quickly highlights not simply that our experiences and habits are different from one another's, but how they are different, and how people associate different meanings with the same activities.

Often, students who have taken the MBA operations management class on process mapping want to know if this exercise involves creating a process map of the steps customers go through when they fly somewhere. Process mapping is a powerful technique for understanding the inputs and outputs of a system, by creating a visual map of it to identify fail points and where quality can breakdown. But trying to understand the interactions and experiences from passengers' points of view provides a different orientation, which is what mapping the user journey opens up.

Approaches to designing experiences

This example of trying to visualize an experience opens up the challenges facing people designing innovative services. The example of the airport illustrated how organizations can be seen as offering multiple and diverse experiences over time, shaped by – and shaping – people's behaviours[50]. For users, customers, employees, partners and stakeholders, organizations are the sum of their experiences with organizations over time.

There is no single way to understand experience, and any attempt to describe it carries with it intellectual baggage. There are several specialisms that claim experience as something that organizations can understand and design. Table 2 presents an overview of the fields that have contributed to current understandings of experience that mobilize different concepts and activities. Although there are many overlaps between these fields, the table captures their main features.

The first of these specialisms, customer experience marketing, focuses on behaviour: how users or customers feel, what they think or believe, and the attitudes, motivations, drivers and barriers that impact on their decisions to purchase particular products or services and their usage of call centres and digital channels. The focus of customer experience marketing is to understand what happens in users' minds, recognizing that previous experiences, current intentions, expectations and associations all shape how people engage with organizations and the choices they make. Developments over the past decade include

3 Behaving and experiencing

understanding how social digital media platforms shape people's relationships with organizations, and which provide near real-time digital data about what customers are doing or are about to do. More recent accounts of customer experience also attend to the unconscious aspects of human experience, things that a customer will not be aware of and may be unable to put into words, but which are also involved in their decision-making[51]. Another development is the hope that using brain imaging technologies will help organizations better understand and predict customer behaviour[52], although like in other areas prefixed with the tag "neuro", it's unclear if the reality can live up to the hopes[53].

A second field concerned with understanding and designing experience is branding. With its origins in graphic communication design, branding has shifted over the past two decades away from a focus on corporate visual identity, to an expanded notion of the relationship between customers and organizations that considers all the touchpoints through which they interact. Key concepts in branding include creating stories, authenticity, and the mediators and interpreters who play roles in constructing brands. For organizations that have several different kinds of offering, the brand is a useful construct that differentiates them with other providers. Sociological accounts of branding emphasize how the symbolic value of brands results from the interconnections between diverse actors. But brand analysis can be too high-level to understand people's experiences in their encounters with the organization and its touchpoints and staff.

A third area associated with designing experiences is systems design. This field is concerned with the design of computer-based systems for multiple users. During the 1980s, researchers helping design software systems began to explore the use of ethnographic approaches to help design teams work out what was going on for users of the systems they were designing. For example, Lucy Suchman's influential study of the use of a photocopying machine[54] showed how human action is constantly constructed and reconstructed through dynamic interplay between the various actors involved. Suchman showed that instead of planning what action to take and then carrying this out, human action in relation to interacting with a machine unfolded through multiple encounters that were situated in everyday life and practical activities. These kinds of studies reframed systems design. Instead of seeing it as the creation of software to enable discrete, intrinsically meaningful tasks, designing computer systems involved the production of new habits and routines. Systems designers began to recognize how people brought their own knowledge, skills and capacities to using software shaped by previous histories of interactions, and in response to local situations.

Fourthly, the relatively new fields of interaction design and service design also focus on designing experiences. Drawing heavily on ideas generated by earlier systems designers, interaction and service designers recognize that they cannot fully design an experience. Rather, recognizing the active participation of users and others in constituting experience,

	Customer experience marketing	Branding	Systems design/participatory design	Interaction design/service design
Leading exponents and authors	Joe Pine and James Gilmour, Colin Shaw, Bernd Schmitt	Doug Holt, Celia Lury, Wally Olins, Erik Roscam Abbing	Paul Dourish, Pelle Ehn, Lucy Suchman, Terry Winograd	Hugh Dubberly, Shelley Evenson, Jon Kolko, Erik Stolterman, Andy Polaine
Key concepts	Behaviour, motivations, attitudes, choices	Stories, relationships, mediators, interpreters	Culture, practices, routines, infrastructures, language games	Interactions, touchpoints, intangibility, aesthetics
Background disciplines	Psychology, cognitive science, behavioural economics	Branding, visual communication, sociology	Anthropology, sociology, philosophy	Human-computer interaction, product design, performance, installation and live art
Emblematic activities and outputs	Quantitative metrics about customer decision-making, customer journey maps	Brand DNA, activity frameworks, values, touchpoints	Qualitative analysis, participant observation, fieldwork, ethnographic analysis	Experience models, customer journey maps, user experience research, experience prototypes
Organizational exemplars	Marketing consultancies, in-house teams	Branding and marketing consultancies and in-house teams	Technology firms, qualitative research consultancies	Design consultancies, in-house teams
Strengths	Identifying opportunities for improvement	Focus on an organization's external world and stakeholders	Analytical rigour; focus on inside and outside organizations	Generative exploratory research able to generate/innovate new concepts
Weaknesses	Less good at generating concepts for innovation; not good at understanding the holistic 'why' for users and collective meanings	Less focus on inside organizations and how to link outside/inside	Significant investment in expertise and time; how analysis is mobilized for decision-making	Emphasis on descriptions of people's activities, rather than deeper analysis

Table 2 Perspectives on customer experience

they can design for particular experiences. Interaction and service designers are attentive to the numerous artefacts or touchpoints that are part of an experience, and to the aesthetic qualities of experiences in which participants become immersed. Within interaction design and service design, experiences are often equated with behaviours, as if they mean the same thing. Influenced by ethnography, designers recognize that their work involves the construction of new meanings as people participate in interactions and services. But at the same time, influenced by cognitive science, designers are also concerned with creating mental models that shape people's interactions with services.

Although this summary has simplified these fields, it highlights that there are important differences in how experience is conceptualized, although there are many overlaps between these areas. Underpinning them are

3 Behaving and experiencing

different academic traditions which need exploring in more detail. By so doing, the differences between the concepts of behaviour, experience and practice can be clarified. This will help people designing services to work out what new kinds of value-in-use their innovation ecosystems might bring into being. Or in other words, it will help them understand the "thing" they are designing.

Behaviour and culture

In British English, the term behave has a slight quality of admonishment. It's the word people often use when they tell children that they should stop being naughty, which typically means doing what the adults, not the children, want. The term behaviour emphasizes what people do and say that can be described and predicted to take place again, which may or may not conform to the regular way of doing things. In this approach, the user or customer exists in an external context, to which they respond. A behaviour-based view emphasizes the choices they make, and how barriers and drivers shape what they do. It is based on the belief that people are rational beings, who are conscious of why they make the decisions they do.

For example, many people have the habit of going shopping at the airport. Major airport operators have invested in building retail spaces and encouraging retailers to set up in them. The behavioural approach might look at people's choices to go to this retail outlet or that one, and what shapes this. It might study what kinds of things people buy as part of their customer experience at the airport. It would highlight people's needs – for example, to buy things they have forgotten to pack or decided to buy at the airport. This kind of analysis can shape decisions to open particular kinds of retail outlet of particular sizes, and where to locate them within the airport terminal. It helps identify areas for improvement based on people's needs, which are assumed to pre-exist, and aims to help them achieve their goals by giving them choices.

However, focusing on the individual and his or her behaviour tends to treat "society" as an externality. Some theories of behaviour make efforts to conceptualize how the wider social world can shape an individual's choices. One example is to say that individual behaviour is shaped by social norms, but where the social norms come from in the first place is not investigated. In general, the behavioural approach stays analytically close to the individual. Further, the behavioural approach takes an etic perspective. This means the starting point is to look at individuals from outside their contexts, which is useful for making comparisons across large numbers of people, but less good at helping reveal the nuances associated with being a member of a social world.

Although shaped by research originating in consumer contexts, behaviour is increasingly on the agenda of policy-makers as something they want to change, sometimes called "nudge"[55]. Its appeal comes from the recognition that human beings are active participants in many of the issues that make up the contemporary world, such as obesity, chronic health conditions, and climate change. The premise for policy-makers is that if people's behaviours can be changed, then positive social impacts will be realized, reducing the load on public services. Efforts to change people's behaviours have lead to a proliferation of frameworks and initiatives, in part because the concepts associated with behaviour are amenable to quantitative analysis.

An alternative lens to understanding customer experience is based in anthropology and sociology. The socio-cultural approach also seeks to learn what an individual does, feels, knows and says. But it sees behaviour as an *outcome* of complex inter-relationships with other social actors situated within collective structures and practices. While a behavioural approach asks what people do, the socio-cultural approach asks what it means for them and how and why that is so. It describes attitudes, feelings, cognitive models, and motivations, but looks at how these exist within wider structures of signification. In contrast to the etic perspective of behaviourism, to understand the meanings of an experience requires an emic or insider perspective. Its starting point is the people who are participants in a social world, viewed from inside that world, rather than importing conceptual categories from outside. While a behavioural approach sees people as existing in a context, the socio-cultural approach sees them as actively *co-constituting* the context.

For example, thinking again about the airport, a socio-cultural approach might look at what it is like to be someone waiting for a flight, and what kinds of spaces airports and planes are. It might recognize that, for most passengers, air travel is a paradox. It offers a kind of freedom, which is accompanied by giving up autonomy as people have to remain in their seats, wait for long periods, follow instructions or behave in particular ways. This perspective might suggest that shopping and consumption activities may distract people from the autonomy paradox. They have the freedom to fly or shop (assuming they have funds and a passport from the right country), but with this comes relinquishing freedom at the airport and on the plane.

A socio-cultural analysis is different from one based on behaviour. It generates opportunities to think differently about what goes on, or could go on, at an airport or on a flight. In the case of the Virgin Upper Class service, the airline captured for business passengers some of the enjoyment associated with the early days of air passenger travel, masking the paradox by changing the meaning of business class flying. Other opportunities include rethinking the social context of strangers being close to one another at airports or on a flight. One example that addresses this is KLM's Meet and Seat service[56]. This allows passengers to find out about other people on the same flight who are also members of Linked In or Facebook, and pick a seat next to them. This service acknowledges the unique, temporary social world that exists on a flight and gives people an opportunity to engage in new ways with this social world or continue ignoring it if they prefer.

This discussion of the distinctions between two major research traditions has exaggerated their differences in order to simplify them, and is summarized in Table 3[57]. The behavioural approach focuses on people's choices, motivations and attitudes, and the barriers and drivers that shape what they do, think, feel and say. The socio-cultural approach looks at how these doings and sayings are constituted, resulting in particular kinds of significance for people. The behavioural approach looks at people's activities from outside the world they exist within, whereas the socio-cultural lens tries to understand people's experiences from inside their world and recognizes their participation in constituting it. The behavioural approach's unit of analysis is the individual who is also a member of society, whereas the unit of analysis in the socio-cultural approach is society, which is made up of many different kinds of participant. The former offers a functional approach in which experience is something that can be commoditized and improved on, whereas the latter highlights possibly surprising and uncomfortable insights about meaning, which can trigger opportunities for innovation.

Behaviour lens	Socio-cultural lens
Focus on individuals	Focus on people as carriers of practices
Experience is shaped by choices and attitudes, drivers and barriers	Experience as an outcome of a dynamic mixture of elements
People and their activities exist in a context	People and their activities co-produce the context
Humans have agency	Agency is distributed
People have choices	People make decisions resulting from their situated activities and participation in a practice
Etic – viewed from outside people's worlds	Emic – viewed from inside people's worlds

Table 3 Distinctions between a behaviour lens and a socio-cultural lens on experience

Breakdowns that open things up

To develop a better understanding of why the socio-cultural approach is particularly relevant to people designing innovative services, it's useful to explore the question of what service ecosystems are made up of. The starting point for socio-cultural research is to discover what the world is made up of from the point of view of people within it, rather than assuming that managers' or researchers' current models of it are right.

The work of philosopher Martin Heidegger has become a resource for many of the researchers trying to understand what goes on as people interact with technologies and other aspects of organizations. Two software researchers, Terry Winograd and Fernando Flores, presented a version of Heidegger's ideas that has shaped many later developments[58]. They explain how Heidegger was grappling with two incompatible ways of looking at the world, that persist today. This dualism goes as follows: either (a) the objective physical world is the primary reality; or (b) the subjective stance of a person's thoughts and feelings is the primary reality. Heidegger's philosophy challenges this dualism. He says that neither view is right: it is impossible for the objective world to exist without subjective experience of it.

A famous example Heidegger gives is someone using a hammer; the hammer becomes invisible and *ready-to-hand*, when they are doing hammering. The person takes the hammer for granted, until the moment when something goes wrong and there is some kind of breakdown in his or her reality. At that moment, the hammer becomes visible as an object, or, in Heidegger's terminology, it becomes *present-at-hand*. No longer providing functionality, the equipment comes more clearly into view and the person is prompted into a more deliberate mode of action.

Winograd and Flores compared a computer system to Heidegger's hammer. The hybrid comprising the software, devices and user activity is taken for granted until there is a breakdown. This means that a breakdown is not a problem to be smoothed over. Instead, it's an opportunity:

> "A breakdown is not a negative situation to be avoided, but a situation of non-obviousness, in which the recognition that something is missing leads to unconcealing (generating through our declarations) some aspect of the network of tools we are engaged in using."[59]

Or in other words, when something doesn't work, it reveals assumptions about what the user thought would or should be there, which is valuable information organizations can use as they try to identify opportunities for innovation, not just for finding problems to be fixed.

Heidegger's concept of breakdown invites people creating innovation ecosystems to pay close attention to what happens when things go wrong. When there is a breakdown, this brings things that were non-obvious into view – they become present-at-hand. Using Heidegger's concept of breakdown offers organizations a chance to get closer to the worlds of users, customers, employees and stakeholders and locate them, *from*

3 Behaving and experiencing

inside their worlds. Finding out what was taken for granted and what the analysis of breakdown revealed is missing is a starting point for innovation, not just for improvement. When breakdowns reveal the innovation ecosystem around a user and the activities he or she is involved in, this surfaces opportunities for creating changes to the configuration, a key service innovation capability.

Experiencing practice

Sociologists and anthropologists have developed various theories of what the world is made up of. Of particular relevance to designing innovative services is the socio-cultural concept of practice. Theories of practice start with the recognition that ways of doing things, routinized behaviours or habits, are arrangements of various inter-connected elements. These elements include physical and mental activities, materials and infrastructure, background knowledge and know-how, states of emotion and symbolic structures and meanings.

One way to understand practice is to consider how showering has changed, a topic considered by social scientist Elizabeth Shove, as part of her research into energy use. In many countries in the Global North, it is now common to shower once or sometimes twice a day.

> "For many this has become such a normal routine that it is socially and physically uncomfortable to wash any less often. This has not always been so. Less than a generation ago, quite other habits were equally firmly in place."[60]

A practice orientation highlights that it was not inevitable that people started showering more often, for longer, and in bigger, more powerful showers. Instead, it is possible to give an account of how showering changed as a result of technological innovation, as showering moved from communal bathing to individual homes, along with reliable domestic water supplies and instant hot water; combined with changing ways of thinking about the body and cleanliness and associations between showering, freshness and invigoration; combined with associations of immediacy and convenience in a time-pressed, fast-changing world[61]. The practice lens suggests that the repeated ways of doing and knowing how to do showering keeps the habit of showering going. But that does not mean showering is fixed. Disruptions within and between the elements of practice can result in new configurations becoming stable. For Shove, social practices – that is, habits and routines that become the regular way of doing things – are the dynamic mix of elements shown in Table 4.

> "Social practices, like driving or cycling to work, taking a daily shower, cooking and eating dinner … all involve the act of integration of elements … [such as] materials, objects, infrastructures, forms of competence and know how, images and meanings … practices are made up of all these three elements. So, cycling to work everyday or having a daily shower involves the integration of meanings, and skills and materials."[62]

In short, practices are the combination of *stories* (meaning, images), *skills* (know-how) and *stuff* (objects, infrastructures)[63].

What this offers to people designing innovative services is a conceptual framework that identifies the dynamic combination of elements involved in configuring a new innovation ecosystem, shaping new kinds of value-in-use. Embedded in a socio-cultural approach, the practice lens acknowledges the social meanings afforded as people experience services and their active participation in creating a context. It offers a holistic picture that provides a way to explain how routinized ways of doing things become the norm, which may yet change. The mixture of elements involved helps explain why it is hard to change behaviours. If existing habits and routines are the dynamic result of stories and meanings, skills and know-how, and stuff and infrastructure, then varying one of these in isolation may not result in persistent change.

Element	Definition
Stories	What things mean, the images and stories associated with doing something
Skills	The know-how, procedures and competences
Stuff	The digital and material objects and infrastructures that are part of something happening

Table 4 Elements of practice (adapted from Shove and Pantzar 2005[64]).

Several organizations using the socio-cultural approach have tried to render the concepts of experience and practice graspable, to help teams designing products and services[65]. For example, the consultancies Doblin and E-lab, which hired mixed teams of anthropologists, designers and technologists, developed the AEIOU framework shown in Table 5, which shows a mixture of elements that they saw as defining human experience. Their version of human activity and experience shares conceptual roots with Shove's work, but operationalizes this for use when designing. The AEIOU framework shares the core concepts of practice of story, skills and stuff, but breaks up the conceptual world – in which users, consumers or employees exist – into elements that are more amenable to designers of services and products. Researchers and designers use these categories when writing notes during fieldwork, or looking at video footage of what people do. Researchers then review and cluster the observations they make, with the aim of finding higher-level themes and patterns, which become the conceptual framework shaping the "thing" they are designing.

3 Behaving and experiencing

Element	Definition
Actions	Goal directed sets of actions – things people want to accomplish
Environments	The character and function of the spaces where things take place
Interactions	Between a person and someone or something else; the building blocks of activities; special or routine
Objects	Building blocks of the environment, sometimes put to complex or unintended uses, changing their function, meaning and context
Users	Consumers – people providing behaviours, preferences and needs

Table 5 AEIOU framework: Elements of experience (adapted from Wasson 2000[66]).

There are many other such frameworks that try to make the concepts of experience or practice accessible, not just as something to be analyzed, but as something to be shaped in the design of innovative services. Before turning to how the concepts discussed here open up the service innovation capabilities introduced in the previous chapter, it is worth taking a detour to explore some of the other terminology often used by people designing services.

Shortcuts for understanding experience

With the take-up of customer experience within new product development and service operations has come a new vocabulary that people use to demonstrate that they are deeply focused on people's experiences. Although these terms have some currency, on closer inspection these shortcuts are confusing. Further, they carry with them some implications that need to be thought about.

The first shortcut is the concept of being *human-centred*. Some design consultancies have introduced this term as a distinction to what is supposedly the alternative – being technology-centred or organization-centred. The first problem with this is that it is very two-dimensional, as if the people advocating being human-centred are the good guys, whereas everyone else will ignore the needs or goals of human users and customers. When design consultancies present the concept of being human-centred to marketing specialists or operations managers, it suggests that the latter's work is not human-centred.

There is an important issue at stake here. In many organizations there is uncertainty about who is best able to represent users' or customers' perspectives and the right ways to do this. Marketing practitioners have developed numerous ways to research customers – from surveys, focus groups, Net Promoter Scores, to "voice of the customer" programmes. The field of operations management has developed methods that try to identify quality from the perspective of customers, and use that to drive the design of processes and operations. The version of being human-centred that focuses on users and how they think and feel, rather than seeing the hybrid in which a person exists in relation to wider social practices, offers a limited picture of the world. What a practice perspective offers instead is a way to link human experiences with organizational activities and wider social and cultural patterns. It recognizes the habits and routines that people are part of. The practice lens emphasizes how having a (human) experience is located, specific, contingent and tied up with the other (non-human) things such as infrastructures, processes and technologies.

The second shortcut found in much discussion about customer experiences is the idea of *empathy*. In a study about empathy in management consultancy and in design consultancy, my colleague and I discovered there were several different versions of empathy[67]. One version is when someone imagines putting themselves into the position of another person, or ascribes to the other person his or her own feelings or likely actions if in the other's place. A second version relates to someone's ability to work out what is going on in the other's mind, or refers to a shared emotional response to a situation – for example, feeling fear or excitement from imagining being in that situation.

While trying to understand what it would be like in someone else's situation is a powerful driver for action, it comes with some implications. Some people get so caught up in their own emotional response as they imagine someone else's situation – "I feel your pain" – or their own projections – "This is what I'd

do" – that they downplay the particularities of the other person's world. So instead of bringing into view the other person's reality, this kind of empathy privileges the experience and perspective of the person being empathetic.

A second complication is how empathy is deployed as having some kind of truth. In contrast, research traditions that try to understand practices from inside users' worlds acknowledge there is only ever a partial view, and that researchers bring biases into representing other people's realities. So although being empathetic can on the surface offer a seductive and quick way in to understanding people's experiences, it is not neutral and does not necessarily reveal what's really going on. Instead, researching and accounting for people's behaviours, experiences and practices develops the organizational capability of understanding value-in-use.

3 Behaving and experiencing

Implications for service innovation

Drawing these discussions together leads to a shift, towards seeing users' practices as what organizations are involved in co-creating by combining resources into new innovation ecosystems. This means that people involved in service innovation are designing something that is complex, dynamic, messy, forever incomplete and never fully graspable. To summarize, the behavioural perspective focuses on how people's choices are shaped by attitudes, drivers and barriers that are seen to exist outside the contexts people are in. The practice perspective is attentive to how new ways of doing things take shape and become routine, seeing them as dynamic combinations of stories, skills and stuff that together produce the context and the behaviours. Both perspectives open up the service innovation capabilities discussed in Chapter 2.

Firstly, the concepts introduced in this chapter offer different lenses to understand how value is experienced and created through the participation of users, customers, and others within an innovation ecosystem, as things unfold in people's lives over time. Together, these lenses offer a deep understanding of value-in-use. Knowing whether a new configuration aims to amplify existing practices, or will try to create new ones, gives designers of innovative services a handle on the object they are designing. It also prompts recognition of their limitations in intentionally designing practices and the pathways laid down by existing infrastructures and embedded processes.

Secondly, instead of seeing customers or users as having pre-existing needs, a service innovation perspective recognises capacities as assets that emerge from, and can be re-mixed into, a new innovation ecosystem. People's knowledge, skills and resources, as well as technological or material assets such as databases, buildings and open spaces, are all examples of such capacities. Understanding these capacities through the lens of practice highlights the complexity of what is involved in bringing new innovation ecosystems into being. For example, a practice orientation provides a holistic picture of what's involved in creating a service that links people who want to rent out their cars when they are not using them to other people. Crafting that service, as RelayRides has done, involves dynamically mixing up *stories* (convenience, low risk, getting value from an asset that will otherwise sit there, impacting on climate change), *skills* (car owners' abilities to become entrepreneurial and engage with drivers, and drivers' abilities to drive unfamiliar cars) and *stuff* (web services to sign up and book cars, legal mechanisms to insure drivers and cars, social mechanisms to create trust).

Thirdly, an orientation to practices opens up a different perspective on what's required to innovate. Instead of thinking of a new service as (mostly) a business opportunity or technological object, realizing that a new service involves new behaviours and practices changes the idea of what is being created, and the time frames over which things take place. This has implications for the service innovation of launching clumsy solutions to learn. If launching a new service or venture results in new behaviours, experiences and practices, then the organizations involved need to put in place ways of assessing the expectations of what will or might happen and what can be learned as things take place over time.

Finally, during a service innovation process, a project team's abilities and expertise to develop concepts and knowledge, and to work inside and outside of the organization's boundaries, can be seen as a collective practice. What team members do, say and know in the skilful application of their knowledge and expertise, what this means to them, and the organizational routines and habits they are part of are not fixed, predetermined or given. This has implications for the service innovation capability that requires moving between concepts and knowledge, and inside and outside organizations. The lens of practice draws attention to the way things currently are in a project team, what comes with the current ways of doing things, and how things could be different.

Case 5 Changing nurses' care-giving practices at Kaiser Permanente

Kaiser Permanente is a US-based healthcare provider with 8.9 million members and 37 medical centres. Looking to improve its customer experience and to save money, in 2003 the company established an internal innovation consultancy[78] team with the help of innovation consultancy IDEO[69]. The brief was to explore the impact a human-centred design approach could have, focusing on the care experience of patients, and the work experience of staff. The team includes designers, researchers and operations specialists. Since its inception, the internal innovation consultancy has tackled issues across care provision, including pain management, administering medication, and the journey home for mother and baby after delivery.

An early project looked at the handover of patient information between nurses starting and finishing their shifts, at four hospitals. During handovers, which happened three times every 24 hours, patients described the unit they were on as a ghost town[70]. From interviewing staff, the innovation team learned that nurses were exchanging information in a quiet backroom or creating audio recordings of each patient's status, as part of the handovers. A quiet space meant nurses could talk without disrupting patients or being interrupted, and recordings ensured there was a record to refer to. However, in practice this meant that nurses spent a significant period of their shift away from patients.

Patients felt isolated, and there was opacity about decisions being made about their care. Further, knowledge exchange was not systematic and sometimes key information was lost.

In response to these insights, the team developed a process called Nurse Knowledge Exchange (NKE), in which the handover between nurses happened at the bedside of the patient, with the discussion being captured visually on the wall next to a patient's bed, supported by new digital systems. These changes made the patient's involvement in their own care more meaningful and offered a more efficient way of creating a record of important information. Having tested the approach and analyzed the outcomes, the service redesign was spread across the 37 medical centres.

Five years later, the issue of shift handovers resurfaced in a new project looking at how to increase nurses' time with patients. The innovation consultancy revisited their earlier work, thinking NKE had solved a large part of the problem. However, on further investigation, the team found that take-up of NKE was variable[71]. Some units were struggling to persuade nurses to exchange information at bedsides, whilst others had taken up the approach and had made improvements to it. They found that for some staff, not doing handovers at bedsides resulted from immediate priorities such as a new patient being assigned to them, or a patient in pain.

However, this did not explain the wide variation in take-up.

The team concluded that not complying with the NKE scheme came down to how staff felt about the redesign. Many staff believed it wouldn't make a difference to patients' experiences. Others were not comfortable doing handovers at patients' bedsides, feeling that they were on stage, performing for the benefit of patients. In short, the service redesign resulting from applying the principles of human-centred design thinking had not resulted in significant behaviour change.

In response, the innovation consultancy initiated a new process. Inspired by stories and observations around the disruptions and interruptions that occurred during shift change, they focused on creating solutions that better supported nursing staff at shift handovers. The team then prepared a roll-out of the new service design, NKE Plus. The redesign established a standardized round for nurses' last hour on shift, and created pre-shift assignments to help units prepare for oncoming shifts[72]. It coordinated roles to minimize disruptions during handovers, and developed new ways to engage patients in their rooms and improve patients' safety.

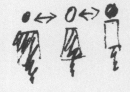

But to their surprise, as the innovation consultancy prepared to roll out NKE Plus with presentations, training and role play, they experienced push-back

and criticism. Although clinical staff were actively involved in creating NKE Plus, and communications and training materials included their video testimonials, other staff were not persuaded. Faced with this, the innovation consultancy turned to the field of change management to help them understand what was going on. They learned they had to help staff understand the reasons behind the changes and engage with their purposes.

In response, the innovation consultancy developed an intensive, three-week "soft-start" roll out that left the design of the solution open and created ways for staff to explore and connect with the issue of handovers. Instead of explaining to staff why they should adopt the new behaviours, they elicited stories and opinions from nurses. They let units tailor solutions to fit in with their particular activities, and established a strong shared purpose.

The innovation consultancy team also created ways for care teams to experience issues from the perspective of an outsider. For example, they developed observation guides to point staff to problems within the current system that had been uncovered from earlier research, and shared interview cards with questions to ask their peers and patients regarding key issues. Through these activities, nurses became co-researchers who were now enrolled in hearing and sharing stories that

Case 5 (continued) Changing nurses' care-giving practices at Kaiser Permanente

underpinned the service redesign, which as a result was more meaningful to them. Further, rather than presenting a finished design and training people in it, the innovation consultancy supported units to finalize their own service designs in relation to the key goals of NKE Plus, which were patient safety and quality patient engagement time. During the go-live phase, staff and patient engagement continued, with devices such as boards in hallways tracking and sharing indicators of progress[73].

After seven months, data showed that in units where the soft-start implementation had been used, nurses were now going into patients' rooms and actively engaging patients in conversation during the shift-change handover 100% of the time. In contrast, in units where the original approach was used, these indicators were 76% (going into patients' rooms at handover) and 60% (engaging patients in handovers)[74]. The team concluded that they were able to meet their goals of increasing the amount of time nurses spent with patients and keeping patients safe, by combining change management with design thinking[75].

The case demonstrates what's involved in innovating in an existing service to improve patients' experiences, which requires changing staff behaviours embedded in organizational cultures. Rolling out a new process based on a redesign required

changing staff routines, involving the stories, skills and stuff of social-cultural practices. Although not everyone can be involved in early stage research, the innovation team found it needed to create ways to involve staff as co-participants so they could connect their own purposes to the project goals, engage with understanding the problem from different perspectives, reflect on their own behaviours and habits, and understand the wider implications of change.

Case 6 Changing behaviours through amplifying positive deviance in Danish prisons

Service innovation involves creating new configurations of actors resulting in new kinds of value-in-use. Viewed through a socio-cultural lens, such innovation involves modifying or creating new practices, as people behave differently, tied up with technologies, policies and infrastructures. But as anyone who has tried to change their eating habits knows, modifying the ways things are done is complex, messy and tied to deep-seated, unspoken collective meanings.

One approach to changing behaviours is known as positive deviance[76] (PD) in the fields of community development and social change. This is the idea that rather than experts driving change from outside of a context, a more successful way to support change is by identifying people within a community who follow uncommon, beneficial practices and, consequently, experience better outcomes than those neighbours or colleagues who share similar risks or face similar challenges, but don't follow such uncommon, beneficial practices. The term comes from researchers, Jerry and Monique Sternin[77], who lived in Vietnam in the 1990s, where two-thirds of children under the age of five suffered from malnutrition. The goal of their work was to address the well-established issue that nutritional gains from feeding programmes tapered off when such projects ended[78].

The Sternins undertook a study to find out what some local families in an area of Vietnam were doing differently. They identified poor families whose children managed to avoid malnutrition without access to any special resources. The researchers called them positive deviants – positive, because they were having a beneficial impact on their children's lives, and deviants, because they engaged in practices most other people were not engaging in. The challenge was then how to spread these positive practices.

With local people, the Sternins designed a small project in which other families were asked to try out the habits of the positive deviants, alongside them, such as foraging for crabs and vegetables, feeding their children more frequently and in the company of other children, and washing their hands before eating. Before starting the project, the parents weighed their children and plotted their weights on growth charts. Able to see the impact on their children over two weeks, the other families were then convinced of the benefits. Many of these families then carried on with the new behaviours. Later studies showed that these children remained healthy over subsequent years[79]. Simplified as local wisdom trumping external expertise, the positive deviance approach is based on two key moves. First, it involves identifying individuals with better outcomes than their peers (positive deviants);

3 Behaving and experiencing

Case 6 (continued) Changing behaviours through amplifying positive deviance in Danish prisons

and secondly, enabling communities to adopt the behaviours that explain the improved outcome.

The positive deviance approach has been explored in other settings. Examples include the Danish prison service and commercial organizations such as Hewlett Packard, which have also adopted the approach[80]. Although the Danish prison system is associated with low rates of recidivism among offenders, it has significant HR issues such as high levels of stress, harassment and burnout among officers[81]. Evidence of these issues includes an average rate of absenteeism of more than one month per year, and an average retirement age of 48[82]. To address what seemed intractable problems, Lars Thuesen of the Danish Prison and Probation Service introduced and developed a positive deviance approach in maximum security facilities[83].

Having initially set up a project as a collective inquiry into absenteeism – a concern of the central prison service – Thuesen and colleagues discovered that staff were more concerned with the risk of violent incidents, improving communication and tackling issues related to gangs. Launching their PD approach, the project team began by asking if there were officers who had good, professional relationships with inmates.

They found several unusual behaviours among members of staff who did have good relations with inmates. For example, deviants did not follow the usual conventions when admitting new inmates to the prison. Instead of sitting down to enter data into a computer with prisoners sitting across the desk, one officer took new inmates on a tour around the facility and engaged them in a conversation. Another example was how an officer responded promptly when inmates rang a bell to call an officer to their cells, jangled her keys to alert them that she was on her way, and knocked and opened the door gently before entering the cell. As a result of these projects, prisoners under their supervision behaved differently, as evidenced by fewer violent threats and greater enrolment in treatment programmes.

Part of the study involved understanding the differences between these officers and other staff members. One finding was higher levels of involvement in social activities outside of the workplace, such as volunteering and sports clubs. As a result of these and other behaviours, these officers were better equipped to deal with the challenges of working inside a prison[84].

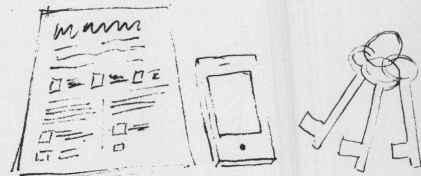

Having identified positive deviant behaviours, the researchers trained internal positive deviance facilitators and created a bottom-up knowledge sharing process. A senior manager commented:

> "The challenge was for us to understand that the employees are the ones with the sustainable solutions. This implies fundamentally new roles, relationships and wider boundaries between staff and managers. And managers need to learn to give up control, stop executing, having answers to every question and taking all the decisions. We need to facilitate processes and let go of our authoritative power. That is the difficult part." [85]

Outcomes of the PD approach included reduced absenteeism among officers, reduced staff stress and burnout, and improved relations between inmates, guards, and social workers. Improved relationships between inmates and staff, based on mutual respect, made programmes to support prisoner re-socialization after release more effective.

Reflecting on five years of implementing the approach in the prison service, Thuesen and collaborator Mark Munger identified five key ingredients for success. The first step involved re-defining the challenge as a community-driven problem rather than a managerial one. Second was letting the community discover the "whats" and the "hows" of the potential solutions that already existed. Third involved relationship-building among community members as a driver for behavioural change. Fourth saw senior managers shifting to roles as facilitators. The fifth step involved combining internal and external change leadership to work towards resilience.

In short, positive deviance challenged the accepted wisdom about how sustainable behaviour change in prisons happens. Instead of consulting experts, appointing champions of change, and importing best practice proven to work elsewhere, it involved identifying positive deviants and bringing their ways of going about things into the mainstream. It is based on identifying assets, rather than deficits. Further, it involved looking broadly at the network of actors involved, rather than staying close to protagonists or the usual suspects[86]. Within the context of service innovation, this approach sees those people with deviant ways of doing things that lead to desired outcomes as a resource.

3 Behaving and experiencing

Method 4: Mapping the user experience

Time involved	Preparation, 15 minutes
	Using the method, 60 minutes
Associated capabilities	Understand value as created in practice
	Increase the variance/bring in new actors
Methods to use before or after this one	Method 5 Creating a persona/storyworld
	Method 10 Telling stories

What you'll need

Masking tape, Post-it notes, Blu-Tack, marker pens

A flipchart

A facilitator to guide the teams

A documenter to capture the results

key question

'What is someone's experience of his or her interactions with an issue, organization or service over time?'

Purpose

Using this method helps a team understand holistically the interactions with a service or organization from the perspective of a user, customer, stakeholder or employee. It helps clarify what the experience is made up of, for that individual, allowing the team to identify important patterns and pain points. You can use this method and the template to describe existing experiences, or to describe future experiences.

Outcomes

This activity gives participants a shared sense of something they usually consider in parts. Thinking about someone's experience of an organization or service over time gives a holistic view of the diverse interactions and touchpoints involved. It also reveals important pain points and gaps that can become opportunities for improvement or innovation. Repeating the exercise for different user segments brings into view differences in process and outcome for particular groups.

Tip

Prompt participants to provide lots of detail, however apparently mundane or unimportant. What is obvious to one person may provoke valuable insights in another.

Preparation

Customize the template to the context you are in. You might want to select a single set of interactions during one visit to a store, a whole customer lifecycle or someone's journey through a public service. It may be important to pull out specific channels through which a user interacts with an organization and its partners, people and resources.

How to do it

Capture ideas. Introduce your adapted user experience template for the issue, organization or service you are working on. Ask people to pick one user, customer, employee or stakeholder and imagine this person in as much detail as possible (preferably via Method 5). Then ask them to use the template to describe the most important steps in detail of the person's journey on a large piece of paper or on the wall, working in small groups. In a simple workshop you might produce two such journey maps – one for a dream user/customer and one for a nightmare user/customer. If you have defined user segments, you can produce journey maps for each of these.

Maintain a strong focus on the person's activities and their interactions with touchpoints during the journey, and describe things in the user's terms. If data is available from research, then share this and invite people to use it. If not, use team members' knowledge to create a rich, holistic picture of a specific user (segment) interacting with the organization or service over time.

Share and tell. If you have created different versions, ask people to share their journeys with the group. Review where the pain points or critical incidents were for users. Where might people drop out or give up? What kinds of knowledge, skill or resources do people have which are part of how they experience an issue or journey through a service?

Reflect. If several experiences have been mapped, what is shared across them? How do pain points and gaps get handled by operations, customer service, research or marketing teams? Discuss how users' capacities, and their practical and emotional responses, are captured and made use of or ignored by organizations. What workarounds do people have when things go wrong?

Synthesize. Consider whether the research that currently goes on captures people's experiences of an issue or with the service or organization over time. Should more research be done to capture experiences for specific segments? Or for people not currently being served?

continued...

3 Behaving and experiencing

Mapping the user experience

Adapt this to describe someone's experience as they interact with an issue, service or organization over time

Whose experience is this? Time ▶	Find out about it	Decide to engage	First interaction with or use of the service	Later interactions	Ending/closing
What the person does, intends, knows, says, feels…					
Touchpoints and devices the person interacts with – eg website, apps…					
Where the interactions happen…					
How it **feels**					
Other people involved – eg service staff, family and friends, bystanders…					
Why the user is interacting with the service…					
What using it means for the person…					
Issues in how things are					
Opportunities How they could be different					

Example

Steve's experience of volunteering

Steve-24	Find out	Commit	Training/prep.	Volunteering	Ending
🯅	Hears from a friend who is volunteering	Attends a 2 hour intro session	Attends a weekend training session	Does the volunteering	Attends a feedback session
Touchpoints	Looks online, asks friends Looks at posters in library and community venues	Fills in application form ▢ Q&A with volunteer co-ordinator	Meets others being trained as well as other volunteers Receives manual & guidelines ▢	Expenses form ▢ Access to member by phone 📞	Feedback form ▢ Reference ▢
Why?	Wants to do something meaningful, wants to build experience, & do something he feels equipped to do	Signs up to move things on but still unsure of implications	Builds confidence, understands monitoring & support process	It's now real but Steve is not confident he's doing the right things. The service gives him backup	Opportunities for self-reflection, and to confirm that he volunteered.
Issues	How to really understand what's involved	Concerns about being able to hop on/off as things change. Likely to be put off	Long gap between app. and training to check references	Has lots of questions but is aware co-ordinator doesn't have much time to talk	How to handle assessment & disciplinary & safety issues
Opportunities	Access to volunteer stories	Better signposting to things he can do & will enjoy	Access to existing volunteers early on to hear stories	Provide continued mutual peer support between volunteers & mentors	How to articulate impact.

3 Behaving and experiencing

Method 5 : Creating a persona/storyworld

Time involved	Preparation, 30 minutes
	Using the method, 60 minutes
Associated capabilities	Understand value as created in practice
	Increase the variance/bring in new actors
Methods to use before or after this one	Method 4 Mapping the user experience
	Method 6 Segmenting by meaning

What you'll need

Masking tape, Post-it notes, Blu-Tack, marker pens

A flipchart

A facilitator to guide the teams

A documenter to capture the results

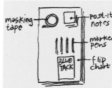

key question

'What is someone's world made up of?'

Purpose

This method helps a group understand the world holistically from the perspective of a user, customer, stakeholder or employee. It helps clarify what his or her world is made up of, allowing the team to share knowledge and identify important patterns.

Outcomes

Gives a team a richer, more rounded picture of individuals they are thinking about in relation to an issue or service. Allows a team to combine data from different sources with their own associations and imaginations. Gives shape to composite characters that provide a focus for other methods.

Preparation

Engage with colleagues who specialize in research to clarify what is known, and what isn't known, about target users, customers, employees or stakeholders (select as required). If you can, make this information available to participants before and in the workshop. Adapt the template to what matters to your issue or organization.

Tip

While facilitating, encourage participants to write down their ideas, getting things out of their heads that might be obvious to them, to share with others.

How to do it

Capture ideas. Invite people to look at your adapted persona template. Ask them to use this format and fill in the detail of the boxes on a large piece of paper, in any order. If data is available from research, then share this and invite people to refer to it. If not, use participants' knowledge, or their imaginations, to create rich, holistic pictures of specific people.

Share and tell. Ask people to share their personas with colleagues.

Reflect. Consider as a group how "real" these people feel. Do you need to add anything to the template structure to capture something important about people's worlds or about their interactions with other people or organizations? Discuss whether users are presented as having needs and/or capacities. If so, what kinds of knowledge, skills or resources do they have? If you have quantitative data about users or customers, how do these personas compare with your data?

Iterate. Invite teams to edit or refine their personas based on feedback from others.

Repeat. Create more personas following the same method. Participants may find it slightly odd at first to jump from person to person, but this can open up their sense of creativity as they begin to bring into view different people you work with or aim to serve.

Synthesize. Stick up all the personas together on the wall. Together, discuss if this feels like an accurate mixture of the people you work with or want to serve. Are there common characteristics? Does anything surprise you? Are there important things missing – for example, have you considered children, older people, people from different cultural, ethnic or national backgrounds, levels of income, or at different life stages? Pick a small set of personas that exemplifies the different profiles of users or customers. Refine these.

Reflection. Does the research you currently have access to help you understand people holistically? How are ventures and services designed right now in relation to the complexity of people's worlds? How might services be different if they were more closely targeted at personas that summarize a segment?

3 Behaving and experiencing

Creating a persona/storyworld

Use this to describe someone in their world

The backstory

My family, study and work background…

Current situation

My name is…My age is…I live in…with…
How and where I spend my time…My work
and income…

Beliefs about change

How I think about the future…

Key insights

Capacities and resources

I can easily…I can't easily…My skills
are…because…

Goals and values

The future I want is…because

Issues and challenges

Workarounds

Strong ties with…

People, places and organizations

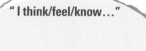

" I think/feel/know…"

Devices and technologies

Things I have with or around me (eg car,
TV, mobile phone)…because…

Relationships with organizations

Formal/informal…occasional/frequent

Weak ties with…

People, places and organizations

Example

Volunteer persona/storyworld

Backstory
She graduated from university BA Media Studies 1 year ago, huge debts, not sure what direction to take, working as shop assistant but considering caring/healthcare

Workarounds
To move on to career next step
- Researching tim-banking & volunteering sites
- Applying for jobs as media assistant
- Thinking of MA study but it's expensive

Beliefs about change
I know I have to make things happen myself but I'm not sure where to start

Insights
- Got some time now, but may not want to volunteer for more than a year
- Tech/phone/camera TV skills to connect with friends & music + going out
- Not used to older people's company

Goals & values
I want to do something meaningful

 TERRI
age 23

Strong ties
Friends, own family, sports club

Weak ties
Where she lives, it's just temporary, not much contact with older people

"I don't know what I have to give an older person, but I can see volunteering might give me experiences that might help me find work"

Devices/tech
smart phone, PAYG tariff, Facebook, Instagram, WhatsApp, Spotify

Organisations
Not many organisational connections, not much work experience, but has university networks.

4 Exploring and analyzing

snapshot

— Problem finding, problem setting, deciding on a research approach, and making interpretations to understand an issue in more depth are habits organizations can practise.

— Big data reveals large-scale patterns about behaviours.

— Thick data helps make sense of patterns by explaining the meanings and identities that shape and are shaped by people's behaviours and collective cultural practices.

— Open data initiatives introduce new actors and new capacities into service ecosystems.

IN 2013 THE UK GOVERNMENT DIGITAL SERVICE began an experiment on the web page that thanked people who had just purchased a car tax disc online, a service visited by 2 million people a month[87]. The aim was to see if people who had completed that transaction would sign up for organ donation. Working with colleagues in the government's behavioural insights team and the national organ donation service, the team tried out eight different page designs. The most basic page design simply said "Thank you" and, below, "Please join the NHS Organ Donor Register", which linked to that online registration process. Another version declared a social norm, "Every day thousands of people who see this page decide to register". Another variant introduced the idea of loss: "Three people die every day because there are not enough organ donors". Others included a picture of a group of smiling people alongside the text, or a logo. Another variant asked, "If you needed an organ transplant, would you have one? If so please help others". These variants were seen by more than a million people over five weeks.

The most successful version (based on actual donor registrations) was the latter, which linked organ donation with fairness and reciprocity. The team estimated that this version will lead to an extra 96,000 donor registrations a year, when compared to the original invitation to sign up. This is an example of big data – access to large numbers of digital transactions (here, click-throughs and sign-ups), opportunities to conduct quick experiments, and the ability to offer people options that result in changes in behaviour.

But what's missing in this story are the reasons why more people responded to a call to action based on fairness and reciprocity. This is the deeper, holistic "why" that has traditionally been the territory of ethnographic research based in anthropology and sociology, which aims to understand human life and experience, discussed in the previous chapter. In short, service innovation requires understanding what people do, as well as why they do it, and it is the combination of big data and ethnographic data that enables this.

This chapter discusses aspects of research that have seen a transformation in the past decade, of particular relevance to people designing innovative services. It presents the emerging tension between big (mostly quantitative) data and ethnographic qualitative data, and then shows how these approaches can be fruitfully combined to support capabilities for service innovation. The chapter also reviews the implications of open and personal data for designing innovative services, in which individuals and organizations, including public bodies and governments, make available their data for others to use.

Two case studies reveal some of the important questions that face managers. The first case study shows how consultancy ReD Associates helped toy manufacturer Lego work out what its business was really about. The second tells the story of a creative research project for a consumer goods manufacturer by consultancy Actant. It demonstrates how exploratory design research based on a socio-cultural approach generated novel concepts that were situated within, and responsive to, people's everyday habits at home in the evening.

The chapter is followed by three methods. Method 6 shows how to use a socio-cultural approach to understand the meanings that exist in people's worlds, to segment target users or customers. Method 7 shows how to combine drivers of change and socio-cultural changes to identify opportunities. Method 8 helps teams articulate the issue that is a trigger for a project and links it to a solution. These methods should not replace research by specialists, but can be used to generate snapshots of analysis at an early stage of a project. Using them can reveal how issues, users' worlds and opportunities are framed, which has a massive effect during the fuzzy front end of an innovation process.

Kicking off research

The first chapter highlighted how innovation proceeds through the creation of new concepts alongside the generation of new knowledge. Both of these processes are required for service innovation. A concept is neither true nor false. In contrast, the creation of knowledge happens through research: the structured set of activities that produces understanding that other people agree has validity. This section outlines some of the key stages involved in undertaking

research and presents new ways of looking at research for service innovation.

Problem finding and problem setting. In many organizations and projects, problem finding and setting is barely attended to. The logic is understandable. Problems are everywhere, and pressing. Action needs to be taken. People should get on with finding solutions. Some problems have champions who are able to pull together resources, which result in an issue being addressed. Other kinds of issue do not find or generate a public that makes the issue something that has to be attended to. The point here is that problem setting is a collective process. Problems do not pre-exist, waiting for someone to trip over them or pay attention to them. Rather, through collective activities, problems are brought into being[88]. They are framed through social processes that make some things matter more than others, that privilege some people's perspectives above those of others, and that box things up in ways that are recognizable to the people who find the resources required to take action. So problem setting results in particular paths being followed, which is why pausing at the beginning of a project, to analyze an issue, and consider how it is being framed, based on kinds of evidence and in dialogue with different stakeholders, is an important step.

Deciding on a research approach. Most textbooks on research start off by saying there is no right way to do research. But in practice, people carry with them a "right" way and are rarely able to consider alternatives. So for engineers in technology firms, for example, research is a formalized activity which involves being systematic about aims, expected outcomes, timeframes, and ways of determining validity and reproducibility. In contrast, people working within creative design and arts traditions, wanting to understand an issue relating to a place or group of people, might leave the studio and go and take photos as a way in to doing research, without having thought about the research question they are trying to answer. These days, many of us start research by searching online, which we imagine will give us a feel for the topic we want to understand. Deciding on an approach is therefore not self-evident or neutral. It carries with it assumptions about what is valid as knowledge and how to go about creating it.

Interpretation and analysis. Within different research traditions, how data are made sense of is handled very differently. For example in research traditions based in the physical sciences, analysts are considered to be outside the process of interpretation in order to maintain objectivity: "The data speaks for itself" and the world exists "out there". In contrast, within traditions called interpretive research, the active role that a researcher plays in organizing, interpreting and communicating findings is recognized. So this tradition has developed reflexivity that prompts researchers to make explicit how their own backgrounds, locatedness and biases will in some way determine research findings. In the former, research is objective and data are found. In the latter, research is constructivist and data are created.

Turning now to developments that are reshaping the research landscape provides a way to rethink how knowledge can be created for service innovation. The differences between the orientations towards research described above play out here. But it is the combination of big data and ethnographic analysis that supports the organizational capabilities needed for designing innovative services. Further, the development of open data platforms and organizational commitments to share data present opportunities to increase the variance of the actors involved in doing research.

How big data is reconfiguring research

The term big data emerged over the early part of the 21st century, as computer hardware and software capacities were invested in – and deployed in – a wide range of contexts. Analyzing big data sets used to require supercomputers, but advances in processing power and connections between computers mean that large data sets can now be analyzed on desktop machines. Instead of seeing this as an inevitable development, it's worth stepping back to note the configuration of actors involved in the development of big data as a phenomenon.

Firstly, there are hardware vendors, which invested in building storage capacity and connections between devices so that server "farms" in several locations can host software used by people from all over the world. Then there are the software developers, which have created new software that uses algorithms to analyze or "mine" data, identify patterns, and bring insights to

4 Exploring and analyzing

the attention of software users. A third kind of actor in the big data ecosystem is consultancies, which help client organizations harness data analysis with the intention of achieving business goals – for example, by developing better knowledge about customers, reducing the cost of serving customers or being able to cross-sell more effectively.

Some of the other related developments include the growing numbers of networked devices, including consumer smartphones and tablet computers that can connect to the "cloud". This involves software storage located on remote servers, often outside an organization's boundaries and sometimes located within countries that do not conform to international law – although the use of the term cloud suggests the data is nowhere at all. Another development is the sensors that gather data, such as the locations of FedEx trucks, or data from devices embedded in people's bodies sent wirelessly to clinical service providers, to devices in the home such as the smoke detectors developed by Nest. This internet of things, and the associated platforms and software capacities, is tied up with narratives about connectivity, immediacy and transparency. Big data is not simply about there being lots of data, but about data of different kinds being brought together in new ways, often for the first time.

Finally, there are the emerging businesses that depend on having access to large numbers of datasets, and the ability to connect data of different kinds. For example, the personal genetics testing company 23andMe offers services based on people undertaking genetic tests, and providing complementary data such as family history. This is based on the premise that provided with such information, people will better manage their own health. According to its founder

Anne Wojcicki, the company's goal is to attract many millions of customers, in order to be able to identify patterns across them[89].

Even this brief overview shows that big data is not simply one thing, but is interconnected to other developments, both technological and commercial. Together, these developments respond to and shape emergent consumer and organizational behaviours. What the term big data does highlight, however, is the massive scale at which organizations can now routinely collect, store, and do things with data, which the next section goes on to explore in more detail.

Creating patterns from big data

The technology usage associated with big data can create new opportunities for organizations, in particular those that are oriented towards innovating in service in the sense of reconfiguring capacities into new kinds of innovation ecosystem. However, as with other matters, it is not the case that bigger is automatically better. More data does not on its own produce better analysis, improve decision-making or lead to innovation. But big data as currently constituted does have several distinctive features, which present opportunities for service innovation.

Many data points. Big data is about scale and combination – the possibility of gathering and organizing vast amounts of data about operations, orders, sales, customer and employee behaviour, organizational processes, and contextual factors in the environment. The embedding of sensors into objects connected to the internet (the internet of things), combined with massive distributed storage capacity (the cloud), and the possibility of accessing software to do things with that data (software as a service) results in opportunities to gather massive amounts of data, of different kinds, from many different locations and make it available for many different uses. Examples are how customers engage with an organization after purchase, helping understand what value-in-use looks like for users in the contexts in which they are engaging with a product, service or organizational function. Some organizations have turned ordinary objects that are part of their supply chain into opportunities for data capture through using RFID tags. Organizations that have captured customers' mobile phone numbers are able to communicate with them wherever they are, enabling data-gathering that extends the relationship into their day-to-day lives and beyond the immediate service.

(Near) Real time data gathering. Digital technologies enable gathering data in near real time. Real time data helps organizations find out things that are happening on the ground in sales, operations, customer service facilities, users' lives and contexts of use. Depending on the kind of operation an organization offers, "real time" can exist within quite different time horizons, from just now to the past hour to the past week or longer. For example, organizations are using big data to identify patterns about demand in order to better prepare to meet it. Power consumption is often a significant expense for providers of data centres, and a fast-growing part of global energy demand, but most managers lack a detailed view of energy consumption patterns. Manufacturers have developed sensors that monitor power use, employing software that balances computing loads and eliminates the need for under-used servers and storage devices[90].

Behavioural analysis. Big data supports gathering data about customer and employee interactions with services and organizational functions. Examples of direct customer activity can include contact with call centres, via phone calls, and web chat, email or social media. Direct customer activity can include service-specific behaviours such as whether users take up opportunities to supply information such as meter readings for a utility company serving homes, or tracking activity in users' accounts in financial services, or analyzing car bookings for a rental firm. There are also opportunities to gather indirect data and identify patterns from things like usage of devices, accessing resources, times when things happen and where they happen, search terms on a website, pages viewed, or micro-activities such as key presses and mouse clicks. Some organizations trawl publicly-available social media to do sentiment analyses about how users posting messages or updates are feeling about something.

Revealing (visual) patterns. Software enables large datasets to be analyzed by algorithms. But software is not able to make people read faster, or increase their ability to take in and process data. So one of the concurrent developments associated with big data is the growing importance of data visualization. Cognitive scientists have shown that data visualization helps free up people's mental resources, by allowing researchers to use their working memory to identify patterns and make interferences[91]. Big data in digital form can be optimized to support people's cognitive capacities to spot visual connections and emergent trends.

Together, these features of big data help reveal the configuring and reconfiguring of multi-actor innovation ecosystems over time. Big data reveals patterns

4 Exploring and analyzing

about users', customers' or employees' behaviours, capacities and usage, based on evidence from many sources, gathered in near real time. However, although at scale, big data can never offer a full picture of what is going on within an innovation ecosystem or in people's day-to-day lives. As the discussion of research issues earlier showed, problem setting, deciding on a research approach and making interpretations emphasize how data-gathering is embedded in organizational routines about how to do research.

In the case of big data, some of the issues associated with it are how it devolves interpretation to software algorithms. It relies on sensors and software that can suit particular kinds of digital data, which configures the research agenda in particular ways. For example, Twitter and Facebook offer limited archiving and search functions. Because it's very hard to get older data from these sources, this skews research using this data to focusing on things in the present or in the immediate past such as tracking reactions to something that has just happened[92].

Further, although it can track usage (what people do) it does not necessarily illuminate why they do particular things. And the ethical considerations that are part of any research project take a particular form in the application of big data. For example, if a retailer learns from analyzing customer purchases that a family has started buying nappies, suggesting there is a new baby, and sends the family coupons for beer based on an assumption there is a beer-drinking family member who is staying at home more because of the baby, this

may be seen as smart consumer targeting rather than surveillance, interference or a public health matter. But other variants of this basic algorithm are more worrying because of the speed, scale and pervasiveness of data-driven targeting. A second development in the research landscape helps address some of these issues.

How ethnographic data is reconfiguring research

Another important change is the growing importance of ethnographic approaches used by organizations as part of strategy and innovation, organizational change, and marketing. The previous chapter gave a brief history of how socio-cultural perspectives became important in technology and other firms. Accompanying this has been increasing use of these perspectives in understanding consumption – not just as consumer "behaviour", but the social and cultural conditions and meanings through which people and organizations come into relation with one another. This section clarifies what this perspective offers, and shows how it contributes something distinctive, and complementary, to big data approaches.

There is a growing community of researchers and practitioners involved in using ethnographic approaches in organizations. Associated with the annual Ethnographic Praxis in Industry conference, blogs such as Ethnography Matters, and mailing lists such as anthro-design[93], this professional community is made up of people who typically have backgrounds in anthropology or sociology. Writers such as Grant McCracken[94], Melissa Cefkin[95], and Christian Madsbjerg and Mikkel Rasmussen[96] have helped explain how social and cultural research prompts organizations to think differently about what they are doing, and what they might do. This section offers a snapshot of recent debates to open up ways of thinking about doing social and cultural research in the context of service innovation.

Although there are many takes on ethnographic research, what they typically share is a commitment to understanding a context or site from the perspective of people within it. Secondly, ethnographic research proceeds through an iterative process of data-gathering and analysis. Tricia Wang is a cultural sociologist whose work focuses on how people use digital tools in their day-to-day lives. She introduced the term "thick data"[97], borrowed in this chapter, to illuminate the differences between data-gathering, which consists of large quantities of usually quantitative data; and the holistic, in-depth, qualitative research associated with ethnography. The term "thick" is a reference to one of the important founders of ethnography, Clifford Geertz, who outlined an influential vision of ethnographic research in his 1973 essay on thick description[98]. Wang explains:

> "Big data produces so much information that it needs something more to bridge and/or reveal knowledge gaps. That's why ethnographic work holds such enormous value in the era of big data...Big data reveals insights with a particular range of data points, while thick data reveals the social context of and connections between data points. Big data delivers numbers; thick data delivers stories. Big data relies on machine learning; thick data relies on human learning."[99]

Doing this kind of fieldwork has often been seen as expensive in terms of resources. People trained in academic ethnography are used to having extensive periods of time immersed in the field to do their research. In contrast, ethnography in organizational contexts has to produce useable but robust analyses in only a few weeks or days. Further, some argue that it requires people who have had extensive training in research methods and qualitative data analysis, typically gained from studying anthropology or sociology at graduate level. Consultancies such as ReD Associates or GFK rest their credentials on hiring such specialists. Others, in contrast, aim to open up ethnographically-informed research to non-specialists. For example, organizations promoting social innovation and public service innovation have published toolkits aimed at non-specialists that describe how to go about doing ethnographically-informed research[100].

Creating insights from thick data

If big data is about scale, real time data, and evidence about what people do, then – at first glance – thick data might seem to be the poor relation. Traditionally, it gathers data from few sites and few users, and creates data that may be from some weeks or months ago, and takes a relatively long time (weeks or months) to do this. However, this opposition neglects what is powerful about ethnographic approaches, and how,

4 Exploring and analyzing

combined with big data, they can provide a complementary analytical and interpretive capability.

Holistic orientation. Ethnographic analysis aims to understand the whole, while knowing what it offers can only ever offer a partial account. With its roots in ethnography, thick data is oriented towards identifying social practices, the usual way of doing things that are often assumed and unexamined. It involves grasping what goes on in a context from inside it. It surfaces many contributory details, including what people do, say, feel, know, the people and things they engage with, where things happen, and the shared social structures, stories and processes these activities are part of. Ethnographic approaches illuminate the differences between what people say they do, and what they actually do. One of the tensions in ethnography that skilled researchers find a way to address is the impossibility of there ever being "enough" data about the whole context, or the whole of a user's life, and the requirement to make sense of what data there is.

Collective interpretation. Thick data emphasizes the shared work of creating interpretations. The ethnographic foundations of thick data result in its value being about the interplay between research and analysis. Researchers construct insights through an iterative process, rather than following a two-stage process of doing fieldwork and then analysis. Thick data approaches pose interpretation as something many people can contribute to and as something that can open up questions for an organization. Firms such as Intel, Microsoft and Nokia use ethnographic approaches to illuminate and challenge assumptions about their core activities, employee cultures, and users and their worlds. For example, user experience research at Intel Labs has helped the chip-maker shift away from thinking of itself as a producer of technology, to being a firm that focuses on enabling people's lives through distributed technologies.[101]

Cultural meanings. Thick data is concerned with describing how a social world and the behaviours within it hang together. Ethnographic research takes as its object of study the worlds of people as they live and experience them through their own categories. Thick data approaches are adept for finding what people take for granted – the patterns and ways of thinking about a social world that are obvious to participants in a world. Like big data, thick data approaches are about describing behaviour, in the sense of what people do, know, say and feel. But the distinctive contribution of an ethnographic approach is to locate behaviours within an understanding of the socio-cultural patterns, structures and collective meanings that hold a service or organization together. For example, Indian innovation consultancy Quicksand undertook a multi-site study for the Bill & Melinda Gates Foundation about how the urban poor in India interact with spaces, services and communities in relation to hygiene and sanitation[102]. The research offered a holistic, rich picture of people's defecation and washing practices and the meanings these have. The resulting insights provided urban planners, public health promoters and policy-makers with resources to help them shape the design of facilities, and service and business models.

Inspiration not just analysis. Thick data offers insights into human experience and cultures – emblematic moments or nuggets of behaviour that exemplify a conundrum in its context. Here, complexity is rendered into something usable, but in a way that allows people to move towards changing the story. Researchers who work with both kinds of data typically emphasize how thick data helps capture the imagination of teams working on new product development and identifies opportunities for innovation. For example, Tracey Lovejoy, an ethnographer working at Microsoft, describes how a research team investigating organizational blindspots uncovered opportunities in new areas:

> "We were floored by how much truck drivers are on the cutting edge of communication technologies and strategies to stay connected wherever they are. We heard over and over that 'when you live your life on the road, connecting with the people you love is essential to maintaining relationships'."[103]

The researchers' assumptions about truck drivers were challenged as they explored the detailed ecosystems drivers built to stay connected. "These were not technology people – but they are driven to use technology in innovative and advanced ways to meet a critical need they have. Ethnography helps uncover these unexpected but invaluable uses of technology."[104]

Patterns from big data	Insights from thick data
What is happening?	What does it mean?
Numbers	Stories
Helps identify issues in the past and present	Helps inspire possibilities for the future
Reliability and generalizability	Credibility and transferability
Algorithms do the interpretation	Interpretation is a collective process
Shows a reality	Constructs a reality
Behavioural analysis – what people do and what drives this	Cultural analysis – how what people do is connected to social meanings
At a distance	Close in
Specific and focused	Open ended
Detailed	Holistic

Table 6 Differences between big data and thick data

Echoing the traditional tension between quantitative and qualitative research, big data and thick data might be considered to be incompatible. Table 6 summarizes some of the main differences. But recent advances in both fields have resulted in opportunities for organizations to combine these approaches, which is of particular value for service innovation. Before moving to look at these intersections, it is worth opening up a third development in research of relevance to people designing innovative services – open data.

Opportunities from open and personal data

When the G8 countries signed the Open Data Charter in 2013[105], this was a powerful signal that the trend towards transparency and openness in some areas of government and business is speeding up. The signatories agreed:

> "We, the G8, agree that open data are an untapped resource with huge potential to encourage the building of stronger, more interconnected societies that better meet the needs of our citizens and allow innovation and prosperity to flourish."[106]

Inspired by the open source software movement, the concept of "open" in open data means content, information or data that people are free to use, re-use and redistribute without any legal, technological or social restriction[107]. In the spirit of this vision, but conforming with conventional legislation around protecting IP rights, the G8 charter recognized the role open data can play in improving public services and governance and through stimulating growth through innovation in data-driven products and services. It has five principles, which are:

- Open data by default
- Quality and quantity
- Useable by all
- Releasing data for improved governance
- Releasing data for innovation.

By late 2013 more than 40 countries had initiatives in place to publish data produced by or for government for others to use and redistribute[108]. The World Wide Web Foundation's Open Data Index rates governments for their open data initiatives. In 2013 it ranked Sweden, Norway, United Kingdom, United States and New Zealand as the top five most open governments out of 81 countries[109]. The UK's open data service includes datasets created by UK public bodies for use by others, that cover things such as healthcare, live traffic data, social deprivation indices, water and air temperatures, flood levels, and government spending. More than 300 apps that use government datasets were listed on the data.gov.uk website in early 2014[110].

An example of using public data to shape service delivery comes from a study by Mastodon C, a big data start-up company, Open Health Care UK, a health technology start-up, and Ben Goldacre, a medical doctor and writer[111]. Over eight weeks, working with publicly available National Health Service (NHS) data, the team looked at the prescribing patterns in NHS primary care practices, focusing on a class of drugs called statins, used to prevent cardiovascular problems. Statins are expensive, but some are much more expensive than others: patented ones can cost 20 times more than generic versions[112]. As a result, the NHS guidelines are that unless doctors have good clinical reasons for choosing an alternative, they should prescribe a generic product in the first instance. However, on looking at patterns of prescribing by doctors across the whole of the UK, the study found much local variation in prescriptions. The researchers estimated that if every NHS doctor had prescribed cheap statins, the UK's drugs bill would have been more than £200m lower. The team, who first met at an NHS hack day, plans to repeat the exercise for other drugs and make the resulting analysis available to doctors and NHS managers[113].

The statins prescriptions example is about using open government data to improve accountabilities around public spending. Other initiatives involving open data aim to support new ventures and services based on open data, especially government data. For example, the Knight Foundation created a challenge in 2013 to spark new approaches to connect citizens and governments[114]. There were more than 800 entries to the competition via the OpenIDEO innovation platform, which were given feedback and refined and evaluated, resulting in seven winning projects that shared $3.2 million to develop their ideas, from public sector procurement, to small business support to community activism.

Alongside some governments' and NGOs' commitments to publishing open data, commercial organizations are engaging with open data. In a 2014 report, consultancy McKinsey saw opportunities in sectors ranging from oil and gas, transport, power, finance, consumer products and education, as well as healthcare[115]. The different roles included being suppliers of data at no charge to others; being aggregators, who combine data within their products and services, and charge others for these; and being developers and

enablers that help other organizations work more effectively with data. However, it is unclear as yet what the economic and business impact of the move to open data is[116].

One of the tensions shaping these developments is concerned with privacy, trust and access, especially when personal data are involved. Do the data created by individuals using products and services or in their interactions with organizations belong to them, or to the organizations, especially public sector ones? Do individuals trust organizations with their personal data? Can people access data that is directly connected to, by or about them? An example that brings this tension to life is the case of Hugo Campos. He describes himself on Twitter as "an e-patient on a quest for access to the data collected by my implantable cardiac defibrillator. Passionate about connected health"[117]. The device is there to monitor his heart rhythm and to prevent sudden cardiac arrest by delivering electric shocks. In the course of doing this, the device produces data that are not available to him but are accessed instead by the manufacturer Medtronic and by clinicians.

For Campos, these data streams are valuable as he believes they might help him manage his own care better. For example, Campos could track whether symptoms he experiences such as light-headedness or dizziness correlate to abnormal heart rhythms. While he consented to the company's data gathering, Campos was frustrated that he had no way of accessing the data or using it for himself[118]. Campos is one of a number of people who want access to personal data; others are campaigners and activists, and entrepreneurs creating a new market in personal data management services.

This brief overview of some of the potential issues associated with open and personal data reveals the increasing complexity of the research landscape. Organizations that think of the data created through people using products and services as a corporate resource, ignore how it is generated through the mutual interactions between the actors in a value constellation. Opening up data to others, as some governments have done, has the potential to enable other actors to find new uses for it by combining it with other resources.

Combining big, thick and open data for service innovation

Drawing these developments together leads to identifying several opportunities to strengthen the capabilities required for designing innovative services.

First, designing innovative services involves combining resources and capacities in new ways that co-create value. Actors in such ecosystems can be people, technologies, organizations, data (including open and personal data) and other organizational and personal resources and capacities. Big data enables accessing and analyzing data from many different actors and sites in the operating environment, from connected devices which are part of people's day-to-day personal

or professional practices, or those that are embedded in the built environment or in organizational supply chains, as well as databases and other digital resources. This plethora of data-gathering, combined with competences to analyze it at scale, and present it in visual formats that emphasize patterns, is a powerful resource for understanding what is happening in an innovation ecosystem. Complementing this capability, thick data provides ways to connect data patterns to people's lived experiences, to help make quantitative phenomena meaningful at the scale of people's interactions with organizations. Open data approaches involve combining other organizations' or individuals' data sets.

Second, designing innovative services requires being attentive to value-in-use, rather than focusing on the moment at which value is created through exchange, as in the goods-dominant logic. As the previous chapter showed, there are various lenses that shed light on what goes on when people engage with things in the practical encounters they have with the digital and material stuff of organizations. The big data approach that combines distributed data-gathering through connected devices and access to algorithmic analysis allows organizations to track behaviour in near real-time, demonstrating patterns in what people are doing and saying. The thick data approach makes sense of these behaviours by identifying the meanings behind the patterns, and the new identities that emerge through people's interactions with organizations and with one another. Personal data and open data on contextual factors such as the environment, transport or crime are additional resources that add depth to understanding value-in-use. Used in combination, big data and thick data help designers and managers of services understand what shapes value-in-use for different actors constituting innovation ecosystems, by identifying and making sense of patterns and developing insights about what is changing and why, leading to changes in how service experiences are configured and delivered.

Thirdly, designing innovative services involves launching clumsy solutions and learning from how they unfold in practice. Service innovators recognize not only that they will never get it right first time, but that they will never get it quite right ever. Launching new services requires creating fast feedback loops to allow managers and designers to respond by reconfiguring resources, relaunching and seeing what happens, and repeating the loop again. This is where big and thick data approaches are valuable. The distributed data-gathering, multiple data points, and analytical power of big data provide evidence of how things are unfolding in practice. The holistic, meaning-creating orientation of ethnographic thick data helps people designing innovative services work out what to pay attention to, and construct insights and frameworks to shape future iterations that will keep a service design team learning.

Fourthly, designing innovative services requires capabilities in increasing the variance and bringing new actors into an innovation ecosystem. The combination of big data and thick data provides ways to identify actors that might be potential candidates to combine into new configurations. Big data, especially when presented visually, presents anomalies and outliers that may signal an emerging pattern or, at the very least, prompt new or different questions about what is currently happening. Thick data approaches based in ethnography's attentiveness to the minutiae of everyday life, which typically goes unexamined, highlight unexpected or unlikely candidates for actors to combine into new hybrids, which may have gone unnoticed previously. An orientation to open data acknowledges the vast diversity of data sources, including government-generated data, which organizations can re-use and combine into services.

In conclusion, it is the combination of big data, ethnographic approaches and open data that supports designing innovative services. The speed, pervasiveness and scale of big data, combined with the depth and holistic framing of thick data, and the variety of open and personal data, support the capabilities for designing innovative services. Together they constitute different kinds of knowledge, provide ways to bridge the inside and outside of organizations, and are likely to require developing new competences when designing innovative services. But an innovation process requires the generation of new concepts as well as knowledge, which prompts a discussion of creativity, to which the next chapter turns.

4 Exploring and analyzing

Case 7 Using thick data about how children play to reframe business opportunities at LEGO

In 2013, LEGO achieved 10% growth in sales of Euro 3.4 billion, with a 9% rise in profits, and media reports suggested it was confident about the future[119]. Ten years earlier the outlook was very different. Although it was the fifth largest toy maker in the world in 2000, the company was in great difficulty. Its bright plastic bricks were well-loved, having been part of many children's lives since the company founder's design for combining bricks was patented in 1958. But in 2004, the company was losing $1 million a day[120]. How did it turn things around?

In 2004 the CEO, Kjeld Kirk Kristiansen, grandson of the company's founder, stepped down and former McKinsey consultant Joergen Vig Knudstorp was appointed in his place. Knudstorp appointed innovation and strategy consultancy ReD Associates[121] to help. Based in Copenhagen and New York, ReD Associates' approach borrows heavily from the humanities and the social sciences, particularly anthropology and sociology, as well as offering more traditional business analysis. Although the story of how LEGO changed its fortunes involves many contributing factors, the insights gained from developing a deep, socio-cultural understanding of its customers and their lives played a significant role. Asked about what was behind the turnaround, Knudstorp said: "Our development teams have been extremely good at reading kids, listening to kids, and really finding the kind of product expressions and concepts and ideas that bring us to the top of the children's wish list".[122]

What does this work of listening to and reading kids entail? ReD Associates co-founders Christian Madsbjerg and Mikkel Rasmussen[123] provide a detailed account of LEGO's approach. This shows how analyzing people's practices through fieldwork, interviews and analysis helps organizations (re)discover what underpins their organization and its relationships with customers and users. LEGO's learning journey shifted the company from asking, "How do we recapture market share?" to "What is play?"[124] On the journey, LEGO discovered that its core assumption that contemporary children wanted simple or digital toys, because they had less time to play, was wrong.

LEGO began a process to collect data about children's and families' lives, by embedding research teams in US and German cities and suburbs. Teams of researchers spent months studying children's play habits and paying close attention to contextual factors such as family relationships and environment. They went shopping with families, and interviewed experts. The researchers used a range of methods, including observation, interviews and photo diaries completed by research participants.

Through this they created a rich database of qualitative data that captured the worlds and habits of LEGO's customers and users of toys. Using software that helped code the unstructured data into themes, the team identified the most significant patterns in the data they had collected. Then researchers came together to discuss the patterns, and to explore similarities and differences in their observations. Together the team began the process of refining their observations down to the most significant insights.

For example, they looked at photos of children's bedrooms taken by participants in New Jersey and other wealthy areas of the US. These photos showed spotless and meticulously curated bedrooms, akin to images from interior design magazines. The researchers felt these photos must be staged. They did not capture the children's rooms during their everyday use. Instead, they showed how parents and carers wanted the children's lives to be. The ways the research participants managed these images represented a challenge to the researchers. How were they to understand the children's lives, if the data they had collected was crafted by people around them? However, rather than hindering the team, thinking about the careful management of these images by parents helped the researchers identify other behaviours they had witnessed.

Researchers had observed that children's lives were as carefully curated as their bedrooms. Their free time after school was full of activities intended to enrich their lives and foster the characteristics parents desired. The team saw that in addition to staging the photos, these parents were in effect "staging" their children's lives. As a result, the researchers started to see these children's experiences through the lens of French philosopher Michel Foucault's concept of the panopticon, in which all activities are subject to rigorous surveillance.

This point was further demonstrated by the widespread use of the acronym POS (parent over shoulder), which researchers observed in online gaming. The researchers began to see that play was providing a much needed way for children to carve out freedom and space in their lives. They saw that children hid things from parents, or were turning to virtual spaces and imaginary environments. This was a way of experiencing freedom and danger that might have previously been enacted through playing outside, or other activities no longer accessible to them.

During their analysis, the team also noticed that they had observed children reciting detailed information relating to play, whether it was memorizing statistics about an imaginary football team, or

Case 7 (continued) Using thick data about how children play to reframe business opportunities at LEGO

obsessively discussing high scores in computer games with one another. This behaviour pointed to the important role that games were providing in determining social hierarchy.

This insight is reflected in one of the most emblematic examples captured during the research. An 11-year-old German boy showed his most treasured possession to a researcher, who was surprised to discover the item was a pair of worn out trainers, instead of a shiny new toy or video game. From talking to the boy, the researcher learned that this pair of shoes was meaningful because it symbolized his mastery of a skateboard trick that brought him admiration among his peers.

This finding reinforced the team's theory about the role of play in hierarchy, but it also suggested a further role for play – that it was about mastering a specific skill over time. This contrasted with the starting assumption that contemporary children growing up in middle-class homes did not have much time. For LEGO, which had been concerned that it could not compete with the instant gratification provided by computer games, this insight was invaluable. It suggested that there was demand for complicated LEGO sets that required significant amounts of time and energy to complete.

Altogether, the LEGO research team developed four key insights – that children play:

- To "get oxygen", that is, escape parents' scrutiny
- To understand hierarchy
- To achieve mastery at a skill, and
- To socialize. [125]

These were simplified into four categories: under the radar, hierarchy, mastery, and social play. These categories helped LEGO revisit its initial assumption that children did not have time for play. Instead, the company began to reconnect with its core users: children who wanted to achieve mastery by playing with LEGO, and LEGO began to explore some of the other categories through innovation initiatives[126].

These insights – extracted from months of research and data gathering – demonstrate the role of thick description and analysis in helping organizations understand value-in-use and identify the actors, identities, meanings and habits involved in the worlds around a product. For LEGO, it resulted in a clearer focus on producing difficult toy sets that had previously been seen as a problem, but would in fact be seen as valued by children as a way to achieve mastery over time and gain social standing. It was this refocus that contributed to the firm's recovery.

Case 8 Playing with cultural probes to generate new concepts in fast-moving consumer goods

Manufacturers of fast-moving consumer goods (FMCG) are shaped by a goods-dominant logic. They design, produce and ship products in vast quantities. Their focus historically has been persuading people to buy things, not the usage that happens after purchase. As a result, they typically have highly developed marketing and communications functions, producing large amounts of quantitative data focusing on how people make purchase decisions. With access to detailed data provided by firms such as AC Nielsen, FMCG firms have increasingly accurate information about what mediates people's decisions to buy things. With the shift away from the idea of rational choice, marketing researchers increasingly began to see decisions to purchase goods as shaped by people's emotions and symbolic factors – what things mean to consumers.

Influenced by the lens of traditional marketing science, these organizations have a style of working which researchers Doug Holt and Douglas Cameron associate with "brand bureaucracies"[127]. Operating within a culture of standardization, FMGC firms do extensive research including concept testing and piloting before committing to a new product. A common framework in FMCG marketing teams is the benefit ladder. This requires articulating how any product concept has an emotional benefit to the consumer. For example, if consumer Cheryl buys a particular product to clean her toilet, she feels as though she's protecting her family and is therefore a much better mum.

This framing reduces the complexity of consumer practices by cutting out the contextual richness. This simplification means marketers neglect the value-in-use that emerges through the situated engagements people have with consumer products over time. However, some firms do explore socio-cultural approaches to understanding people's engagements with and use of products after purchase, as a starting point for innovation. Simon Blyth of UK-based design and innovation consultancy Actant explains:

> "Any innovation has to sit within an already existing set of social practices and cultural meanings. It has to both make reference to what's currently going on and bring about some kind of change or disruption. So we have to be able to map the 'now and normal' as well as imagine and prototype the 'new and innovative'".[128]

The projects Actant work on frequently emerge from a client identifying an issue by analyzing large data sets. For example, a client's brand might be under-performing within a specific consumer group. Actant helps clients locate their products within consumer practices and supports them to identify opportunities for innovation. Using methods drawn predominantly from interpretative social science and design research, Actant aims to bring

4 Exploring and analyzing

Case 8 (continued) Playing with cultural probes to generate new concepts in fast-moving consumer goods

clients closer to the complex and messy worlds of people. It helps them shift towards thinking about innovating in washing practices, for example, rather than washing powders. A project for an FMCG client, which aimed to generate new concepts for families at home in the evening, brings this to life.

The approach Actant took was to combine ethnographically-informed research and generative design research. The goal was to quickly generate new concepts through interactions with families in their homes. First Blyth trawled through the firm's quantitative and qualitative research. "Where I usually get hotspots and hunches from is narrative, qualitative research. The thing I am looking for is the context, the stories around the occasion – the rich picture of the consumption." After reviewing the existing research, Blyth clustered his notes into themes and generated around ten areas for further exploration. Together with the client, he reviewed these against the brand lens and they selected some to take forward.

Actant then customized two methods to understand evenings in family homes and the associated habits and meanings. Blyth added: "We went in with a particular idea of what evening means – that it's about families chilling out. What we learned was that evenings are associated with tight time

management. It's about being productive, and involves choices and dilemmas, not just chilling out."

The first method used wearable cameras to generate photos automatically. Actant recruited family members to wear cameras during the evening. They then accessed the photos that were taken, sorted through them, selected some, and went back to talk to the people about the events of the evening. This visual data offered a different way to approach accessing and interpreting the participants' practices at home in the evening.

The second method used was cultural probes[129]. This involves creating a small number of custom-made objects that people in the home environment were invited to use or play with. The cultural probes approach is about generating research insights and concepts by opening up conversations and seeing how people engage with objects that are not routine in their context. Blyth explains: "We developed 11 objects that we put in to five different households, which they engaged with and returned to us afterwards. We asked them to report back to us about their experiences of using them and creating stories with them". Each of the probes was associated with an opening hypothesis drawn from the research review.

A cultural probe to stimulate creating fictional stories about secrets

For example, one of the research aims was to find out more about people's secrets. The probe created for this was a paper cup with a photo of a couple at one end, connected by a piece of string to a USB microphone at the other end to record sound. Actant asked the families they worked with to choose an internal wall in their home and place the cup on it, and record audio. Blyth explains:

> "Our research hunch was that having private shared knowledge was one of the things we thought created intimacy amongst couples, and we wanted to explore this. We did not want people's actual secrets or to hear what their real neighbours did. We wanted fictional stories about this imaginary couple in the photo – what the participants imagined they would be talking about and their secrets."

After leaving the probe with people for several days, Actant then transcribed the audio pieces and analyzed them. Having summarized all the research outputs from the families, Actant developed seven concept areas, traceable back to the insights and to people's creative engagement with the probes. Actant spent a day with the client to share the findings and concept areas. In addition to sharing the 11 probes with the client, Actant created posters with observations (what they noticed about what people did or said) and insights (why that was happening). By the end of this study, the client had a set of concepts nearly ready to go into testing, grounded in the habits of people in their homes at evening time, and inspired by the ways they engaged with the cultural probes that might lead to new habits and meanings. The client also had research collateral in the form of stories, posters, objects, photos and video. Such objects are often displayed around managers' desks, embodying the practices being explored and the new ones that might be brought into being.

What this approach did was help the client to generate concept areas grounded in practice, through a quick piece of creative fieldwork. It produced a rich understanding of what goes on in family homes in the evening. But it also generated novel concepts that directly emerged from participants' responses to the objects they were invited to play with in their homes. As well as bringing into view existing practices among families at home in the evening, it resulted in concepts derived from people's activities in situ, which hinted at emergent or future practices and new kinds of value-in-use.

4 Exploring and analyzing

Method 6: Segmenting by meaning

Time involved	Using the method, 90 minutes
Associated capabilities	Understand value as created in practice Move between concepts and knowledge, and inside and outside organizations
Methods to use before or after this one	Method 5 Creating a persona/storyworld Method 7 Opportunity mapping

What you'll need

Blank sheets of paper, Post-it notes, marker pens

A flipchart

A facilitator to guide the teams

A documenter to capture the results

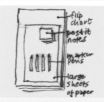

key question

'How can the similarities and differences between target users be made sense of?'

Purpose

If you do not have access to people trained in qualitative research, this method helps create a framework distinguishing between key users, customers, employees or stakeholders. The main idea is to divide up people based on understanding the meanings, identities and habits that shape – and are shaped by – interactions with actors in an innovation ecology.

Outcomes

Creates a framework that helps a team focus on the groups of people they aim to engage in a project or venture. Involves a diverse group in sense-making.

How to do it

Study the research findings. Make available to participants any research available about the experiences and perspectives of people affected by an issue or those engaging with a service or organization. Include qualitative and quantitative data. If there is no research available, use the user experience maps from Method 4 and personas created in Method 5.

Tip

Be open to being surprised by what surfaces. Forming an analysis is a creative activity.

Pull out themes. Invite people to jot down on sticky notes themes, ideas and categories that jump out at them as they read through and discuss the materials. These could be meanings, behaviours, specific acts, events, activities, strategies, practices or tactics, states of being, participation, relationships, conditions, constraints, consequences or settings where things happen. Participants might produce about 20–30 individual sticky notes each with a word or phrase that captures these.

Share themes. Invite people to share what they have noted down on the sticky notes. Organize these into affinity groups on a wall or on a flipchart by clustering together things that seem similar to participants. Together, build up the themes and then identify the ones that are most resonant for the current project.

Create a structure. Now select themes that the group finds most resonant relating to the groups of people connected to your issue or service. There are lots of different ways of making sense of the themes. There is more art than science to this.

The template suggests some different structures you can consider, but you can use others. You might find you are able to use a 2x2 matrix, or a 3x3 version. For example, you may find that some of the themes participants generated can be divided up in terms of intensity or scale – for example, more or less, or very or not very. Alternatively, it may be better to use different themes at each end of a single axis of a 2x2 matrix – for example, people are shifting from one kind of behaviour to a different kind of behaviour. An alternative way of creating a segmentation is to identify key themes and then define segments of people that have these variables in different combinations.

Decide on the best structure to use to divide up the different kinds of people you are focusing on, using the themes that have emerged through the collective sense-making process. You may need to try several different ways of doing this until you create a segmentation that makes sense to the group.

Review the segmentation. Now step back and see if the analysis you have created makes sense to participants in the group. One way to test it is to see if any of the personas you created in Method 5 fit within the segmentation. You can also test it by presenting it to other colleagues or partners. How does the analysis compare with previous ways of segmenting users or customers? What research would be useful to deepen the team's understanding of people involved in the issue, service or organization?

4 Exploring and analyzing

continued...

Segmenting by meaning

Use or adapt one of these structures to divide up particular segments based on themes derived from your discussing research findings

	Variable 1	Variable 2	Variable 3
Variable 4	A	B	C
Variable 5	D	E	F
Variable 6	G	H	I

	Variable 1	Variable 2
Variable 3	Segment A	Segment B
Variable 4	Segment C	Segment D

	Summary	Variable 1	Variable 2	Variable 3	Variable 4	Variable 5
Segment A						
Segment B						
Segment C						
Segment D						
Segment E						

Example

Possible segmentations

Volunteers

many connections,
lots of social capital & resilience

1 "Confident Carls" Low time/short commitment in a hurry to move on up	"Busy Brendas" **2** Organisers, active, generous over-committed
3 "Committed Katys" Want to give what they have – time – and build networks & skills	"Patient Peters" **4** Not so confident but want to keep active & connected

very early career

few connections,
not much social capital & resilience

Older people

deteriorating situation

early retired

few connec-tions

Segment A	Segment B

many connec-tions

stable situation

Method 7: Opportunity mapping

Time involved	Using the method, 60 minutes
Associated capabilities	Recombine capacities into new innovation ecosystems Move between concepts and knowledge, and inside and outside organizations
Methods to use before or after this one	Method 2 Visualizing drivers of change Method 8 Problem/proposition definition

What you'll need

Blank sheets of paper, marker pens

A flipchart

A facilitator to guide the teams

A documenter to photograph the results

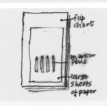

key question

'How can we make sense of changes and see them as opportunities?'

Purpose

This method prompts a team to crystallize its understanding of changing socio-cultural practices and behaviours, and other drivers of change over a specific time horizon. It produces a simplified framework that orders the team's current understandings and assumptions.

Outcomes

It brings into view the relationships between changing behaviours and other changes in the operating environment and involves a group in collective sense-making. It surfaces important points of agreement and disagreement among members of a team.

How to do it

Explore the shared issue. Introduce the issue you aim to address using your current research materials. If you have visualized drivers of change (Method 2) or created persona storyworlds (Method 5), have these available for people to explore and share. Ask people to share their perspectives on how change happens. Identify the time frame over which you are considering change.

Tip

Involve a diverse group of people in using this method – people who enjoy and are good at synthesizing, and those who do/are not. The latter may resist or struggle, but they need to participate in the sense-making to feel a shared responsibility for the concepts and activities that will later follow from it.

Identify key shifts in behaviours. Get people to review the research available about how people's behaviours are changing. These might not be existing users or customers but could be other groups of people. Aim to simplify these shifts into statements of the form "people's behaviours are changing from this" to "something else". Produce several of these pairs, and then together agree one or two that seem more important or relevant to the issue you are aiming to address. This will be for the y axis.

Identify a key driver of change. Now, ask people to share their views on what is changing in the wider operating environment over the relevant time horizon. Again, simplify some of the complex data or opinions you have into the form "the operating environment is changing from one situation" to "another situation". Again, produce several of these pairs, and ask participants to select one or two of them that are most important or relevant. This will be for the x axis.

Create the framework. Use the template to create a 2x2 matrix that combines some of these shifts in behaviour and socio-cultural practice, with something that is changing in the operating environment. This is more art than science and will involve considerable discussion among participants. You may require several iterations of creating frameworks to generate something that is meaningful to participants.

Explore the framework. Review how existing products, services and ventures map into the framework. For example, you may find that there are several organizations addressing two of the quadrants, but that one is quite empty. Explore how any potential solutions the team has come up with map onto the framework. It may be important to reject a framework and start this method from the beginning.

Synthesize. Review the framework. Articulate any key assumptions and where knowledge and data are lacking.

4 Exploring and analyzing

continued...

Opportunity mapping

Use this to identify opportunity spaces over a particular time horizon

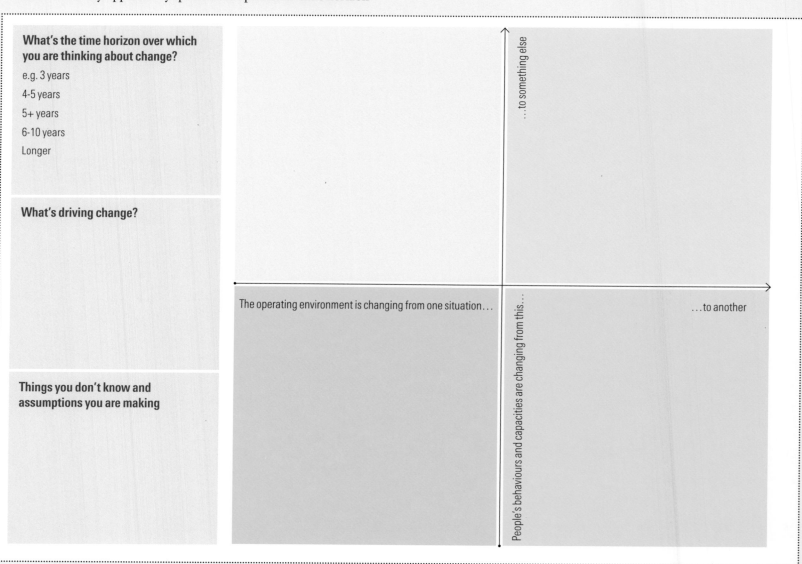

What's the time horizon over which you are thinking about change?

e.g. 3 years

4-5 years

5+ years

6-10 years

Longer

What's driving change?

Things you don't know and assumptions you are making

…to something else

The operating environment is changing from one situation…

People's behaviours and capacities are changing from this…

…to another

Example

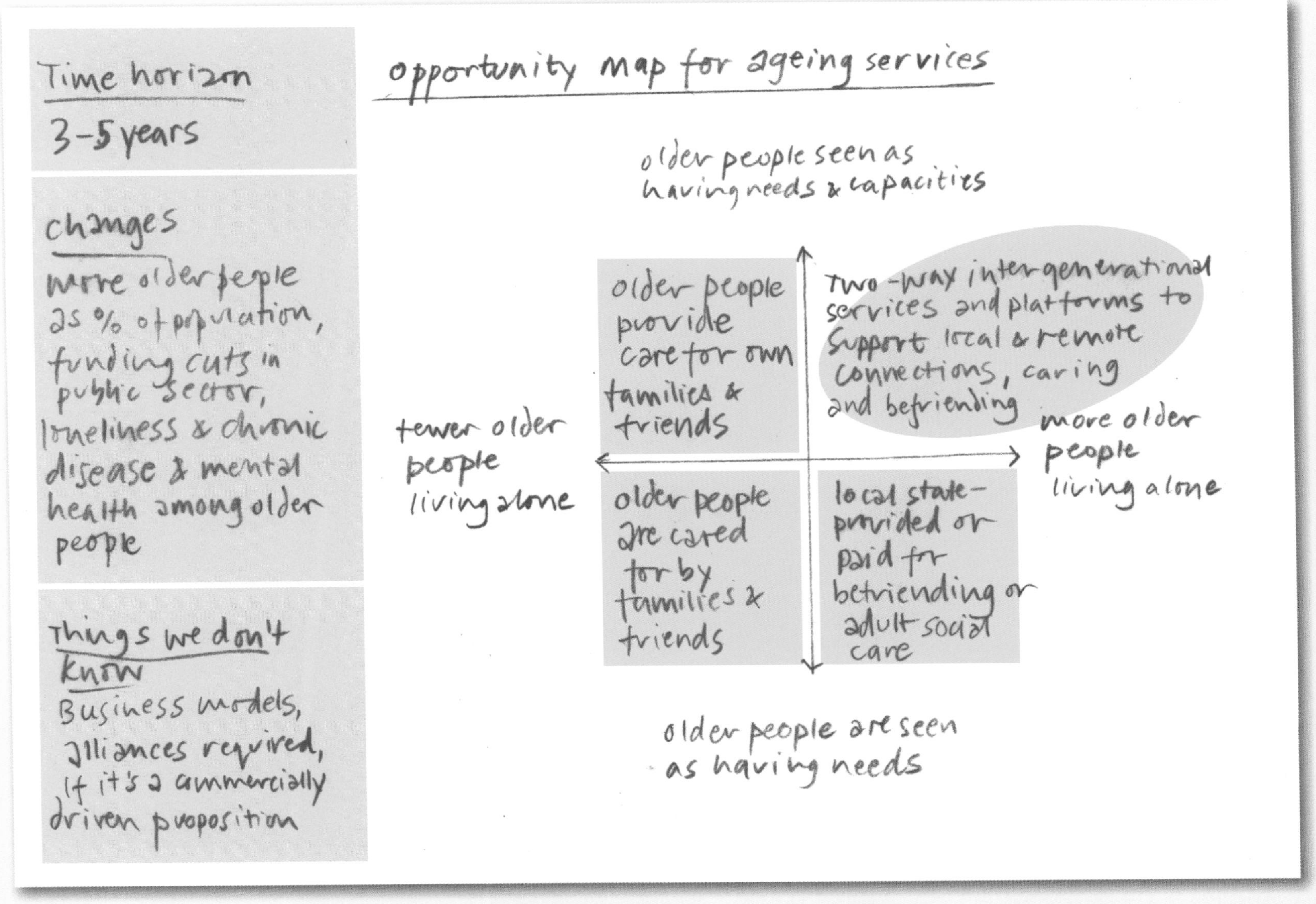

Time horizon
3-5 years

changes
more older people
as % of population,
funding cuts in
public sector,
loneliness & chronic
disease & mental
health among older
people

Things we don't
know
Business models,
alliances required,
If it's a commercially
driven proposition

opportunity map for ageing services

older people seen as
having needs & capacities

older people
provide
care for own
families &
friends

Two-way intergenerational
services and platforms to
support local & remote
connections, caring
and befriending

fewer older
people
living alone

more older
people
living alone

older people
are cared
for by
families &
friends

local state-
provided or
paid for
befriending or
adult social
care

older people are seen
as having needs

Method 8: Problem/proposition definition

Time involved	Using the method, 60 minutes
Associated capabilities	Understand value as created in practice Move between concepts and knowledge, and inside and outside organizations
Methods to use before or after this one	Method 7 Opportunity mapping Method 10 Telling stories

What you'll need

Blank sheets of paper, marker pens

A flipchart

A facilitator to guide the teams

A documenter to capture the results

key
question

'What is the issue and what is a possible solution?'

Purpose

This method prompts a team to clarify its understanding of an issue, reflect on how it is framed, clarify who it is an issue for, and explore how a possible solution relates to this problem and the impacts it might have.

Outcomes

Brings into view what the issue is represented to be and a possible solution to it at a particular moment in time. Prompts a team to link generating concepts for solutions, to representations of problems.

Tip

Use this method after solution concepts have been suggested, to clarify how they relate to the issues to which they are a proposed solution.

How to do it

Summarize problems and solutions. Ask people to work individually or in pairs to use the template to summarize their current understanding of the issue, and any current solution concepts. They should explore each possible issue/solution pairing on a new sheet of paper.

Share and tell. Ask people to share their issue analyses and possible solutions.

Discussion. Review the different problem/proposition pairs. Do all the solutions relate to the same issue, or are some of them solutions to different problems? Do the different versions suggest that participants agree on the key users and stakeholders and on the resources available? Do you have sufficient information at this stage to define the problem in ways that make sense to everyone relevant? What research could you do to clarify understanding of the issue for the different publics or stakeholders involved?

Do some of the solutions make you think about the problem in a new way? If you have people from different personal or professional backgrounds in the group, discuss how these backgrounds shape their understanding of the issue.

Is the issue being framed in ways that make sense to everyone? How could you reframe the issue?

End the exercise by agreeing on one or more versions of the problem/proposition statement.

continued...

Problem/proposition definition

Use this to define the issue and possible solutions

Proposition definition

It's a …
(kind of thing)

That is/has …
(characteristics)

Which results in …
(the change we want to take place)

User segments

Aimed at/co-created with…
(the target user segment(s))

Who want/need to…
(purposes, tasks)

And are able to…
(capacities)

And who benefit because…
(outcomes)

Problem/issue definition

Addressing the issue of…

Which is shaped by …
(social, economic, other factors)

For which we have evidence that shows that …
(research findings)

Which matter because …
(insights)

And which we are framing as a …
(kind of issue/opportunity)

Organizational/wider resources

Which is resourced and co-created by involving …
(organizational and other resources)

Resulting in…
(organizational and/or social outcomes)

Example

Problem / proprsition definition

The proposition
It's a service/platform that connects and supports older people & volunteers (young people + early retired) via befriending, tech support of home & trips out resulting in reduced loneliness...

...Aimed at
older people in stable situations but with not many meaningful connections

and
young people with time and with tech/phone skills who need some work experience to move towards employability

and
recently retired people who want to stay active & have a sense of purpose & build connections

...which is resourced by combining...
older people's groups, community groups, colleges

and Broadband providers, phone providers

and public sector providers - eg social workers, housing providers, employability enablers

Resulting in Reduced isolation, better mental health, reduced use of acute emergency services, lighter burden on carers/families, early warning of issues.

problem
. dealing with (i) the loneliness & isolation of older people with reduced or few meaningful connections and (ii) difficulties in establishing careers and work for young people with few connections/social capital

Because evidence shows loneliness is a significant factor in well being and mental health

Framing this as about inter-generational connections not just befriending older people and seeing them as having capacities, not just needs.

5 Inspiring and generating

snapshot

– *Creativity during designing innovative services is distinctive because service innovation concepts are multiple, temporal and involve many actors.*

– *Inventive habits for service innovation are:*
  · *Making the strange familiar and the familiar strange*
  · *Moving between excess and simplicity*
  · *Zooming in and zooming out*
  · *Connecting and disconnecting.*

– *These habits open up the tensions between the particular and the general.*

HERE'S A STORY THAT HAS BEEN AROUND FOR a decade or so: *The internet of things will present huge opportunities to tackle social, environmental and organizational challenges. Connecting billions of devices to the internet, and thus to one another, will create platforms for important service innovations.* In 2002 the interdisciplinary conference Doors of Perception asked, "What is the question to which the internet of things is the answer?"[130]. Over a decade later, it is still not clear what the answer to the internet of things question is. Despite billions of dollars of investment in the research and development of technological platforms, services and devices to support the internet of things, it's not yet clear how it will impact on people's lives.

Instead, the story that has become most closely associated with the internet of things is usually summarized in a sentence, here re-told by Intel[131]: *Imagine an automated message from home adding milk to the shopping list because the refrigerator recognized that the carton was almost empty.*[132] For a story to work requires making connections and meanings for and with audiences. The storytelling that excites us when we read great literature, watch a well-constructed and directed film, or hear a speaker talk from the heart, is that which joins up with our own anxieties about what it is to be human.

But the story about the internet-connected fridge ordering milk connects positively and negatively with people's anxieties about what it is to be human in a fast-changing, techno-scientific world. The story of the fridge makes the highly technological familiar, even banal. All that techno-science, and it's about ordering milk, not remote brain surgery, saving the world from climate change or improving children's health. But the intelligent fridge evokes the terrifying prospect of algorithms making (even more) decisions for people, perhaps harmless in the case of ordering milk, but more alarming when algorithms routinely make decisions that people used to think of as requiring judgement.

This story captures a challenge central to service innovation. Designing innovative services involves configuring actors and capacities within new value constellations. Value-in-use unfolds through actors' participation in the interweaving of stories, skills and stuff over time. So generating concepts for service innovation is about complex hybrids of actors and technologies. What does this mean for creativity?

There are three ways that generating service innovation concepts is different from coming up with new concepts within the goods-dominant logic. First, as the example of the connected fridge shows, a service innovation concept is not a singular entity. Instead, a service innovation concept is a nexus connecting a hybrid of actors. Without all the other bits of infrastructure and the practices of end users and other actors, the connected fridge cannot exist and the concept has no meaning. Second, the connected fridge is interwoven with socio-cultural practices that unfold over time. So service innovation concepts have a temporal dimension. Third – unlike in

5 Inspiring and generating

the goods-dominant logic, in which people inside organizations (or their consultants) come up with ideas for new offerings – service innovation involves distributed actors who have a stake in an innovation ecosystem, and who participate in generating value-in-use. Service innovation concepts are therefore multiple and temporal, and the creativity involved in generating them is distributed among many different participants. This makes creativity, in the context of designing innovative services, distinctive, and is what this chapter will explore, and what the next chapter on prototyping will add to.

Like others writing on innovation, I will draw on the approaches of creative practitioners. Artists, designers and performers have a special place in contemporary culture. They are recognized as being creative, even if what they do and produce is not well-understood or appreciated at the time. Descriptions of "design thinking" over the past decade have made the approaches of some designers accessible to managers aiming to generate and develop novel ideas[133]. Notwithstanding criticisms that much of designers' work reinforces existing unsustainable taste regimes and ways of doing things, even if they claim to be critical, the currency of such approaches remains high[134]. This chapter focuses on how the inventive habits of creative practitioners offer something distinctive and relevant to the challenge of generating service innovation concepts that are multiple, temporal and that result from distributed creativity.

First, I briefly visit the origins of contemporary art schools and the studio inquiries that enable particular kinds of creativity. Then I summarize what is distinctive about these practices as opening up the particular, at the same time as saying something general. I then identify four inventive habits of particular relevance to service innovation. These are: making the familiar strange and the strange familiar, moving between simplicity and excess, zooming in and zooming out, and connecting and disconnecting. I explore each of these in turn, using examples from contemporary practitioners' work to bring them to life. I then summarize what these four inventive habits do for people designing innovative services.

Following this, two cases highlight ways organizations use such inventive methods to go about service innovation. The first shows how developing Google Glass involved not just technological innovation, but also ways to bring into view the possible value-in-use the device could co-create with people using the new eyewear in their daily lives. The second case shares the ways a group of interaction designers and software developers involved in the Frugal Digital project developed service concepts for rural India through material and digital tinkering.

Two methods then make these ideas actionable for managers during the fuzzy front end of a service innovation process. Method 9 supports people – who are not skilled in creating visuals – to sketch, as a way of generating and sharing ideas. Method 10 structures a way of telling stories about new services that brings ideas to life in forms that can be explored and shared in organizational contexts.

What happens in studios

In his book *Why Art Cannot be Taught*[135], art historian James Elkins presents a history of the main ways art has been taught in Western Europe. Greek and Roman workshops taught crafts, but there was not a distinct category of people known as artists or designers. Medieval workshops enabled practitioners to develop expertise over long apprenticeships, which focused on learning skills and techniques and specified the forms and content that people could use. Later, the Renaissance saw the emergence of academies. In contrast to the formal established sites of learning associated with European universities, academies were often set up by groups of people, with a patron, who wanted to offer training in a particular style or approach. Building on these traditions, later academies set up during the Romantic period began to emphasize the individuality and freedom of students, rather than the visions and expertise of teachers.

What became important here was that teachers did not try to foist a uniform standard on each student.[136] Instead, art schools supported students to find their own ways of making art. The legacy of this commitment to fostering individuality and autonomy is still evident today in the design and art schools that share a backstory in such academies, rather than in universities. Later buttressed by the ideas of philosopher John Dewey, the theory of learning that became dominant was that students' interests, not teachers' preferences, should drive choices about what should be learned. Further, it was students' interests that began to drive what were the appropriate forms and content for making art. Through the emergence of studio-based learning, students' creativity became closely tied to replicating particular kinds of autonomy and individuality.

Today, what many art schools still share, according to Elkins, is a lack of a fixed or agreed curriculum for teaching art. There is no hierarchy of styles, no fixed sequence of courses, no coherent body of knowledge or unified theory of what art or design practice is. Despite this apparent lack of coherence, art schools continue to attract students, people sustain practices as working and exhibiting artists, and the institutions of art – such as museums, galleries, media, funding bodies and collectors – continue to seek and invest in new kinds of art. Thus, student-led studio practices play important roles in nurturing and developing the particular generative creativity associated with contemporary art schools in the Western tradition.

There is a close alignment between this way of teaching and some (but not all) design schools. Educational institutions such as Illinois Institute of Technology in Chicago, Politecnico di Milano and Central Saint Martins in London all offer teaching and learning experiences rooted in studio inquiries. These institutions are part of ecosystems that include individual practitioners, small design studios, big consultancies, in-house design teams and many other kinds of project and organization. Although the different design fields such as graphics, product design, interaction design, textiles, fashion and architecture have different concerns and drivers, their roots in the studio inquiries of art schools – sometimes simplified into "design thinking" – mean they have some shared habits which will now be explored.

Opening up the particular

The creative practices associated with studio inquiries have three attributes that make them good candidates for generating clumsy solutions at the early stages of generating service innovations. Firstly, they make things specific, but in these particulars constitute something about universal truths[137]. In art, this piece of metal is combined in *this* way with *this* piece of wood to produce *this* sculpture, which resists being subsumed under universal concepts. This pixel is coloured with *these* values for red, green and blue located next to another pixel coloured like *this*. This dancer moves *just so*. Some creative acts involve re-interpretation – think of the skills of theatre performers who do two shows a day. But the act of creating involves combining things in new ways that results in something specific, which alludes to but resists generalization. The new configuration or ordering of things might be just a sketch, but it serves to move things forward by fixing possibilities, right then and there.

Secondly, studio practices are inventive[138]. As a result of the tradition of art education described above, which lacks a unified theory of what art is or how to make it, many artists and designers become adept at developing their own structures and methods when they create new work, rather than applying the tried-and-tested approaches of others. When an inventive method is applied to a context or issue, it changes the situation by opening up the particular. It brings into existence new configurations of things that are partly a result of the creator's intent and skills, but also the contingent result of the capacities or properties

of materials or people in that context, as well as of chance and serendipity. Originality lies in the (re)configuring, rather than being a quality inherent in or tied to a particular object.

Thirdly, the new configurations that come into being through creative practice are not reducible to one of their elements in isolation. They are multiple, not singular. The sensuous material excesses of a sculpture by Anish Kapoor, for example, cannot be separated from a viewer's experience of it and the place in which he or she encounters it. The symbolic is inseparable from the material and the particularities of when, where and how someone engages with an artwork.

In short, when generating something novel, artists and designers don't simply apply a method from elsewhere and feel confident that they will get a certain kind of result. Instead, people working within the tradition of studio inquiries consider a particular situation or opportunity, develop a method to engage with it, and respond to the contingencies of what emerges through its application, which is likely to throw up unexpected results. With inventive methods, specificity is valued, opening up generalization but without being subsumed by it. The capacity to instantiate and open up something particular by bringing a new configuration into being makes it available for others. At the early stage of generating and exploring new innovation ecosystems and new kinds of value-in-use, using inventive methods helps open up the specific, showing something about what engaging with a new concept could be like.

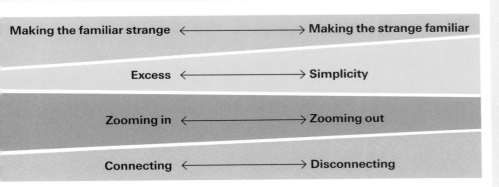

Making the familiar strange ⟷ Making the strange familiar

Excess ⟷ Simplicity

Zooming in ⟷ Zooming out

Connecting ⟷ Disconnecting

Figure 5 Four inventive habits for service innovation

The inventive habits of studio inquiries

There are four habits associated with the inventive practices of studio inquiries, which have particular relevance to service innovation. Each of these involves a tension between two extremes, as shown in Figure 5.

The first inventive habit relevant to service innovation involves exploring the tension between *making the familiar strange and making the strange familiar*. Think of the important works of modern and contemporary art, which often make the familiar strange. For example, Picasso's Cubist paintings from the early 20th century rejected conventional ways of representing the world. The subject of a Cubist painting is usually just about discernible. Figures and objects were fractured into many smaller components, and then reassembled to evoke those same figures or objects. In music, composer John Cage's composition 4'33" invites the audience to listen to apparently nothing for the duration of the title of the piece. It draws attention to the ambient noise in the environment in which the audience members find themselves, for 4 minutes and 33 seconds. Such artworks invite audiences to see or hear things that they no longer notice in new ways.

The opposite of making the familiar strange is making the strange familiar. It too is a common device associated with studio inquiries, and especially associated with design. Influential industrial designer Dieter Rams argues that good design makes a product understandable[139]. It has to create opportunities for someone using an object to recognize its possibilities – demonstrating sufficient novelty to draw someone in, but sufficient familiarity so that they know how to engage. When Thomas Edison developed electric lighting, he made sure that the new technological system he brought into being was familiar to customers used to gas lighting[140]. So for service innovation, shifting between the familiar and strange is productive. It enables seeing actors and capacities taken for granted in a new light; it also ensures that novelty is rendered accessible to people encountering it for the first time.

The second inventive habit associated with service innovation involves moving between *excess* and *simplicity*. Apple's products and software user interfaces are often said to be simple – intuitive and enjoyable for people (at least, for those who are familiar with Apple) to use with little visual clutter. Similarly, the international Red Dot design awards – covering product design to games to communications – include among the criteria the requirement that designs submitted for consideration are "thoroughly thought out and stripped of superfluous details".[141]

But simplicity is not a self-evident characteristic of good design or art. It is associated with the social and cultural movement of the early 20th century known as Modernism. This was a loose collection of ideas

5 Inspiring and generating

that came to dominate industrial manufacturing and architecture in Europe and North America, which aimed to reject history, and brought with it excitement about fast-moving modernity. This is the style associated with clean lines and a lack of ornamentation in the work of architects like Le Corbusier and Mies van der Rohe. The production and enjoyment of smooth surfaces and clean lines is not inevitable. It is tied to narratives about the future and associated with a particular influential cultural movement.

Further, what ends up as smooth and sparse usually has a messy backstory: a hidden excess of inspirations, concepts, sketches, and models that are associated with and dependent on creative practice. The purposelessness of art, identified over two centuries ago as one of its defining characteristics by the philosopher Immanuel Kant, creeps in here, shaping the studio inquiries through which concepts are generated. Creating what looks like simplicity involves generating and encountering excess. This can take the form of coming up with many ideas during a service innovation process, not just sticking with the first one that seems reasonable. Or it might take the form of a creative team going off topic as they resist instrumentalist rationality and revel in generating ideas that do not seem to have a purpose or relevance. This inventive habit supports service innovation. Service innovation comes as a result of apparently wasting resources on generating novel, but not useful, concepts. Further, achieving simplicity requires people who have developed a taste for things that look simple or that behave simply, even if they are not.

A third inventive habit is *zooming in and out* between the big picture and the detail. Matt Jones of the Google Creative Lab, an interaction designer who co-founded design consultancy Berg London (both discussed later), explains how exploring concepts at different scales at the early stage of a project helps clarify the nature of the concept being developed:

> "One thing that we talked about a lot in what we did at Berg was scale hopping…Right at the beginning of a project, you deliberately consider the tiniest detail and the biggest macro scale around the problem domain you are in. And try and scamper between the two of them, almost like tweening like an animator or like the Eameses in their film Power of 10, seeing the connecting tissue and the linkages at each scale. Doing that really quickly at the beginning of a project stood us in good stead."[142]

This inventive habit is also part of the work of professional service designers. In an ethnographic study of service designers at specialist consultancy livework, I found that one of the distinctive ways they did things involved paying attention to the apparently small details of a service, such as packaging or signage, as well as to the value proposition and business model in relation to which these touchpoints existed[143]. These designers seemed adept at moving fluidly between both positions. One moment they were discussing the detail of text on a webpage. A few minutes later they were taking apart the service model and who it created value for – not just staying close to the users' experiences of the service. There's a parallel here in studies by management researcher Rosabeth Moss Kanter[144], who proposes that good leaders have the ability to zoom in and out. Sticking with one perspective is limiting. Too close and you don't see how everything fits together. Too far out and you miss nuances. It is the willingness to move between these two positions that marks a creative approach relevant to service innovation that requires seeing both the whole, and the parts.

The fourth inventive habit relevant to service innovation is shifting between *connecting* and *disconnecting*. If creative practice involves assembling new kinds of configuration, this involves repeated efforts to move things forward, first by adding something, and then taking something else away, or moving things around. Think of how a sculptor works, or a writer. They don't have a single idea they stick to and realize, from start to finish in one smooth journey. Instead, they fiddle around, try ideas out, reject them, through an iterative practice of combining, taking away and recombining. In the context of service innovation, in which there are multiple actors such as different kinds of touchpoint, user and staff roles, and organizational functions and partners, handling this complexity becomes easier if the contingency of these configurations is recognized. Things that are currently connected can be disconnected, and actors can be connected together in new kinds of combination. Designing innovative services requires recombining and disconnecting actors as new ecosystems are configured.

These four inventive habits can be practiced to generate concepts that are multiple and temporal and which emerge through the distributed creativity of diverse actors. Four examples from design, the arts, and comedy illustrate how these habits play out in creative practice. This is followed by a summary of what these habits offer to people designing innovative services.

Making artefacts from the future

Design is explicitly about giving shape and form to concepts for future things. One strand of contemporary design practice centres on crafting objects that might exist in the future, embedding these objects in speculation and imagination about the future worlds that might exist. Encountering these artefacts opens up discussion as to what different futures might be like. Work by the Near Future Laboratory shows how creating and exploring artefacts from the future helps surface possibilities, by making familiar things strange, and by making strange things familiar.

The Near Future Laboratory is a team of four people working in California and Europe. Describing itself as a thinking, making, design, development and research practice, its goal is to understand how imaginations and hypotheses are given shape and form to "swerve" the present into new, more habitable worlds in the near future. Its members and collaborators come from different backgrounds including computer science, design and ethnography, and combine these to create a variety of conceptual and creative platforms to

5 Inspiring and generating

explore the future. One of its ways of working is to create design fictions, about which the Lab says:

"This is the platform best suited for taking a sideways glancing blow at a set of open issues, exploring unknown unknowns, working through turbulent alternatives, contesting the status quo and walking down strategic alternatives."[145]

For example, its *Winning Formula* project from 2014 (a World Cup year) explores the intensifying relationship between data and football. Realized in several formats including a printed newspaper from 2018 and a data visualization displayed at public exhibitions, this exploration looks at the implications of the ways that data is changing football for players, fans, commentators, managers and clubs. By creating an imaginary European newspaper from several years into the future, the Near Future Laboratory locates its strange imaginary developments within something mundane and familiar. Newspapers usually carry reports and advertisements about football as sport, politics, business or celebrity gossip. But this fictional newspaper's sports section, dedicated to football, offers an excess of the specific, presenting readers with many different possible ways that data might affect football. This artefact from the future makes speculation about the future accessible, even if the implications, on closer inspection, are not palatable.

Another project by the Near Future Laboratory resulted in a short video, *Corner Convenience*[146]. This project started with the observation that the trajectory of all great innovations is towards the counter of your corner convenience store. In order to explore

the cultural implications of this idea, the Near Future Laboratory first created a newspaper and then organized a design fiction workshop at Arizona State University's Emerge conference[147]. The resulting ideas were then produced in a five-minute video showing a typical US convenience store, piled high with groceries and domestic items.

In the near future presented in the video, products on sale at the store include sweets with pheromones, panda jerky, a scratch card that allows you to win a million followers on Twitter, and glasses that display editorial content. The video shows a customer at the counter in the store, thinking about what he is going to buy. The screen then shows a close up of a display unit of pairs of glasses pre-loaded with digital material – *Vogue*, *Cosmopolitan*, and *Big Booty Bitches Magazine*. He reaches for the latter and puts the glasses on. The audio track then mixes in the sounds associated with female pleasure in heterosexual porn and the man begins to focus on the lenses of the glasses, not his current location. The shop assistant gets his attention by waving at him. She points out a sign on the display that says "No browsing". This video brings possible futures into view by making things that are familiar strange and the strange familiar. By showing possible future products in the context of an ordinary US shop and in relation to existing products and services, it renders them familiar and at the same time questions whether they should exist.

Both these projects involve making the strange familiar and zooming in and out. The newspaper and the video allow people to zoom into the detail of a possible future which is recognizable but not yet familiar. The newspaper's stories, fictional adverts and the products in the convenience store of the near future prompt you to zoom out again and see the whole that they are part of. The opportunity for designers of innovative services is to create future artefacts that make the unfamiliar familiar, and that offer a way to zoom closer towards some of the actors in a future innovation ecosystem.

Videos that choreograph simplicity from excess

Berg is a London-based company founded in 2005 that develops connected products and a software platform for the internet of things. Berg describes its platform as "the world's friendliest and most complete platform for web-connected products"[148]. Examples of the Berg Cloud put to use include Little Printer[149], a smart printer for the home connected to the web with a consumer-friendly mobile user interface. People use this to receive and print messages and photographs sent via the web, or online updates they have chosen to route to the printer.

Perhaps unusually, this technological innovation capability came from what started as design consultancy. The two founders, Matt Webb and Jack Schulze, combined knowledge of digital technologies with the creative culture of interaction design. Then, joined by Matt Jones, the firm morphed into Berg, which worked on strategy and digital products for clients such as Google, Intel, Bonnier and Dentsu.

But then the team self-funded and launched its own connected consumer product, Little Printer. Its success, measured in sales and in recognition – such as the London Design Museum's Designs of the Year award in 2013 – resulted in a switch of focus towards developing its internet of things platform for others.

Some of the creative exploration that is core to Berg's culture is evident in its early projects. For example, in 2009 Berg worked with film-maker Timo Arnall to explore near field communication such as RFID, specifically the concept of digitally-enabled objects connecting to one another without touching. This exploration resulted in a short film entitled Nearness, which plays with "the problems of invisibility and the magic of being close", as Schulze put it on the blog[150]. This is a film that explores proximity through a studio inquiry that imaginatively shows what near field technologies might, could, or even should offer. However, rather than embedding this exploration within a human-centred story communicating some benefits to a user, this is a film that draws in viewers in the mode of purposeless art, not purposeful design. Paying explicit homage to the film *The Way Things Go* by artists Fischli and Weiss, Nearness shows things happening without any reference to making things easier or more useful for humans.

This is a beautiful one-minute film in which "touch without touching" takes place. A contactless smart-card is swiped, causing an arm to rotate. A phone sends a text message to another, which triggers a light coming on that is picked up by a sensor. An electro-magnet is de-magnetized, which releases an arm that swings up and triggers another RFID reading, and so on. The film offers a digital and physical choreography that draws in viewers, even without a human narrative, by showing interconnections between objects.

This practice of creating exploratory videos exemplifies two inventive habits. It makes familiar things strange, by taking device-to-device communication and turning it into something sensuous and captivating. Further, in its one minute of apparent simplicity, crafted as a result of many earlier sketches and trials, it hints at the excess that is the internet of things – a future in which billions of devices are connected to billions of others. The opportunity for designers of innovative services is to use such habits to configure new ecosystems by rendering them in unfamiliar ways – for example, by creating non-human narratives or reducing an excess to something simple, even if strange.

Making the mundane strange and the strange familiar in data art

The emerging field of artists who use data as a material illuminates some of the creative opportunities from living within a world of constant data-gathering, and the need to make sense of and question it by rendering it in new ways. These artworks move between simplicity and excess, and between the strange and the familiar, as the artists grapple with large data sets and

repurpose the data within formats that can be experienced as creative works. Although not yet part of the mainstream art world, some of this work is finding an audience – for example, at TED[151], and through support from the Data as Culture programme of the Open Data Institute, from which many of these examples come[152].

Metrography[153], a project by Benedikt Groß and Bertrand Clerc, is a map of London. It looks somewhat familiar to anyone who knows the map of the London underground, and yet it also appears strange. The artists created the map by combining two data sets – the station locations on a map of the London underground and a more standard geographical map of London. The resulting visual mash-up appears familiar but also confuses. It turns the original map, famed for its simplicity and accessibility, into something that more closely matches travellers' experiences of walking through the city.

Martin John Callanan's *Text Trends*[154] uses Google's data about the content of search queries over time. By plotting the frequency of search terms such as "me" and "you" in a simple time graph, the artist artificially simplifies the complexity of people's searches. His images show how two search terms vary over time, inviting viewers to wonder what was happening among the population of people who use Google in English when searching for these terms. Zooming in on particular search terms, and combining them into graphs, the artist prompts reflection about why these terms were chosen, their inter-relationships and interactions, and the mass of other possibilities that Google's open data platform enables.

James Bridle's *Watching the Watchers*[155] is a series of photographs taken from publicly-available digital satellite maps of unmanned aircraft at training bases in the US desert and installations in Afghanistan, Pakistan, and elsewhere. Although these military technologies were designed to operate without being seen, they are nevertheless accessible to the gaze of contemporary civilian networks, thanks to Google Earth. By rendering them visible, Bridle opens up their operations and their politics, turning open data about things that are supposed to be secret into something as yet unknown.

Some of the artists working with data as material create works that emphasize the way data is produced, rather than using it as if it is a found material. Julie Freeman's installation *The Lake*[156] comprised 16 fish swimming in a lake in England, whose movements were tracked via electronic tagging systems. The resulting real-time data were transformed into a musical composition and an animation. Visitors were invited to come and listen to the fish composing their own soundscape whilst watching an animated representation of what was happening under the water. By recognizing other life forms as creators of digital data, this piece expands the possibilities by including unlikely actors in a creative process.

My own book *Audit*[157] resulted from a year-long project in which I distributed questionnaires to people who know me, asking them in many different ways to answer the question "What am I worth?" I combined the resulting qualitative and quantitative data from the questionnaires into a book. This overlaid the data with my comments on people's responses, giving hints as to the social context around the production of the data. Further, the book embedded the data visualizations within quotes from my discussions with specialists about how we make sense of our value, from an economist and an auditor, to a psychoanalyst and a real estate agent. This project appropriates the conventional organizational activity of doing an audit, and makes it strange by doing it about a person.

By appropriating or creating data, repurposing it within different contexts, or pointing to the circumstances of its production and circulation, these art projects invite paying closer attention to data. They connect things that are not usually put together, and disconnect some things from their contexts and make strange the familiar and mundane. Such inventive practices are an opportunity for people designing innovative services to take something that others might have overlooked – such as data about usage or billing – and reframe this as an organizational resource.

Neurological disruption and improvising unexpected connections

The improvisational skills involved in stand-up comedy offer another approach to service innovation. Tim Dingle is a trainer and – at weekends and some evenings – a stand-up comic. His one-day workshops provide a supportive but challenging space for people to try out what it's like to do stand-up comedy. Over the course of the day people learn how comedy works, develop their own material, practice some of the skills, and finally deliver a five-minute set to the other participants. Having taken this workshop twice, I can confirm it's excruciating but also exhilarating. Doing stand-up comedy is terrifying because the only things that matter are your ability to relate to your audience and your ability to make them laugh, right then, right there. Three exercises are worth exploring in more detail.

The first is an exercise to warm people up. Dingle asks participants to speak for one minute on a topic, in front of the other participants, alternating every word they want to say with a swear word. For the performer, it's difficult to do because it disrupts the way the brain usually works. For the audience, it's fascinating and sometimes hilarious as it triggers unexpected new connections between words.

A second exercise involves generating material by making unexpected associations between concepts. Dingle asks participants to pick something that annoys or bothers them. People typically pick things from their daily life like "big corporations", "bad drivers" or "my family", and write down this central concept on the middle of a large piece of paper. They then write down as many words or phrases as they can that they associate with the concept in a circle around it.

Creating the first of these circles generates associations that many other people would note down. For example, if we take big organizations, the first circle of annoying things might include lots of emails, lazy colleagues, expenses forms, or security guards who enjoy pulling rank. What's important at this stage, Dingle says, is not to reject or filter out ideas.

The next step is to take one of these words or phrases from the circle, and repeat the process of generating associations so that a second circle is created around it. For example, continuing with the theme of organizations, associations for security guards might be bodybuilders, bullies, Charon the ferryman who rows people over to the land of the dead, or fashion mannequins. None of these are right or wrong. They emerge from the creator's unconscious and should be accepted, not filtered, at this stage.

But this is where things get interesting. In two steps, the exercise produces associations relating to the topic that will be unconventional for most people. This is the starting point for comedy: creating unexpected connections. What happens next in the workshop is that participants select a couple of their second level concepts to explore further. By the time they get up on stage to share their material an hour later, what they have is the ability to make an emotional connection with the audience ("I find big organizations very annoying") and some concepts that are apparently unrelated but which produce humour through being put together in novel ways.

The third exercise involves improvising this material in relation to a live audience. The skill here is remixing in real-time – for example, referring to what another performer said earlier, picking up a cue or responding to a heckle from a member of the audience – and mixing that into the material. Here, the excitement for the audience is seeing how the performer's brain recombines these materials in unexpected ways on the fly, creating unforeseen associations that go against the grain and provoke laughter.

Thus, stand-up comedy offers a particular take on creativity. Its inventiveness involves a mixture of preparation and seeing what unfolds with an audience in real-time. Laughter comes from sparking unforeseen connections between concepts, linked back to an emotional driver that makes it meaningful to performer and audience. With its focus on disrupting neurological patterns, stand-up comedy suggests how service innovators can try to avoid the conventional associations and instead combine capacities together in unexpected new ways.

Combining inventive habits for service innovation

The four inventive habits associated with contemporary art, design and comedy are resources for organizations generating new concepts in a service innovation process. Two of the service innovation capabilities introduced in Chapter 2 are of particular relevance.

Firstly, the service innovation capability that involves understanding value-in-use as people engage with a service over time is enhanced by these inventive habits:

- Generating concepts for novel service experiences requires repeatedly shifting between the strange and the familiar. Proposing future value-in-use for participants within an emerging ecosystem can proceed by looking differently at things that are currently familiar, and by introducing things that may initially seem strange. One example is taking capacities and actors that are established in one context and imagining what might happen if they existed in another.

- The process of coming up with, exploring and making sense of concepts involves moving between excess and simplicity. The divergent phases of the creative process involve generating many ideas for future value-in-use, which may result in concepts that are ridiculous or irrelevant. The convergent phases recombine, reduce and refine concepts, disciplining these creative excesses into manageable simplicity that is required to show benefits to the participants involved in an innovation ecosystem.

- Creative teams shift between zooming in on the detail – an aspect of the service encounter, user interface, or user behaviour – and zooming out to consider the relationship between these objects or events and the value constellation they are part of. Zooming in and then out offers a way to grapple with the multiplicity of service innovation concepts.

Secondly, the service innovation capability that recombines capacities into new ecosystems is enriched by these inventive habits:

- Being able to configure new value ecosystems is supported by the habit of zooming in and out between the detail and the big picture, and the parts and the whole. Zooming in enables being attentive to the particular capacities of an actor. Zooming out offers a way to see its situated inter-connections with other actors within an ecosystem, and grasp, if only partially, the whole.

- Configuring new value ecosystems involves combining actors and capacities in new ways. The habit of connecting and disconnecting highlights the iterative and ongoing activity of actors being combined into new combinations over time. Instead of making the most obvious connections, people designing innovative services can configure connections that result in unexpected value ecosystems that are harder to imitate.

- Moving between excess and simplicity helps illuminate what is involved in creating value constellations. Configuring an excess of actors and capacities within a value constellation is part of the creative process, as is moving towards simplicity. Service innovation concepts result from distributed creativity through the active participation of diverse actors. Navigating between too many actors and capacities, and between too few, is part of the process of generating novelty.

Although this chapter began by examining the origins of contemporary art schools in order to understand the studio inquiries associated with creativity, it is not the case that these habits are only available to artists, designers and other designated "creatives". Rather, the point of the discussion about art schools was to illustrate how some habits related to creativity and concept generation have been associated with particular cultures through the evolution of art education over time. People designing innovative services can practice these habits by trying out methods associated with them, and building team cultures in which such approaches become the regular way of doing things. The next chapter discusses how prototyping and design games open up creativity to a wider group of actors at the early stage of service innovation.

Case 9 Prototyping value-in-use by storytelling at Google

Google is a leading innovator in technology-based services. With the acquisition in 2005 of the Android mobile operating system, Google developed a vision of multiple connected devices including desktop computers, phones, tablets, and wearables.

One development is Google Glass, a head-mounted computer that resembles a pair of glasses, developed by the Google X experimental research team. As with similar devices being launched by other firms, it's not clear how people might use these new technologies. In its beta release in 2013, the initial functions of Google Glass included allowing people to record video and take photos. When connected via WIFI to the internet, Glass can broadcast online what is visible to it[158]. If online, people wearing Glass can search Google, use maps, and interact with other people using Google's social media platform. Users interact with Glass using voice – addressing it as "OK Glass" – as well as via a touchpad.

The Glass device looks distinctive; it has a small light that comes on at the front when it is filming. But it potentially allows the wearer to record *and broadcast* video and photos in real time, without many other people in the immediate environment knowing. It is this ubiquitous wearable connectivity that has raised ethical and social concerns about privacy[159]. Should people around someone wearing Google's device be informed and give consent for being filmed and broadcast? How will use of Glass change social practices if this becomes more routine?

In developing Glass, Google can be seen as undertaking technological innovation based on pushing something to the market, without an established consumer need. But the lens of service innovation brings a focus on understanding value-in-use and increasing the variance of actors involved in an innovation ecosystem. First, Google used video narratives to create visions of future value-in-use. Second, Google launched clumsy solutions with a range of possible users outside the firm – known as "explorers" – to further explore use.

Google's Creative Lab started exploring how people would use the device through video storytelling, during the early phases of designing of the device. The Creative Lab is a team of people from backgrounds in advertising, film-making, design, art and animation. In the words of Kevin Proudfoot, the lab's executive creative director: "Stories allow us to try on a future for size".[160] Richard The, a senior designer in Google's Creative Lab, explains the approach:

> "We make the ad before the product exists. Very often we talk with an engineering or a product team and we have no idea if [what they are creating] will be a product or a feature. So we treat it as if we have

Case 9 (continued) Prototyping value-in-use by storytelling at Google

figured it all out and we can make the ad about it. We make the posters and videos. The general rule at the Creative Lab is to make as much stuff as possible and then you have something to deal with and something to talk about".[161]

Without much of a budget and starring members of the lab rather than actors, this is what The calls "gonzo film-making".[162] Working in well-defined media forms in an information-saturated environment provides additional constraints and focus. He explains, "If you make an ad that is 60 or 30 seconds long, it better be self-explanatory and easy to understand".[163]

In the case of Glass, Google X briefed the Creative Lab team to develop stories for the device when it was still at an early stage. The recalls: "It was a crazy apparatus strapped to a helmet, half cell phone, half I don't know what. They had some idea of what it could be doing, and what it could not be doing".

The Google X development team were prototyping interactions with Glass, exploring questions such as what kind of display it would have, and would it have a camera, and how to control it. The response from the Creative Lab was to make a video showing how someone like a creative in their team might use it in his day-to-day life. Since Glass did not yet exist, the film-makers mocked it up by wearing a helmet mounted with a camera and took footage from the wearer's perspective, which is what the video

shows. Originally intended just for an internal audience, this video was later released to a wider public.

The team designing Glass then incorporated some of the ideas shown in the video into the design, and subsequently invited the Creative Lab to be more directly involved in designing the user interactions and scenarios of use. For example, the team contributed to the principle that using Glass is about focusing on one thing at a time in the now, in contrast to how people use smartphones, laptops, or data in the cloud. Later, a member of the Google team compared what was in the original video, and the features that made it into the version of Glass released to the public. Although the video was "50 percent fantasy" according to The, some of the features and much of the vision in the video shaped the first public version of Glass and what is likely to be in future releases. In effect, the Creative Lab team became involved in designing Glass, by making videos showing someone using the device, before it existed.[164]

Having developed the device to a beta prototype, Google set up ways for wider publics to start using it in their day-to-day lives. In addition to targeting software developers expected to develop apps for Glass, Google created a scheme for members of the public, known as "explorers", to sign up to buy Glass. This gave Google access to a living lab

through which it could learn what kinds of usages people found for the device[165]. Google launched the process to find explorers in early 2013, resulting in a first cohort of people who each got the device for $1,500[166]. Ed Sanders, head of marketing responsible for Google Glass, described this as a new way of doing marketing:

> "Rather than pulling it behind a curtain, it's pulling it out in front of the curtain...It's a risk, saying to people, here's the product in its current form, help us shape the brand, not the other way round".[167]

The stories of how people on the explorer programme used and made sense of their devices were shared within Google and online. One video, for example, tells the story of Alex Blaszczuk[168], who was left paralyzed after a car accident in 2011 and remains unable to use her hands. Her Glass explorer story describes how the device enabled her to do things through using the voice activation functionality – a classic story of technology as an enabler for someone with particular needs. Other people in the Explorer programme discussed their positive and negative experiences using Glass, using channels such as Twitter and the news media, often highlighting the unwelcome consequences of the device's ability to do real-time surveillance without other people nearby noticing.

In creating a video about someone using Glass, the Creative Lab made the strange familiar, and their concepts for value-in-use directly shaped the design of Glass. Through the explorer programme, Google increased the variance of the participants involved in constructing Glass. In short, Google prototyped the hardware and software over many iterations to get the device ready for launch, exploring the question "does it work?" What the video scenarios and explorer programme did was discover how people engaged with and used the device – prototyping value-in-use began to answer "what's it for?"

Case 10 Recombining socio-cultural capacities through tinkering and improvisation at Frugal Digital

Vinay Venkatraman[169] is an interaction designer, originally from India, now based in Copenhagen. One of the co-founders of the Copenhagen Institute of Interaction Design, a start-up educational institution, he is also co-founder of the Frugal Digital initiative[170]. Frugal Digital's work is concerned with making change happen by making digital devices, resting on an analysis of socio-cultural patterns and a political commitment to inclusion and access[171]. Much of the team's work involves combining capacities into new product or service concepts, and launching clumsy solutions to learn, rooted in the creative habits associated with design studio practice. The team funds its own activities, through its members' consultancy activities.

On a trip by members of Frugal Digital to Mumbai, the team studied practices of salvaging computer parts by skilled local people who are not well-educated in formal terms. They found an informal but well-established set of processes by which unwanted CRT monitors were salvaged, and components were combined with TV tuner kits to create retrofitted TVs. These were then packaged up and transported on passenger buses (when there was room on them) to rural parts of India, and sold for around €30. Expanding beyond this informal TV-making economy, Frugal Digital's fieldwork included visits to markets and workshops,

and interviews with – for example – people who fix electronic devices such as mobile phones.

On their trips round markets, the Frugal Digital team also found many different kinds of printed instruction manuals about how to fix things. Often these materials were highly visual, making them accessible to people who were not very literate. User experience research often focuses on micro-social analyses of users' world and neglects wider socio-cultural patterns. In contrast, here the team's research analyzed the socio-cultural practices people's activities were part of. This research helped the team identify resources based on an asset-based model of society, which recognizes capacities rather than seeing people such as the rural Indian poor as only having needs. The team identified the key actors and resources that gave rise to what Venkatraman called in a TED talk the "new technology crafts".[172]

While this analysis of tinkering and fix-it culture is not unique, the team's work opened up new possibilities when they took this analysis, and responded through a studio practice that remixed what was readily available. Venkatraman explains:

> "We went to the markets to buy samples of small products that were easy to get hold of. We ended up with a bag of cheap gadgets. We had a wide range of products and we were toying with them, opening

them up and discussing them, and ideas for solutions emerged from the hands-on tinkering."

Although they did not have a clearly defined user need, the designers wanted to combine resources in new ways that might lead to novel products and services. He explains:

"Studio making is critical. For me, the creative angle does not come by building concepts in the air. It comes from improvisation".

With backgrounds in interaction design, the team members are comfortable with opening up the "black boxes" of digital devices, and connecting and disconnecting components in new ways. One of the readily available devices the team explored was the cheap and ubiquitous alarm clock. By adding sensors and a micro-controller, the team turned an everyday, low-tech object into a multi-functional digital tool that could be used in different ways. For example, adding different sensors turns the hacked alarm clock into a device for measuring things such as blood pressure or pulse rates. A further step was to add a USB port to it, and to develop a simple SDK (software development kit) to allow other people to write and build code for the micro-controller inside and add new sensors to create other kinds of digital device. Venkatraman explains the creativity that led to this:

"The guys who do the fixing and salvaging of electronics were focused on making a living. Their work is

concerned with mobile phones or electronics, so they wouldn't really think of the alarm clock as connected with what they do. We had a different mindset, which is about connecting things. The key thing is the ability to improvise by combining things in new ways. We don't get stuck in domain expertise, but look for the crossovers."

Having made some rough prototypes of the device, the team took it to low-fi electronics fabrication workshops to get them to make improved versions. Venkatraman explains the constraints:

"There was a lot of back and forth. The ideal scenario would be co-creation and we would all be together within the same space. But there's a lack of space in their tiny shops and working with us would disrupt their core business with customers."

In their practical fieldwork, the Frugal Digital team had explored the key roles of front-line healthcare workers who support families close to or in their homes, rather than in the public health centres that are typically 7-15 km away. The team identified an opportunity to enable healthcare workers to help patients decide if it is worth giving up a day's wages, and investing in traveling to the nearest health centre, when someone is ill. The team created a scenario of a triage system to enable healthcare workers to help families make such decisions, thus changing the flow of patients to, and load on, public health centres.

5 Inspiring and generating

Case 10 (continued) Recombining socio-cultural capacities through tinkering and improvisation at Frugal Digital

As part of their scenario for the new triage system, Frugal Digital created Clock Sense, based on the hacked alarm clock. Here, the clock dial was replaced with a simple graphic. This device would enable healthcare workers to establish how urgent a case was, to help people decide if the person who was unwell needed to travel to the health centre. Scaling the proposed healthcare scenario built on three capacities: the Indian fix-it locally culture, resources for cheap fabrication, and strong visual literacy. Within this scenario, distributing and using the hacked alarm clock device as part of healthcare triage could change the economics of rural public health services in India.

Venkatraman sees Frugal Digital's role as being researchers and designers of new digital products and services, who share their solutions through open source models, rather than delivering them at scale themselves. In dialogue with foundations and companies, the team continues to develop further iterations of the clock and other devices and champion the role of local improvisation in digital designing.

Frugal Digital's healthcare screening tool Clock Sense

Method 9: Sketching

Time involved	Using the method, 60 minutes
Associated capabilities	Understand value as created in practice Launch clumsy solutions and learn
Methods to use before or after this one	Method 8 Problem/proposition definition Method 10 Telling stories

What you'll need

Blank sheets of paper, marker pens

A facilitator to guide the teams

Someone to photograph the results

marker pens

large sheet of paper

'What could a touch-point that is part of the solution look like?'

Purpose

This method can be used in lots of different ways, individually or in groups. The basic idea is to generate through sketching many different aspects of a possible solution. Depending on the context, people can sketch touchpoints that are things users or customers would interact with within the new innovation ecosystem. These could be web pages, leaflets, smartphone apps, emails, text messages, signage, products, packaging or media adverts; or environments and places such as homes, offices, clinics, cafes, schools or shops; or public spaces such as parks, sports or community centres or bus stops; as well as mundane things in the built environment such as posters or bins.

Outcomes

Generates ideas and gives them shape and form.

How to do it

Sketch. Distribute templates. Sketch. Compare. Repeat.

Review. Review the sketches. Do they all relate to the same issue and solution?

If the emphasis on the sketches is on digital touchpoints such as apps or webpages, is this right for the intended user or customer segment? Are there other, non-digital ways of making the service proposition real for users?

If you have previously used Method 8, identify which problem/proposition combination the sketches relate to. Do some of the sketches suggest new ways of understanding the issue being addressed and possible solutions? Are some of the touchpoints mutually incompatible?

Tip

Remember that sketching *generates* ideas through the activity of drawing, as well as making ideas easy to share.

5 Inspiring and generating

continued...

If you have previously used Method 10, how do these sketches fit into or challenge the stories you created about future services and impacts? Do they suggest new stories?

If you have previously used Method 3, how do these touchpoints compare with the map of the service ecosystem as it currently is, or how it could be in the future?

If you previously used Method 5, how do these touchpoints fit within the target user or customer's storyworld of objects, organizations and people?

Combine. Identify the important features in the touchpoint sketches and discuss whether it is worth trying at this stage to combine some of these concepts into a smaller number of sketches.

Example

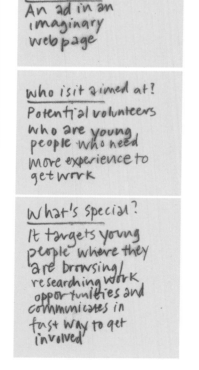

Sketching

Use this to capture and share future service touchpoints

What is this?

What does it do/show/change?

Who would use or engage with it (user segment or stakeholder)?

What is distinctive or special about it?

Method 10: Telling stories

Time involved	Using the method, 60 minutes
Associated capabilities	Understand value as created in practice Increase the variance/bring in new actors
Methods to use before or after this one	Method 4 Mapping the user experience Method 9 Sketching

What you'll need

One table per group

Large sheets of paper, Post-it notes, Blu-Tack, marker pens, old magazines to cut up

A facilitator to guide the teams

Someone to capture the results

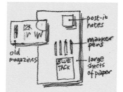

key question

'How could things happen differently?'

Purpose

The method supports people to create stories that follow the well-established three act structure.

Outcomes

The result of using this method is stories that have a clear structure and which include the elements that constitute practice. The method prompts paying attention to the organizational and technological resources that are implicated in changing how things happen. Using the method helps a team gel by involving them in creativity and sense-making, and by using the outputs to think through the implications of different things happening in the future.

How to do it

Generate stories. Invite people to pick a character to tell a story about. This does not have to be a user. It could even be an object. Depending on what you are working towards, you might want to pick as a character to tell a story about someone who is not currently connected with the organization or service you are thinking about. Ask participants to work individually or in pairs to use the template to tell a story about that person or thing. The template will help them think about structure, but they can use whatever method they feel comfortable with to communicate their story. This might be comic strips, short stories, play scripts or role play. To get into character, people can refer to the personas created in Method 5 or generate new ones using that method.

Tip

Before starting the method, watch video clips or invite people to share personal stories to orient them to storytelling.

Although the story template suggests three acts, a narrative might unfold in many episodes or phases. If you have already done some sketching (Method 9), people might want to refer to some of these touchpoints in the stories.

Share and tell. Invite people to share their stories. Ask participants to take notes while listening to the other stories and give one another feedback.

Review. Ask people to identify surprises, concerns, opportunities for doing things differently and ideas to take forward.

If you have previously used Method 8, identify which problem/proposition combination the stories relate to. Do some of the stories suggest new ways of understanding the issue being addressed and possible solutions? Are some of the stories mutually incompatible or impossible?

If you have previously used Method 9, how do these stories relate to the touchpoints you sketched? Do any of the stories require new touchpoint sketches?

If you have previously used Method 3, how do these stories relate to a future map of the service ecosystem?

If you previously used Method 5, how do these stories challenge or enrich the target user or customer's storyworld of objects, organizations and people?

Combine. Identify the most important features in the stories and discuss whether it is worth trying at this stage to combine some of these concepts into a smaller number of stories. For example, you could produce short comic strips to illustrate how someone would experience things differently through a new service.

continued...

Telling stories

Use this structure to tell a story about the change you want to happen
Use as many scenes as you need in each act to tell the story, resulting in perhaps 10 scenes

Act 1

Set up the issue/challenge and how and why it matters to someone

Sketch what happens

Describe what happens

Who is involved (people and organizations), what they do, know, say or feel, where things happen, what touchpoints or technologies are involved?

Implications for the organization(s) involved

Implications or requirements for the technologies involved

Act 2

Describe the change

Sketch what happens

Describe what happens

Who is involved (people and organizations), what they do, know, say or feel, where things happen, what touchpoints or technologies are involved?

Implications for the organization(s) involved

Implications or requirements for the technologies involved

Act 3

Describe the result of the change

Sketch what happens

Describe what happens

Who is involved (people and organizations), what they do, know, say or feel, where things happen, what touchpoints or technologies are involved?

Implications for the organization(s) involved

Implications or requirements for the technologies involved

Example

STORYBOARD from sign up to start for the Tech Friends Befriending service

DAY 1

Jenny   Friend Karen

Jenny decides to sign up as a tech friend to get some work experience

She's worried about how long she'll have to commit for, if she gets a job or moves

DAY 2

Jenny does an online face to face interview
⊛ Fast response to sign up

DAY 3

Back office

Back office team check Jenny's references & review her skills

BLOG

meanwhile Jenny looks at blogs to learn more about befriending services and what to expect
⊛ online case studies

DAY 21

trainer

Jenny attends a training session (expenses paid) which includes role play about handling difficult situations

Jenny has a one-to-one session to review what she wants to contribute and get out of it

DAY 24

Back office

The Local service matches Jenny with an older person
⊛ up to date database

DAY 28

Jenny visits Fred in his home for tea. Next time she'll help him skype his grandson

Jenny's local mentor debriefs her, makes sure she's back safe and they plan the next visits

6 Prototyping and playing design games

snapshot

– *Exploratory prototyping brings a future innovation ecosystem into partial view and creates concepts and actions that shape value-in-use.*

– *Design games involve participants in creating concepts and activities that connect how things are done now, with new capacities and resources, resulting in future practices.*

– *Blueprinting helps different organizational functions see how their activities and capacities co-create value-in-use for different actors in an innovation ecosystem.*

– *Role play stimulates creativity by getting people to approach things in new ways.*

AT THE END OF THE 1990S, MOBILE PHONE operators in many countries were busy designing the third generation of services, known as 3G. By the end of the decade, the technical specifications for 3G services were well-defined. Operators engaged in bidding wars to secure access to the radio spectrum that would carry these services. But managers, researchers and designers remained unclear as to what kinds of services consumer and business users would value.

To focus the many ideas being generated inside their organization about what people might want from 3G services, the Swedish mobile operator Telia organized a research project with university students[173]. The students were given access to mobile devices that simulated 3G functionality, such as internet services on a mobile phone. After 12 days, participants generated 374 ideas, which were then assessed by the company. However, the Telia experts who evaluated the ideas found that either they were not original or not feasible, or both. Disappointed with the results, the team decided to go back and take one more look at the ideas that were original, but unfeasible.

One example was the following: "For the third time running, the delivery man made a mistake and gave me the wrong newspaper. It would be good if the telephone could send a 10,000V electric shock to teach him not to do it again"[174]. For ethical, technical and legal reasons this idea was not feasible. But on revisiting the student's suggestion, however, something happened. The Telia team realized that they were modelling future mobile phone services as a connection for voice and data exchange. In contrast, the delivery man concept was more like a remote control system that enabled users to undertake action at a distance.

What this realization offered was a way to reframe the organization's assumptions about what 3G telecommunications could be. So the outcome of the research project with the students was not a set of original and feasible service concepts for Telia to develop. What it did, however, was open up a new conceptual space within which they could design 3G services. Such reframing is a core activity for service innovation – part of the moves that happen as new concepts and new knowledge are generated. Creating service concepts is productive, not just because some of them might be realizable as service offerings, but because sometimes they disrupt current assumptions.

This chapter grapples with the issue of how to make sense of concepts generated at the early stage of a project. It uses familiar words like prototyping, but shows how they mean something different in the context of service innovation where what needs exploring is new kinds of innovation ecosystem, not new kinds of object or software. To do this, it illustrates how workshops – a format for people to come together to achieve some kind of advance in a project – can be events that unlock individual and group creativity and sense-making, as well as being opportunities for sharing information or making decisions. Design games, hackathons, blueprinting and role play offer ways to

6 Prototyping and playing design games

do exploratory prototyping at the fuzzy front end of an innovation process, when service concepts are still unstable.

Two cases show how prototyping turns concepts that could take lots of different forms into something that is specific that then invites deliberation. The first case describes how the Danish government innovation unit MindLab used a design game with teachers to generate concepts for a web resource, to shift them to a new way of working based on achieving learning outcomes. The second case describes how consultancy Engine helped Mercedes-Benz prototype a proposed new design for the after-sales service for customers. Together, these cases show how organizations can learn through giving shape and form to new service hybrids that reconfigure relationships between actors and develop languages and concepts that create future value-in-use.

Following this chapter, two methods help work out how to use these approaches at the early stages of designing innovative services. Method 11 helps synthesize insights from research and connect them to emerging concepts that need further exploration. Method 12 guides service blueprinting, which helps organizational functions and partners to work together to see how their activities and resources co-constitute value-in-use for the actors involved.

Prototyping at the early stages of designing innovative services

At the early stage of a project, especially before there's a budget and team, it's hard to work out how to take things forward. There may be research findings, an analysis of an opportunity, and initial concepts for new kinds of innovation ecosystem that bring together actors in new ways, constituting value-in-use – resulting in a desired change. But teams often find it hard to make sense of and prioritize the ideas they have come up with.

As many designers, entrepreneurs and business writers have argued, prototyping is a powerful way to help a team explore ideas and engage with stakeholders. Lean start-up is based on the premise of entrepreneurs repeatedly creating hypotheses and designing ways to test them, to help a new venture work out what to do[175]. IDEO's Tom Kelly says, "Give your management team a *report*, and it's likely they won't be able to make a crisp decision. But a prototype is almost like a spokesperson for a particular point of view, crystallizing the group's feedback and keeping things moving"[176]. In agile software, one writer argues, "A prototype is worth a thousand lines of code"[177]. But what does prototyping look like at the very early stage of service innovation?

Service innovation brings into being a new ecosystem or hybrid of actors. But it's not possible to prototype anything at a systems level. By their nature, services involve many kinds of actor. Value is constituted in use, rather than being fixed in time and space. Services are dynamic and unfold over time. Any perspective on an innovation ecosystem can only be partial; it's not possible to have a holistic, detailed view that knows everything about everything in the service system, especially when it is constantly in flux. That would resemble the short story by Luis Borges called *On*

Exactitude in Science, which imagined an empire in which cartographers created a map of it at a scale of 1:1. So the activity of prototyping in the context of services needs to be re-imagined.

One key distinction to make is between *exploratory* prototyping during the fuzzy front end of a project and, later on, when *hypothesis-driven* prototyping is used to isolate particular questions that need answering[178]. Both require people with different kinds of expertise and from different organizational functions, as well as people who are, or can stand in for, end users, customers and other stakeholders. Exploratory prototyping can help a project move forward when resources are limited or not yet committed, time is short, and uncertainty about what direction a project might take remains high. Exploratory prototyping at the fuzzy front end of a service innovation process is useful because it brings into view aspects of a new innovation ecosystem and of future value-in-use.

Methods for doing exploratory prototyping have been used for decades in the field of computer systems design, which, like service design, is concerned with creating new behaviours and different interactions between people, organizations, and resources such as technologies. Three well-established methods are particularly useful. The first – playing design games – comes from the field of participatory design associated with the development of software systems. The second – service blueprinting – originates in services marketing, and contributes to creating a shared vision of value-in-use that helps align actors such as organizational functions involved in constituting it. The third method, role play, allows people to work collectively in creative ways to mock up and perform aspects of a new ecosystem such as service encounters or team behaviours.

All of these methods provide a way of partially prototyping services to bring into view at an early stage what the service might be like, to reveal hidden assumptions and surface conflicts, and lead to discussion of implications. But unlike product prototyping, they don't just show what it would be like. Where exploratory prototyping, in the context of service innovation, is distinctive is that it helps create the concepts and activities that constitute a new service. As with the example of Telia's 3G research, the collective generation and exploration of concepts helps reframe what is actually being designed.

How design games open up the particular

Think about a workshop you have attended. Was it well-organized? What did that look and feel like? How effective was the facilitator? Did you find yourself engrossed in the flow while you participated? Or did it feel like you were presented with a list of tasks to work through, which you did not really get into? How did other participants behave? Overall, did the workshop feel productive? Did it move things forward for some of the participants? How did you feel straight afterwards, and a week after?

Workshops are a hidden problem and an opportunity in many organizations. Well done, they pull people together, forging new connections that are interpersonal as well as combining resources. Like a theatre performance or concert, people have a shared experience of being there and doing something meaningful together. During a well-designed and facilitated

6 Prototyping and playing design games

workshop, people give themselves up to being in the flow, as psychologist Mihaly Csikszentmihalyi[179] calls the experience of creativity. It feels enjoyable and productive. During a badly-designed or poorly-facilitated workshop, it doesn't. In a workshop that does not get people into the flow, participants are restless. They question or challenge the facilitator. They don't engage fully with the tasks. It feels like a waste of time. Designing and running workshops is an important skill that some people have developed, which remains curiously neglected by many organizations. The concept of design games provides ways to work out what a powerful and productive workshop experience could look like in the context of designing innovative services.

The term "design games" comes from the field known as participatory design. This developed in Scandinavian countries in the 1970s. At that time, democratic initiatives to involve employees in decision-making in the workplace converged with efforts to involve users in software development. One researcher, Pelle Ehn, developed ways to combine these two different approaches and, in so doing, he contributed to the emergence of the new field. Ehn's research has provided an important resource for these developments[180].

In one project, Ehn worked with typesetters at a printing company, who were going to be impacted by the introduction of new software. As the software did not yet exist, Ehn and colleagues wanted to find ways to make it possible for the typesetters to be able to experience something resembling what the software

would be like to engage with. Ehn used cardboard and cut-out paper shapes to give shape and form to the possible software's user interface. This low-fidelity "paper prototyping" allowed the participants to manipulate some of the proposed future features.

One possible design approach would have been for the designers to show the workers what the software would be like for them to use and ask for feedback. Instead, the designers set up ways for the workers to play with and manipulate the paper prototypes. This allowed all the people involved – designers, researchers and workers – to develop a shared language and concepts about how typesetting would be reconfigured when some of the activities were done using software. Playing the games allowed the typesetters to integrate their existing ways of doing things, in which they were expert and which they took for granted, with new possibilities introduced by the software.

To help make sense of this, Ehn drew on the work of philosopher Ludwig Wittgenstein and his concept of language games. The central idea here is that language does not simply describe the world. Language is a web of interlocking concepts and activities – language exists through people *doing* things in the world. Reworking language games as "design games", Ehn showed that what mattered was creating ways for participants to engage in and speak about such games, without the concepts having to be a representation of reality that was isolated from what went on in their daily work[181]. So the value of a design game during exploratory prototyping is for a group of people to collectively create the language of concepts and activities that underpins a new service. Instead of concept generation in a vacuum, design games support the collective generation of concepts that spring from and relate to deep knowledge of current practices.

By giving shape and form to concepts at an early stage, design games produce something specific, which says something more general too. Playing games generates particular proposals for how things could be, for the various stakeholders involved to engage with and assess. But rather than these sketches of future possibilities being designed predominantly by a development team, the space of the game allows people who resemble or are the users of the future service to co-create this language together. Design games operate on the boundary between inside and outside organizations. The resulting solutions are therefore a hybrid of the users' existing concepts and ways of doing things, reconfigured to include new capacities and possibilities.

Broadening participation in designing

There are two contemporary versions of design games that take some of the principles described above, but also broaden participation in designing. The first of these, hackathons, emerged in the culture of software developers, who come together to work intensely over a short period of time to write, test and review code. Open hackathons typically have a host organization, or sponsor, that wants to engage others to address a particular issue. For example, Australia's volunteer-run GovHack annual weekend events involve hundreds of software developers across the country, collaborating to combine open data in new ways, and create new visualizations and apps[182]. Some technology firms such as Facebook and Google use hackathons to engage with a diverse community of developers outside of their organizations who write software that connects with or uses their platforms.

Beyond software, other kinds of workshop have adopted and adapted these formats, often in relation to public and collective challenges such as ageing, climate change, young people's alienation from education, or healthcare. Hackathons, makeathons, hackdays or jams share aspects of the design games discussed above. They involve small mixed teams of participants in generating and developing concepts collectively in response to an issue or challenge, with fast feedback cycles to expose concepts to scrutiny, and a strong emphasis on giving shape and form to concepts through sketching, fabrication, mocking things up and role play. When participants include those who have a stake in an issue, or are deeply knowledgeable about it, concepts that are generated are more likely to combine existing resources and knowledge, with new capacities that change the situation.

A second contemporary version of design games are online, crowd-sourced, concept generation platforms. These allow a diverse range of people (who have access to the web) to participate in generating concepts in relation to a problem or challenge, typically set by an organization. As with web platforms that crowd-source funding for community or arts projects, collaborative creative platforms build in opportunities for anyone to respond and to expose their ideas to others for feedback and assessment. Online collaboration platforms can involve huge numbers of people and increase in the variance of those involved in developing new concepts and activities to address an issue or challenge[183]. However, since they exist online, they are not able to connect new concepts directly to socio-cultural practices they aim to intervene into, as can happen when workshops include people directly involved in an issue.

Some companies use concept generation platforms as part of innovation initiatives across an organization. For example, IBM has been organizing and hosting "innovation jams" since 2001. One of its online brainstorming sessions brought together more than 150,000 people from 104 countries and 67 companies. As a result, 10 new IBM businesses were launched, with seed investment totaling $100 million.[184] Another example is IDEO's open innovation platform, which has partnered with groups such as Amnesty International, Coca-Cola and the UN. OpenIDEO enables participation in four phases – inspiration, idea generation, refinement and evaluation. A project with the Mayo Clinic started with the question "How might we all maintain wellbeing and thrive as we age?" This resulted in 317 contributions to the inspiration phase, and 133 ideas, of which 20 were further refined, leading to a shortlist of six[185].

Such platforms help organizations that have identified an issue to work on to engage productively with those outside of it. But while they support the involvement of potentially large numbers of people, in locations or contexts that are far removed from one another, the emphasis is typically on concept generation, which may be significantly disconnected from a problem being addressed. So while hackathons and online platforms open up participation to broader publics, the

early-stage concepts that result still need to be related back to and recombined with the issue that was the starting point. Further, people assessing concepts for new services need to explore how they unfold temporally and how the various actors involved relate to one another, which the next sections go on to discuss.

Sketching value-in-use through service blueprinting

A second approach to exploratory prototyping in the context of service innovation is blueprinting. Originally associated with architecture, the blueprint shows in outline how something is structured. It does not aim to show the detail or (in architecture) the surfaces and materials of a new structure. Its purpose is to allow the various specialists involved to see the intended form, to allow them to plan their own contributions to its realization.

Blueprinting in the context of designing innovative services has to do something different. If services unfold over time through the participation of diverse actors in an ecosystem, teams designing services need to create a structure that captures how things might change over time. Service blueprinting resembles the activity of mapping the user journey discussed in Chapter 3, which orders in two dimensions how people engage with an organization or service. But it forges a stronger connection with the organizational and wider capacities that, together, constitute a value constellation and shape value-in-use for different actors. User journey maps focus on people's experiences (see Method 4), whereas blueprints link experiences with organizational resources, functions and underlying infrastructures connected to other actors (see Method 12).

As a tool for service design, blueprinting emerged in services marketing in the early 1980s[186]. Later taken up by consultancies specializing in service design and customer experience such as Engine, Fjord and live-work, service blueprinting is now widely used at various stages of designing a new service. As a method, it can be used to analyze an existing service. But it can also be used to give shape and form to future value-in-use. The template in Method 12 at the end of this chapter combines concepts from early versions of blueprinting in services marketing with more recent versions of this approach, influenced by the social and cultural research traditions discussed in Chapters 3 and 4.

Some approaches to service blueprinting emphasize the multiple channels through which customers or users contact an organization[187]. For example, down the vertical axis of the blueprint, they might list call centres, email, smartphones, face-to-face encounters or printed materials. This can be useful for an organization that structures such channels into different silos, which often do not have effective means of engaging with one another. In this case, doing collective service blueprinting enables different teams, each with their specialist focus in an organizational silo, to see how their concepts and activities connect to the shared matter of concern – the value-in-use that

is co-created with a user segment. This method can also be useful when there are several organizations involved – for example, when arranging care for an older family member, in which families have contact with numerous specialists and touchpoints from different organizations.

One of the tensions associated with blueprinting at an early stage is not knowing enough about operational delivery. Blueprinting does not replace process mapping, but is a method that precedes and works alongside it. Operations managers use process mapping to analyze and optimize the resources required to deliver particular levels of quality and functionality. Process mapping is a simplification that reduces the complexity of an operation to a data-driven framework that helps managers plan investment and activities, when the nature of a service is clear and there is a specification describing it. In contrast, at the fuzzy front end, when concepts are still being explored, the value of blueprinting workshops is in helping a group of people realize a specific unfolding of an aspect of the service, revealing assumptions and aspirations for value-in-use.

To illustrate how blueprinting achieves this, I will use an example from a workshop I ran for a small IT services firm. This firm provides technology support and development services to local small businesses that are typically fewer than 50 people in size, usually by phone, and sometimes in person when installing new hardware and software. Its fast growth over the past few years showed it had built a culture of providing quality services to customers that did not have an IT specialist on staff, in a marketplace with extensive, fragmented competition. The firm was now trying to work out what new services to launch, such as providing hosting in the cloud, broadband, data back-up and recovery.

I ran a workshop with five members of the team, including the CEO, the head of technology, customer-facing service engineers and a marketing specialist. First, we created personas based on staff experiences with "dream" and "nightmare" clients. We then created a 2×2 matrix dividing these different customers into four segments based on two axes: customers who understand/don't understand IT; and customers who see IT as a strategic resource they want to invest in/those who see it only as a cost. Then, on the wall, I created a blueprinting framework similar to the template in Method 12, adapted to the specifics of the IT support business. Over the course of a couple of hours I led the participants through the activity of filling in the detail on the wall relating to existing services for one of the four segments: customers who don't understand IT and see it only as a cost.

Initially, some of the participants were not sure why I kept drilling down to the detail of the touchpoints and interactions they had with customers. Each time I asked "And then what happens?", they shared with me what was obvious to them, but unfamiliar to me, and not always familiar to their colleagues. But something interesting happened when we were discussing a situation faced by a customer one month, when it changed its web hosting provider without

mentioning this to the IT support company. The result of the client changing its domain name and hosting provider was that suddenly staff were not able to send or receive emails, as their mail software was not set up with the new details. The IT provider's engineer stepped in and spent billable time updating staff software. Since in the workshop we had included finance as one of the organizational functions along the horizontal axis of the blueprint, this prompted us to think about the end of the billing cycle. As a result of the domain name change, the client's invoice was much higher than usual and the client's managing director wanted to know why.

At the workshop, the staff explained that they invested resources in telling their clients to keep them updated about all IT matters, to avoid problems such as service interruptions resulting from customer mistakes, and that they sent regular email updates to all clients to help them get the most from their IT services. But the domain change story, and other examples they shared, showed that customers did not read these updates or really understand how the different elements of their IT services and systems interconnected. The workshop team came up with the idea that the person who does read at least one thing is the managing director who approves the monthly invoice. This led to their rethinking the invoice as an opportunity to communicate with the customer who pays the bill and is incentivized to take action to avoid extra billable hours. The workshop team suggested creating simple, visual reports to help customers understand the bill, and ways to save money in future. They also suggested training for customers in this segment to get the most out of their IT service.

This brief example of a small business-to-business service provider shows how a blueprinting workshop allowed the IT firm's staff to see that, for some of their segments, they needed to find ways to help their customers with different kinds of knowledge of and orientations to IT investment to become more knowledgeable and skilled, in order to deliver a sustainable and profitable service. Second, creating a blueprint together highlighted how their various and often interdependent interactions with the client organization together constituted value-in-use. Although the firm was proud about the quality of the interpersonal and technical services it offered clients, the blueprinting method showed how it required customers to be customers-with-capacities, which not all their segments were. Finally, the blueprinting method allowed various operational and strategic members of the team to hear and make sense of each other's perspectives, through the lens of the value they were co-creating with different actors in the client organization.

Approaching things quickly and differently through role play

A third approach to prototyping at the early stages of designing innovative services borrows from the fields of theatre and performance. If service innovation highlights the need to understand how value-in-use unfolds over time, then organizations need ways to explore what this could be like. There are two key areas to explore: first, the interactions that take place in user-organization encounters, and second, the teamwork and collaboration between other actors within and across organizational boundaries. Performance offers a powerful set of techniques that organizations can use to invent possible service encounters and team behaviours quickly and cheaply.

Examples of different kinds of role play during early-stage explorations of designing new public services come from La 27e Région, a French public innovation lab created in 2008[188]. It aims to bring values and cultures inspired by social innovation, service design and the social sciences into France's regional public administration. Its activities include involving civil servants and regional stakeholders in finding new solutions to local issues through citizen participation, co-design and experience prototyping[189]. Role play is used regularly to engage participants in exploring and generating concepts for public services.

The first way La 27e Région uses role play is to get workshop participants to briefly explore another person's point of view and lived experience[190]. For instance, in Corbigny, the team wanted civil servants to understand how rural train infrastructures and services are experienced by specific people. The team gathered a dozen participants including elected representatives, professionals and inhabitants and gave them a role and a task to complete. For instance: "I'm Jean, I just moved to Corbigny and I want to go to Dijon. What information can I access about train travel?" Ahead of the workshop, the team had

6 Prototyping and playing design games

prepared online and analogue information tools and touchpoints as props to be used by the person playing Jean and others in the role play.

A second use for role play is when the innovation team wants people to project themselves into a situation that does not yet exist, or when there is not yet a shared vision for what it could be. For instance, in Lezoux they ran a project about future uses of the local library. During a workshop, professionals and members of local organizations imagined several new uses for the library. To make this more concrete, they described services from the point of view of future users through role play, which surfaced practical difficulties that people would face in accessing the new services and equipment. These unfolding narratives resulted in discussions of architecture as well as the organization of possible library services.

Laura Pandelle, a designer at La 27e Région, describes the benefits of role play as helping participants explore an issue collectively:

> "It helps a group to consider the totality of a service, not only the user's point of view, but also other people's perspectives, the logistics and infrastructures and the decision-making process. We use it because it's easy to set up and anyone can do it. You don't need to be an expert in anything, as what you have to do is describe a reality in the most authentic way you can. Another benefit is that it triggers creativity and it's playful and compelling and builds a shared purpose."

Asking local politicians to play the role of farmers or business people in scenes of existing or future service encounters prompts participants to experience things from someone else's perspective, which brings aspects of value-in-use to life. Rather than just talking about what an existing or future service could be like, role play quickly gives participants the embodied experience of being someone else, giving them temporary and partial access to someone else's world and how infrastructures and touchpoints connect with people's behaviours.

As well as opening up understanding of users' encounters with services, role play stimulates ways of thinking about how organizations themselves perform. An example from a project at Lancaster University illustrates how. As part of a project to support knowledge exchange between different organizations[191], three members of university staff organized a workshop on physical problem-solving. This was designed for managers of small and medium-sized enterprises, to take them out of their comfort zones and explore how groups work collectively. Researcher Leon Cruikshank explains: "We wanted them to explore how to solve problems by physically moving their bodies and to reflect on what this might mean for organizational creativity and collaboration"[192].

Led by choreographer Alice Booth, participants were asked to work in small groups, without speaking. Their task was to work together to simulate a complex piece of machinery like a car or a lift. Cruikshank explains:

> "Each person had to be one of the components and do an activity that connected with the other components, but they had to do this in silence through bodily

negotiation. Because they were all taking the lead, it took a while before they realized they needed to look at each other's physical cues, realizing, 'oh you're the door, you're the wheels', so they could work together."

In the end, the teams were able to perform the activity harmoniously. The Lancaster team recorded video of participants' reactions after the workshop had finished. The participants, who had begun the workshop feeling very sceptical, discussed how they had approached the task in the workshop and made links back to teamwork in their organizations. Cruickshank recalls, "One manager wondered if he just crashed through things and expected people to pick up the pieces. They began to think about the signs in people's behaviours that they did not see, and how they go about collaboration". The use of techniques from performance in this workshop moved all the participants out of their areas of expertise and into a space of physical exploration. Although the task they were presented with seemed simple, not being able to talk to other people disabled them temporarily. This required them to approach things differently in order to achieve the task. This physically embodied experience of doing things differently helped the managers surface their own unexamined ways of doing things.

In summary, while role play may make some people feel uncomfortable initially, it is a quick and cheap activity that brings aspects of services to life. Well-facilitated and supported with the right props, it can stimulate people's creativity, resulting in a richly imagined set of embodied activities that highlights

the worlds in which service encounters exist, and what happens inside organizations. As with design games, role play connects the way things are done right now, or are thought to be done, with new possibilities, and helps participants generate shared concepts and activities that connect their individual agendas and knowledges to a wider collective purpose.

Making sense of prototyping

This closing section ends the discussion on prototyping at the early stages of designing innovative services by reviewing how the approaches discussed in this chapter contribute to the service innovation capabilities. Exploratory prototyping is both creative and analytical and involves creating concepts and knowledge. It does not test ideas – that comes later in hypothesis-based prototyping. Instead, it helps a team trying to innovate in services to generate, explore and make sense of particular versions of future possibilities.

Firstly, design games, blueprinting and role play offer complementary ways to create and explore new kinds of value-in-use at an early stage of service innovation. Design games involve participants in combining existing concepts and activities with new resources, resulting in new concepts and activities that have a family resemblance to how things are done or understood now, manifesting in new ways of doing things. Blueprinting helps different organizational actors understand how their concepts and activities relate to, and support (or possibly get in the way of), the value-in-use a service creates for specific user segments.

Role play techniques that enable physical exploration of future service encounters or other aspects of organizational activities highlight the embodied work in creating and delivering new services.

Secondly, these approaches increase the variance and involve a broad range of actors in the process of designing innovative services. Design games – when well-designed and facilitated – involve participants whose perspectives and capacities might otherwise not be engaged with. Online platforms and hackathons can attract and create opportunities for meaningful participation involving diverse people, at scale and in many different locations. Blueprinting, carried out as a collective visual and performative workshop activity, brings into view the hidden or assumed resources and infrastructures that are part of a service. Role play, with its physical explorations unfamiliar to people who are not usually engaged in performing arts, gives access to what cannot be put into words, and prompts humour and discomfort.

Thirdly, these approaches navigate between generating concepts and knowledge, and working inside and outside organizations – an important service innovation capability. As the example of Telia's experience of designing 3G mobile services showed, designing innovative services requires thinking about things differently by reframing opportunities, not simply by generating concepts. Design games involving potential users and stakeholders can generate concepts, but such concepts are grounded in the everyday worlds of participants' ways of thinking and doing, combined with new capacities and resources such as software.

So design games bridge concepts and knowledge of a social world outside an organization. Using blueprinting to sketch out how resources could be combined to constitute future value-in-use allows participants with expertise of particular functions inside organizations to connect their knowledge with that of others, and recombine it into new service concepts that engage with users and stakeholders outside organizations. Embodied role play involves unfamiliar ways of doing things that can prompt participants to rethink something they take for granted. In different ways these approaches help teams designing innovative services bridge concepts and knowledge and the different worlds that exist inside organizations and beyond, in the day-to-day lives of users and customers.

As a result, exploratory prototyping in the context of designing innovative services requires the creativity discussed in the previous chapter, but shifts towards exploring and assessing the impact that a new service could have. Design games, blueprinting and role play mediate between the inventive habits associated with creative practitioners and the wider environment of participants in a social world. Understanding how proposed service concepts could change the issue that was the starting point for a project now comes into view, which is what the next chapter goes on to discuss.

Case 11 Combining existing concepts and activities with new ways of doing things through design games at MindLab

MindLab is an innovation unit within the Danish civil service.[193] Part of three ministries – the Ministry of Business and Growth; the Ministry of Education; and the Ministry of Employment; and one municipality, Odense Municipality – it also works in partnership with the Ministry for Economic Affairs and the Interior. Through this group of stakeholders, MindLab covers the policy areas that affect the daily lives of virtually all Danes, from education, employment and entrepreneurship to digital services. Founded in 2002, MindLab has worked on a range of projects that use insights about citizen behaviours to shape the design of public services. Its 15 members of staff come from backgrounds in design, political science, sociology and anthropology. Combining approaches based in design thinking, qualitative research and policy development, MindLab aims to bring the lived experiences of members of the public, business owners and employees into the development of public services.

One project involved supporting the Ministry of Education to simplify a new process and framework, known as the common objectives for curriculum, knowledge and skills, into an online planning tool for Denmark's 61,000 school teachers[194]. The common objectives programme aimed to streamline the existing curriculum and improve Danish schools by helping teachers focus on students' learning outcomes. MindLab and the ministry

agreed that the innovation team would help find out what was needed to make the new framework a regular part of teachers' day-to-day activities.

The project began with six interviews and two workshops with experts on learning, and with staff at the ministry. This helped identify barriers and possible resources to help teachers focus on learning outcomes. This was followed by fieldwork to understand teachers' terminology and ways of doing things relating to situations in which the new framework would be used. The team then identified two scenarios in which it was particularly important for teachers to focus on students' learning outcomes. The first scenario was for the teacher to understand what success looks like in the classroom when the common objectives were met. In the second, the teacher should understand the difference between a focus on student learning and a focus on teaching. This was followed by a workshop with the ministry to clarify if the insights and scenarios developed to that point had implications for the framework as a whole. Further workshops provided expert and practitioner feedback on the insights and scenarios.

The next step was to co-create with teachers new concepts and activities that combined existing work practices with new resources that drew on the common objectives. To enable this, the MindLab team translated the teachers' everyday and technical terminology and activities into a design game. This

6 Prototyping and playing design games

Case 11 (continued) Combining existing concepts and activities with new ways of doing things through design games at MindLab

was created to enable teachers participating in the game to be creative in the process of coming up with ideas about how to use the new framework.

Laura Winge, designer in the MindLab team, describes the challenge she faces when working with people who are specialists in an area with which she is less familiar:

> "The teachers are experts in their field. They bring their ingrained working habits, skills and views on their own practice about which they are extremely well-qualified to speak. But if we have to think in new ways and change our ways of doing things, that means we have to question our habits. As a designer, I constantly ask myself how we can make something better. Our job is to ask the right questions and do this at the right times and with sensitivity."

MindLab introduced the game at two schools with a task and guidelines that "anything was possible". The task was to design a conceptual framework for a future website, and tutorials to help teachers use the common objectives to prepare an annual teaching plan, and to help them understand what doing this well looked like. Three teachers worked with the game for two hours, discussing it throughout with an employee from the education ministry.

The game included terms familiar to teachers, such as *learning objectives, students, grades* and *lesson plans*. But it also introduced speculative devices, such as a "magic straw", which gave participants

access to all the knowledge in the world. Another element of the game was a funnel, which allowed teachers to cut corners. A third, in the form of a wooden fork, was a "grabber", to help teachers think about how to extract the important information on a topic. Finally, the "translation-machine" could be used to help translate the curriculum into learning objectives.

These familiar but strange metaphors helped the teachers question assumptions about how to plan lessons and expectations about the new framework, and to come up with new ideas. One of the results of playing the design game was that the ministry decided to switch from assigning learning objectives from annual to three-year cycles, to enable teachers to address students' needs over longer periods, and to have a differentiated approach to addressing different learning levels in the classroom. Playing the game revealed to the civil servants when the teachers preferred the multi-year learning goals, and when they preferred the best-practice examples of lesson plans in the proposed website design.

Although using metaphors like the magic straw introduced a risk of making the activity seem trivial, Winge was practiced enough to feel it would stimulate participants:

> "I was very curious to see what the magic straw could bring into the meeting with the professional teachers

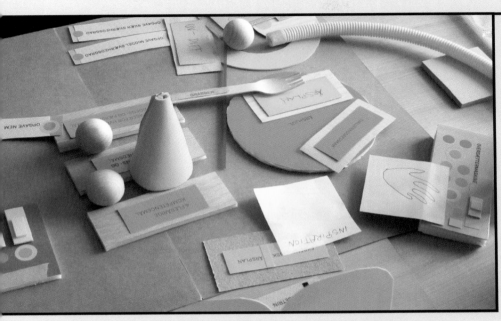

MindLab's design game developed to support a national education initiative

and people from the ministry, and I was confident it would support their creativity. Although the game seemed extremely open, it was quite structured as to how it brought in these disruptions, which were meticulously planned and selected beforehand, even if we could not predict what people would do with them."

What's interesting about this approach is that it carefully combined concepts and activities recognizable from the teachers' worlds, with unfamiliar items that de-centred expectations about what

was the regular or right way of doing things. Winge expands:

> "The designer's role is to gently push and disturb habits and current ways of thinking, adding a bit of magic to our rational ways of dealing with things. If you as a teacher are going to plan the next annual cycle of work – and you simply have to use a magic straw – the chances are that you will laugh at the same time as taking it very seriously, and that you will find a new way of doing it."

Following the game workshops, the civil servants digested their observations. This led to MindLab creating the brief for a design agency to develop the common objectives website. The outcome of playing the game, shaped by the interviews, fieldwork and workshops, was to generate the new concepts and activities to be built into the common objectives website. To shift teachers' practices towards a stronger focus on planning their teaching based on students' learning outcomes required unbundling existing ways of doing things, and creating new concepts and activities that resembled them but were, in effect, new habits for teachers. The use of the design game staged a practical encounter between the teachers' expertise and familiarity with teaching, and the unknown future ways of doing things, and generated the concepts that linked the two.

6 Prototyping and playing design games

Case 12 Prototyping a new after-sales service at Mercedes-Benz

Many organizations understand the value of doing practical experiments. They prototype technical systems and user interfaces, and pilot processes and initiatives. But rarely do they prototype in detail customer and staff experiences to explore early on what future value-in-use might look like, before committing to design decisions. Engine is a UK-based service design consultancy, which helps clients research, design, prototype and deliver new services. As part of a project to research and design a new after-sales service for Mercedes-Benz, Engine created a way to prototype at scale aspects of the new service concepts they had proposed and previously prototyped in part[195].

The first reason for doing this was to communicate and explore variants of the end-to-end experience a customer would have within the new after-sales operation. This included new channels for customers to book services, new customer-staff interactions within the existing process and new devices and roles for technicians. Oliver King of Engine explains:

> "For example, one of the service concepts proposed using number plate recognition, so they knew whose car it was driving in, asking the customer to park in a specific bay, and having a member of staff walk out and greet them by name, so we mocked all that up."[196]

This approach emphasizes the "thick" experiential detail of what it is like to be a participant in a service.

King says: "We wanted to explore the detail of the conversations a customer would have if a service manager called up, or if a customer entered the dealership". The second reason was to engage senior stakeholders and owners of dealerships within Mercedes-Benz. King says:

> "They'd only seen storyboards previously, so we wanted them to be there to experience it for themselves and to see customers experience it. It was a way for the penny to drop, to see that some of the things they thought were big and scary were not that hard to do. And it enabled them to make suggestions and advocate for the changes we were proposing."

The prototyping project involved several months of work. This included designing, orchestrating, staging and delivering the two-day prototype and gathering and synthesizing data created during it. King found it useful to use the metaphor of theatre to help explain it: "I likened it to putting on a stage show. There were stage managers, directors, people filming, actors, grips, and scripts". The investment of around £200,000 covered preparation, one week setting up and running the prototype, and the analysis that followed, which shaped the service roll-out in the UK and later across Europe.

Engine created what King calls a "low-fidelity" but detailed, full-scale prototype: "It was what you might expect from people doing amateur dramatics when rehearsing for a play". Engine designed several scenarios of specific customer-staff or

"Full scale" service prototyping in action

customer-system interactions they wanted to explore variants of. These were carefully choreographed to take people down specific journeys, which they wanted customers and staff to respond to through role play, as if in real life. Sharing the scripts in advance and then following these in the prototype helped ensure that the variants they wanted to explore were covered.

The prototyping sessions took place at Mercedes-Benz World, a brand centre and museum with plenty of space, where the team were able to create sets for the scenarios they wanted to explore, including a customer's home, a dealership and a call centre. Having these all near one another, but

separated by foam board, was more cost effective than creating the interactions in separate locations.

To materialize the scenarios within the proposed new service, Engine created paper mock-ups of some of the touchpoints, such as paper versions of digital interactions. One of the service concepts Engine proposed was issuing technicians with a smart tablet to help them diagnose issues with cars, and to give them contextual information about customers. They mocked this up by creating a series of paper screens showing the digital interface for users to flip through when role playing in the scenarios. Engine also created materials such as welcome packs, which customers would receive.

Case 12 (continued) Prototyping a new after-sales service at Mercedes-Benz

By using low-quality production values, these mock-ups communicated that they were sketches to be refined, rather than investing in producing a glossy, branded version that looked finished.

The participants in the two-day prototyping sessions included ten heads of various functions and area managers within Mercedes Benz, the owner of a dealership who later went on to host the pilot, 12 customers based on three different personas, and three members of staff from dealerships. One of the challenges when preparing for service prototyping is to engage stakeholders, especially premium customers of a premium brand. But Engine found that the customers they engaged with were excited by the new service concepts, as well as deeply appreciative that Mercedes-Benz had asked them to be part of it. King comments, "They are accomplished, busy people but their cars have a special place in their lives, so they made time for participating. This might not be the case if we were prototyping financial services".

To stage manage and run the prototype, Engine had a team of eight service designers and an ethnographic researcher, whose role was to accompany and observe participants through the experience. To gather data, service scenarios between real customers and members of staff were filmed. Customers were interviewed before and after they entered the prototype, as were stakeholders from the business. "This was great evidence Mercedes-Benz UK could take to headquarters in Stuttgart to explain the new service concept and its benefits."

In terms of impact, the prototyping did not lead to big changes to the proposed after-sales service concepts. After months of smaller-scale prototyping, the service concepts explored in the full-scale prototype were validated by customer and stakeholder responses. But there were many small changes and revisions. By doing this prototyping early on, when things were still fairly flexible, change requirements identified during the prototyping were easily absorbed.

The prototyping sessions explored a proposed service concept by staging a scene in which a Mercedes-Benz technician examined a customer's car at her home. Through observing this staged scene, the team concluded that many technicians typically do not have the customer service skills and training suitable for engaging with customers. They decided that servicing cars at people's homes, away from a dealership, required competences the organization did not have. Instead, the organization decided to focus on another service concept of picking up and delivering cars needing a service, which built on existing customer service competences in dealerships.

Some months after the prototyping analysis was complete and the service concepts were revised, a year-long pilot at a UK dealership took place. This 2010 pilot resulted in customer satisfaction ratings up by 50%, with increased retail visits, and more time spent by customers at dealerships. Further, Mercedes-Benz attributed increased car sales of 4.5% compared to the year before to the improved after-sales experience. In 2012, the MyMercedes-Benz after-sales service was rolled out globally, shaped significantly by the upfront detailed service prototyping.

6 Prototyping and playing design games

Method 11: Planning prototyping & design games

Time involved	Using the method, 60+ minutes
Associated capabilities	Understand value as created in practice Increase the variance/bring in new actors
Methods to use before or after this one	Method 4 Mapping the user experience Method 5 Creating a persona storyworld

What you'll need

Blank sheets of paper, Post-it notes, marker pens

A flipchart

A facilitator to guide the teams

A documenter to capture the results

key question

'What do we need to know more about and how are we going to get answers?'

Purpose

This method helps a team work out where it is, and what it needs to explore further, in a structured way, to answer questions it has. It provides a framework to shape future exploratory prototyping, exploring emerging concepts and knowledge.

Outcomes

Highlights important questions, and supports a team to organize to answer them through prototyping, by iterating concepts and building knowledge relating to new service ecosystems and new kinds of value-in-use. Ensures that a team is clear what prototyping activities are going to explore and why answering some specific questions matters.

How to do it

Summarize the findings. Depending on what other work you have done, and your access to any research done by specialists, you should get the team to elicit its main observations about the issue or service. These should be based on close observation of people's worlds, and from their perspectives. You might want to target specific segments of people.

Summarize the insights. Now ask people to articulate the insights that come from these findings. These are easily confused. The findings are based on observations about what people say or do, in their worlds. Insights occur where patterns begin to form, such as through descriptions of habits or shared behaviours, or even explanations.

Tip

Involve designers who are skilled at creating and learning from prototypes.

Summarize the concepts. If you have already started to generate possible solution concepts, capture these.

Summarize the questions you have. You should be able to articulate the main uncertainties in relation to each concept. Prioritize these.

Suggest ways to answer the questions. This will require much deeper and longer discussion about what approaches will be the best way to explore the questions and find answers to them. Methods to do this include role play, experience prototyping or playing design games. It's unlikely at this stage that you will be ready to "test" your concepts. You will want the team to define collectively how to move towards reducing important uncertainties.

Synthesize. Use the template to organize your thoughts – for example, along a wall if several people are involved in using this method. The aim is to structure an argument about what you need to explore further.

Review. Iterate your plan on a flipchart so you can start exploring in more detail how you will carry out the exploratory prototyping.

6 Prototyping and playing design games

continued...

Planning prototyping & design games

Use this to clarify the connections between what you have learned so far, and what you want to explore further

	Findings:	Insights:	Concepts:	Questions:	Methods:
	Observations you have made, things you have noticed	What these tell you	Possible opportunities or ways to do things differently	What you want to explore further through prototyping or design games	How you might carry out the exploration
Issue 1					
Issue 2					
Issue 3					

Example

Planning prototyping

	Findings/ Observations	Insights	Concepts	Questions	Methods
Issue ①	Older people don't want to only mix with people their age or be treated as old	There's no such thing as "older people" with needs homogeneous	Ways to connect older people with others based on shared interests or passions, in which they have something to offer	Would some older people (or their families) pay for a befriending service?	-Design game to co-design a befriending service with carers and families -Home visits to explore a mocked-up form & online site for a paid-for befriending service -Role play a sales call
Issue ②	Many younger people have mobile phone/computer/ tech skills & help out friends & family	Young people's digital literacy is taken for granted but can be seen as a resource	Young people as "tech friends" for older people to help them use their phones/ tv/pc to connect with friends/ family/interests	Should the service focus on providing friendly tech support or more general befriending?	-Role play younger people doing a home visit to assess someone's tech setup -Home visit to "walk through" how a service-encounter might work -Mock-up leaflets & posters & web ads -Role play job interview (after volunteering)

Method 12: Service blueprinting

Time involved	Preparation, 10 minutes Using the method, 90 minutes
Associated capabilities	Understand value as created in practice Increase the variance/bring in new actors
Methods to use before or after this one	Method 4 Mapping the user experience Method 5 Creating a persona storyworld

What you'll need

One table per group

Long rolls of butchers' paper or similar, scissors to cut it, Post-it notes, Blu-Tack, marker pens

A facilitator to guide the teams

A documenter to capture the results

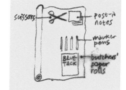

key question

'How do proposed future experiences connect with organizational operation backstage and with underlying infrastructures?'

Purpose

This method brings into view how a service exists in time and space through the interactions of users or customers, people in their day-to-day lives, service personnel and others, and functions of the organization(s) involved. Blueprinting can be used to analyze an existing service, or to sketch out a possible future one. It highlights what a specific user segment experiences and how the segment's capacities connect with the operations and infrastructure of the organization(s) involved. This helps service teams work more effectively together to understand how their various roles, functions and resources are combined into co-creating value in practice with user segments.

Outcomes

Brings a service journey into view, and connects it to organizational and other capacities. By creating a blueprint, gaps or issues in a service proposition can be identified and worked on.

Preparation

Unroll butchers' paper and fix it to a wall, creating a drawing surface of approximately two to three metres long.

Tip

Involve people from different functions and backgrounds.

How to do it

Select a focus. You can use this method to analyze the current service experience and operation, or to sketch out a proposed new one. In either case, the template pushes you to highlight the key resources, capacities and processes that are required in the main service encounters. Ask participants to pick a specific user or customer segment and to use the template to create a blueprint. This will show how their experiences result from their interactions with touchpoints over time, supported by backstage and infrastructure provided by the organizations and other people involved.

There are three areas to explore through service blueprinting:

- *Experience:* what the user segment will do, say, know and think during the service encounters as they engage with touchpoints and with other people and how their own knowledge, skills and other resources are involved;
- *Backstage:* what happens inside the organization(s) involved, including resources and capacities such as service staff in call centres, or responding to customers via email or social media;
- *Infrastructure:* what other organizational resources are required for the service experience to exist, which might include mobile broadband, payment systems, monitoring or verification processes.

Analyze. Review the blueprints. Identify the important:

- *Decision points:* when users or customers, or staff or touchpoints in the service ecosystem, have to make a decision;
- *Fail points:* the moments when things could go wrong and how this can be recovered from;
- *Capacities:* what are the essential knowledge, skills, understanding and other resources required by users and customers, other people in their day-to-day lives and front-stage and back-stage staff, in order for this service vision to work?

Synthesize. If participants have created several blueprints, combine them to create a smaller set that represents the experiences, backstage resources and infrastructure for specific segments.

6 Prototyping and playing design games

continued...

Service blueprinting

Adapt this to describe the experiences of a segment of users or customers as they interact with a service over time, showing the main resources and functions involved

User segment	Time ▶	Find out about it	Decide to commit	First interaction with or use of the service	Later interactions	Ending/closing
Experiences						
What a person does, intends, knows, says, feels						
Touchpoints and devices a person interacts with – eg website, forms, apps, places						
Other people involved – eg service staff, other users, volunteers, family, friends and bystanders						
Backstage						
Marketing, sales and communications						
Operations						
Technology						
Finance						
Infrastructure						
Taken for granted networks, assets and structures that support the service						

Example

Tech Friends service blueprint: Detail of first visit

	Arrival	Introducing	Tech needs assessment	Planning & goodbye	Debriefing
Experiences • Volunteer older person (O.P.) Family member/carer Mentor	SMS or app to confirm arrival	Get to know one another, mutual nervousness	Volunteer goes through app or form to do a light tech needs assessment and understand current usage or issues in discussion with O.P. and carer/family	Volunteer & O.P. & carer/family member agree next visits (activities, dates, times)	Call between volunteer & mentor after visit ends
Backstage Operations/IT Training/support	Details provided in advance to volunteer & O.P. Based on script/role play for less confident volunteers		Data needs to go to OPS team Any skills gap for this volunteer? can others help?	Action plan created for next steps	Confirm safe return Expense claim for travel Reflective journal to track learning
Infrastructures	Assumes volunteer has smart phone & good mobile coverage		ways to get data to service provider if digital and/or paper		Safety/monitoring record keeping

7 Understanding impact

snapshot

– Measurement and evaluation are not neutral – they are part of an audit culture, which is not necessarily right for creative early-stage innovation and which does not always lead to what was intended.

– Designing for outcomes can allow participants in a service innovation process to self-organize and to learn.

– Outcomes should be based in actors' day-to-day contexts and should be crafted, not just borrowed from other contexts.

ONE DISEASE AT A TIME IS A HEALTHCARE organization set up by Sydney-based doctor, entrepreneur and philanthropist Sam Prince[197]. Its first goal was to remove scabies in indigenous communities in Australia, where in remote locations it affects seven out of ten children before their first birthdays. Based on similar initiatives in Africa, healthcare professionals had the view that the best way to treat the condition was by mass administering drugs to the entire population of a community in a short space of time. One Disease partnered with a university to undertake a pilot, which, if successful, would lead to spreading the programme more widely. Alongside this, One Disease's team undertook visits and did interviews within local communities to understand scabies in situ.

Through this fieldwork it discovered that in one community, an elder with a very severe form of scabies was living in a tent behind the house. This relative was never treated, and so repeatedly re-infected the children from the family who did receive treatment and then came home. The team from One Disease realized its plan to mass administer drugs to a local population was not going to work, as there were other factors that resulted in spreading the condition. The organization faced a dilemma. It could continue down the route it had promised funders and partners, knowing this would most likely not achieve the impact it hoped for. Or it could shift its focus to dealing with patients with very severe scabies, who re-infected other relatives.

This brief story reveals some of the challenges in using different kinds of data-gathering and analysis to understand impact. To secure the investment in resources required to make a project come to life, analysis is needed early on to make sense of hoped-for future impacts. Approaches that simplify causes and effects tend to reassure investors and funders that their investments will lead to the desired results. But anomalies that come into view through looking at an issue holistically, often through fieldwork, can lead to reframing what an issue is, and to what impacts can be achieved. This results in a tension between defining and explaining in advance what will happen, and being open to seeing what happens on the ground and adapting to it. Implicated in the first of these two positions are capabilities such as measurement, monitoring, evaluation and audit, which have become closely intertwined with a rationalist agenda that seeks to understand and control things "out there". Connected to the second position are action research, systems thinking and organizational learning[198]. Such approaches recognize the mutual dependencies between actors within an ecosystem and the contingencies that shape what happens as things unfold.

This chapter helps people at the early stage of designing innovative services think their way through the assessment regimes they plan to put in place, and alerts them to some of the implications that come with this rationality. It introduces two approaches to counter the rationalist agenda that dominates contemporary organizations. The first is scenario planning, which highlights the importance of constructing

7 Understanding impact

multiple accounts of possible futures to help make decisions in the present. The second approach is designing for outcomes, which requires active collaboration by participants in a design process as they self-organize to work towards achieving specific results.

Two cases illustrate how the concept of outcomes has been used in organizations aiming to innovate in services. The first describes a project in which a telecommunications company's marketing department focused on outcomes that were meaningful to future users when designing bespoke business-to-business software. The second case describes how Fiat's ability to gather data about driving habits was identified as a resource for behaviour change, but how this did not lead to the desired results. These contrasting stories show how designing for outcomes and the associated data-gathering are a key part of service innovation, but how this does not always play out as planned. Method 13 helps teams sketch out an outcomes framework, not in lieu of doing it properly with specialists, but as part of staging an early conversation about impact and data-gathering. Method 14 prompts a team to articulate the design principles that will underpin its work. Seeing outcomes frameworks as "tools for thinking" highlights their role in helping teams develop and iterate a nuanced understanding of what they are trying to achieve[199].

Assessing impact

In the language of many organizations, if there is a vision, then what it should lead to is impact. Impact can be thought about at the levels of organizational strategy (what do we aim to achieve and why?), marketing (what is our offer, to who or what, and how do we engage and co-create value with them?), finance (what are the costs and revenues, and is a particular investment and set of activities an efficient use of financial resources?), operations (how do we produce and co-deliver an offer effectively and efficiently?), and organization design and behaviour (how do we combine and develop resources to achieve our goals?). Keeping a focus on impact helps managers assess whether activities are leading towards achieving goals and whether the organization is living up to its vision and values. But impact is too diffuse a concept to be useful. Instead, thinking about *outcomes* helps articulate what kinds of impact a project might have, seeing these as situated in every-day practices that are meaningful to end users, customers and organizations, communities, functions and other actors.

The dominant way of thinking about impact is return on investment (ROI). This is typically used to help organizations assess the (financial) impact of undertaking (financial) investment and resource allocation to achieve a particular purpose. There has been extensive criticism of ROI – in particular, highlighting the limitations of trying to reduce the complexity of organizational life to quantifiable values and its neglect of factors such as environmental impact. However, it remains a shorthand used widely in many contexts. To address these shortcomings, people working within environmental activism, corporate social responsibility and social innovation have experimented with different ways to assess impact and understand evidence.

One influential attempt to include a non-financial perspective is the concept of the triple-bottom line (3BL)[200], first proposed by John Elkington, a campaigner working on sustainability and corporate social responsibility. Now widely used, 3BL aims to consider people, planet and profit – for example, including

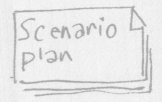

Scenario
plan

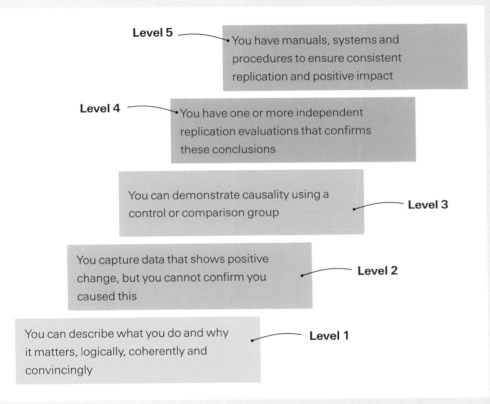

Level 5 — You have manuals, systems and procedures to ensure consistent replication and positive impact

Level 4 — You have one or more independent replication evaluations that confirms these conclusions

You can demonstrate causality using a control or comparison group — Level 3

You capture data that shows positive change, but you cannot confirm you caused this — Level 2

You can describe what you do and why it matters, logically, coherently and convincingly — Level 1

Figure 6 Five levels for different standards of evidence (Puttnick and Ludlow 2012) [204]

Closely tied up with understanding impact is the need for producing evidence. In this logic, evidence that is quantitative and verifiable independently by others usually trumps other kinds of evidence. The UK innovation foundation, Nesta, produced a simplified framework, helping distinguish between different kinds of evidence and what each kind implies[203]. Figure 6 shows the five levels of evidence Nesta identified. This moves from level one, which has a low threshold for evidence and is appropriate for early-stage innovations, to level five, which involves having demonstrable evidence that is independently verified about the intervention having a positive impact at multiple locations. At the early stage of a service innovation project it is useful to distinguish between kinds of evidence about future impact that will be required at the different stages of project.

Unpicking audit cultures

It's worth stepping back for a moment to explore the drive to produce measurable outcomes, which is so embedded in contemporary organizations that it is rarely thought about. Measurement and evaluation – or as some social scientists call it, the audit culture[205] – do not come without consequences. Such approaches are tied to a rationalist agenda that assumes managers are outside a context that they can control, and that people are independent of it, rather than implicated as actors within a complex innovation ecosystem.

Briefly, critics of audit culture point to how managing in commercial and public contexts is now tied up with ways of calculating value and impact. Performance indicators and benchmarking are routinely used to measure services, based on the belief that they improve the productivity and conduct of

human and natural capital in full-cost accounting. Other attempts to broaden the scope of ROI include social return on investment (SROI), which aims to capture and describe the (non-financial) impacts of organizational activity, and in particular those that result in outcomes for particular target groups or in relation to collective matters at local, regional or global scales[201]. For example, the New Economics Foundation developed a guide for organizations to describe their social return on investment[202].

organizations and individuals across different professions and contexts. This includes those services that are non-commercial such as universities, public services and healthcare. This pervasive culture derives its legitimacy from claims that measuring and publishing performance data enhances transparency and accountability, and is one of the drivers behind open data, discussed in Chapter 4.

This culture has now spread beyond organizational contexts to interpersonal interactions. For example, commercial web-based services enable people to assess and make public their own and others' participation in value constellations in which they and other people exchange resources – for example, through giving and receiving feedback from other users of Ebay or Airbnb. Services that have no immediate monetary value to most users, such as Facebook, Twitter or LinkedIn, also build in aspects of audit culture. For example, the user interface of the Twitter web application shows at a glance how many tweets are associated with a user account, how many followers it has and how many other accounts it follows. To be "social" in these social media involves being counted and rated, and habitually rating others, and doing so in public, usually without the ability to turn off this functionality.

Sociologists have shown how with audit culture come some unexpected and unwelcome implications. One is that the insistence on producing evidence about impact means that measurement takes priority over delivering or improving services. As social innovation adviser Jon Huggett puts it, the focus in audit culture is on proving, not improving[206]. The quest for indicators replaces active management – measuring things becomes what managers do. Instead of managing as guiding and shaping things to achieve some purpose,

management in the audit culture is concerned with producing evidence for others. This leads to infinite regression. If managers have to produce data for audit, which is then audited by other experts, who then audits these auditors?

A second implication is that conformity to what worked yesterday (based on the evidence), rather than being open to what might now emerge, reduces creativity and innovation. For example, for a service provider operating a call centre, focusing on answering customers' calls within a particular number of rings can become a metric that staff work to blindly to ensure they meet targets. By focusing on meeting the target, they may ignore opportunities to learn from the detail and tone of customer interactions that provide richer information about what is going on in a service as it intersects with their lives.

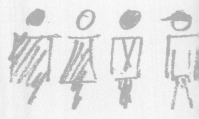

Thirdly, defining outcomes is not neutral. It involves making choices about how change is framed and whose point of view shapes this. For example, for public health officials and educators in the Global North, reducing the number of teenage pregnancies is a well-established goal. But the individual young women who get pregnant and decide to continue with their pregnancies may think about their lives and the meaning having a family has for them very differently from civil servants and experts. So goal-setting should involve discussions about whose meanings and experiences matter more in shaping how impact is framed.

Fourthly, the culture of producing impact data is sometimes associated with a lack of trust by investors, policymakers and senior managers. The audit culture leads to resentment and alienation among team members being monitored and benchmarked. Top-down audit culture is an inappropriate mode of governance

Feedback loop

share

for the digital era, with its multiple connections and flat hierarchies[207].

This short discussion highlights some of the dangers that come from the relentless measurement of impact embedded in contemporary life. People designing innovative services will have articulated the impacts they aim to have, and set up ways to gather evidence in order to understand the outcomes that result. But at the same time they should be attentive to the baggage that comes with audit culture. Tightly defined processes and metrics determined in advance, which drive particular organizational processes and behaviours, often do not adequately capture the impact of a venture or service as it unfolds. At the early stage of a project, when a new innovation ecosystem is being assembled and value-in-use is not well understood, focusing on particular metrics may result in missing what is important. The intended outcomes and the associated measures that were initially agreed on may not be the right ones for different actors involved. Further, as with any research activity, tracking outcomes can capture only a partial view of what is going on. This, then, foregrounds outcome identification, data gathering and interpretation within collective sense-making that is open to diversity and flexibility. The two approaches that follow offer different ways to do this.

Bringing the future forward through scenario planning

One way to approach thinking about impact, that reduces the risk of it turning into data-gathering for the sake of it, is to use scenario planning. This is a capability developed in large organizations dealing with long investment cycles and time horizons, such as oil producers, governments, and technology firms. Scenario planning is used when organizations want to think through possible futures and their implications, in order to shape a strategic conversation and decision-making in the present and near term[208].

At first glance, scenario planning is often considered to be similar to forecasting. Both aim to help organizations consider future developments to help managers prepare for them. However, there are important differences. Forecasting aims to think about the future by extrapolating from current conditions, based on carefully thought-through assumptions, to provide models about the future that managers can assess and plan for. In contrast, scenario planning acknowledges how organizations and managers are actively involved in co-constructing futures. It offers multiple stories about different possible futures for interpretation, rather than models for analysis.

An important principle from scenario planning is that there is not a singular future lying just ahead into which organizations are headed. Instead, scenario practitioners assume irreducible indeterminacy and ambiguity. They draw on quantitative and qualitative data about the past to create and develop accounts of events and activities that are yet to happen, often in the form of a set of narrative scenarios based on different variables. Although data about trends are used in creating scenarios, there is recognition that scenarios are constructed. They are acts of imagination and speculation about the future, not analyses about the past ported into the future.

Once a set of scenarios has been created, the next phase is using scenarios as a resource to engage stakeholders inside and outside of organizations in a collective discussion about what might happen if the events and activities in different scenarios were to unfold. Typically, this takes the form of a series of workshops in which people consider the implications of a set of scenarios supported by skilled facilitation. Sometimes a scenario planning project involves creating and engaging with tangible or digital artefacts that bring aspects of the future into view, as discussed in Chapter 5. Through scenario planning, organizations can surface differences of opinion and different underlying assumptions and values that exist in the present. This collective sense-making that comes from discussing competing accounts of future developments shapes how an organization proceeds with strategy, innovation management and planning.

It is useful to borrow from scenario planning how it combines different sources of data and insight together with imagination and speculation, in order to construct collective, multiple accounts of future events and their impacts. Scenarios surface differences and can trigger productive conflicts, as teams begin to articulate the possibly inconsistent visions and intentions to which they are committed, individually and collectively. Faced with alternative scenarios about what might unfold prompts a team to articulate shared visions and responses, which can help orient an organization as it finds its way through what is to come.

Organizing for outcomes

Another approach relevant to people designing innovative services is outcome-based commissioning.

Research shows that organizations giving up some of the control they associate with specifying how to do things can lead to achieving the outcomes they want. Concepts and activities that emerged in manufacturing are also found in complex service systems, based on the recognition of the mutual interdependencies between actors involved in a value constellation.

The shift towards more effective collaboration, during a project's early design phase, developed in lean manufacturing in the auto industry. The Toyota Production System improved production quality and operational effectiveness by doing things that looked, at first glance, less efficient. Its principles included changing over manufacturing processes more frequently than at other firms, empowering workers to identify and respond to production issues, using distributed data to enable workers and managers to track what was going on, and just-in-time production. Many of the principles associated with Toyota's approach have been incorporated into other areas of organizational life or have emerged in different forms, such as lean entrepreneurship and value stream mapping.

One less well-known aspect of the Toyota Production System is its use of set-based design. The researchers who identified this called it "the second Toyota paradox".[209] They found that Toyota considered a broader range of possible designs and delayed certain decisions longer than at other car firms, yet had faster and more efficient vehicle development cycles. Elsewhere, vehicle design practice tended to converge quickly on

a solution that was modified until it met the objectives set by the product team. For example, many US car manufacturers made decisions early, and then froze them. In contrast, Toyota practised what the researchers called set-based concurrent engineering, taking longer to finalize a design. This started with lots of possible solutions (the sets) within clearly defined constraints, which were gradually narrowed down to converge on a final one. The researchers were surprised to find that Toyota avoided freezing specifications early, based on a principle of "make each decision in its time" [210]. This had implications for suppliers, who had to find ways to deal with this extended uncertainty. One aspect of this was that Toyota specified details such as ranges of performance and interface requirements, and cost and weight targets for components they wanted, leaving suppliers to get on with working out exactly how they should produce the required items within each set. Research showed that this management approach supported reliable and efficient communication and allowed Toyota and its suppliers to work together relatively independently and with fewer and shorter meetings [211].

In adapting these findings for people in the early stages of designing innovative services, there are two principles. The first is not converging too early on a single solution, but working in parallel on several possibilities. The second is specifying what the organization wants to achieve but freeing suppliers and partners to work out how to achieve this, with close and regular dialogue between an organization and its partners and other actors. The latter principle is now increasingly evident in a range of industry contexts, two of which are now explored.

The shift towards a service-dominant logic and an orientation towards hybrids, described in Chapter 2, recognized that manufacturers are implicated in complex value-creating systems of products, people and activities – what some researchers call the servitization of manufacturing [212]. For organizations that are "pure" providers of services, the service-dominant logic highlights how they, too, are implicated in and are co-dependent on combinations of capabilities and physical and digital assets to which access is provided through service. Outcome-based contracts between service providers and their suppliers and partners are one way that organizations involved in such ecosystems instantiate how the combination of their capacities and resources co-creates value.

A study by Irene Ng and colleagues illustrates how contracts with firms that have sold equipment to an individual or to another company have changed [213]. Traditional service contracts were based on the idea of billable time and materials, such as spare parts needed to maintain or repair equipment. In such contracts, there was no incentive for the supplier to repair and maintain the equipment to reduce the likelihood of future breakdowns, since breakdowns and faults generated income. A consumer example is the servicing that is required to keep your car in good condition on the road.

In contrast, contracts that specify outcomes make the usage and ongoing functioning of a piece of equipment a shared concern. One example is how Rolls-Royce has developed a service to maintain airplane engines, remunerated on the basis of how many hours the engine is in the air, known as "Power by the Hour®". Such outcome-based contracts focus on achieving required results rather than on meeting a set of prescribed specifications[214]. Ng and colleagues show that what is distinctive about such contracts is that they require close collaboration between buyer and provider. The service provider's revenues come only from the collaborative performance of the activities, even if the provider has no control over what the customer does. In the Rolls-Royce example, the number of hours a plane is in the air depends in part on where the customer is flying to, which affects environmental conditions such as airborne sand, as well as the customer's ability to use the engine with care while flying.

Designing contracts based on achieving outcomes is becoming more common in public sector commissioning of services. Outcomes-based commissioning in the public sector has been led by government policy agendas to try to increase efficiencies in service delivery, reduce costs and improve impacts, as well as being shaped by political agendas to reduce the role of the state[215]. Some commissioners of public services, such as housing or healthcare, are shifting towards inviting bids from suppliers who are required to deliver particular outcomes (see Table 7 for some examples). Suppliers are then paid if they achieve the results and make payments to the commissioner if they do not. As with the Toyota example, commissioners adopt the principle of allowing suppliers to organize themselves to achieve the outcomes. One of the concerns associated with this approach is whether civil servants in central or local government who commission services have sufficient skills and knowledge to define outcomes appropriately. Defining the outcomes is linked to being able to adequately define in the first place the problems they seek to address[216]. A second concern is the challenge to public sector ways of organizing, to shift them towards a co-production model in which the responsibility of achieving outcomes is shared across several actors. A third concern is whether public sector bodies have adequate competencies in being able to review and revise specifications and contracts regularly on the basis of new data.

To summarize, (co-)production processes, commissioning and contracts in manufacturing and services have shifted towards specifying outcomes, and away from the detail of how to get there. Proponents of such lean approaches argue there are benefits when organizations do not try to tightly define the activities through which teams, suppliers and partners should organize to achieve specific outcomes. Instead, this approach emphasizes how the actors involved in a project are mutually implicated and can self-organize and collaborate to work towards achieving the outcomes to which they have jointly committed. But the implications include having capabilities to collaborate and communicate effectively with partners, being able to define issues well at the outset and being able to maintain learning cycles.

Domain	Example outcomes
Customer service operations	Reduced customer effort to resolve issues, increased customer loyalty, increased customer satisfaction, resolution of an issue in one phone call
Healthcare	Quality adjusted life years, increased access to universal services by under-represented groups, reduced stigma for those experiencing mental health, excess weight in adults
Crime	Reducing reoffending for those with a history of substance misuse, reduced fear of crime, a reduction in youth offending and anti-social behaviour
Community and built environment	Making somewhere a great place to live, an increased feeling of safety outside the home at night, an increase in recycling, increased feeling of pride in living somewhere, increased energy efficiency in the built environment
Education	Increased educational attainment for children in families with complex needs, increased school attendance, reduced numbers of children excluded from school
Social care	Increased participation in activities for people experiencing mental health issues, fewer admissions to acute care, increased emotional wellbeing of looked-after children

Table 7 Example outcomes in different service contexts

Framing outcomes

If organizations are moving towards designing for outcomes, on what basis should outcomes be created? What are the underlying concepts that outcomes are based on? As with any management topic, there are fads and fashions that shape how to answer these questions, influenced by different views as to what matters and what should be attended to. People often reach for two long-established concepts – efficiency and effectiveness. It is worth exploring in more depth the different concepts that underpin outcomes, to help clarify if the most appropriate outcomes are being articulated for a given project.

One recent development is the growing interest in business models, driven in part by the way digital networks and the internet are reconfiguring many industries and organizations[217]. Focusing on business models helps managers and researchers make sense of the different constitutive elements of an organization and establish how well they fit into a whole, and how they exist in relation to customers, partners and suppliers[218]. Conceptualizing business models involves drawing together the various specialisms and functions involved in organizing that usually remain separate – strategy, marketing, finance, human resources and operations. A second emphasis in business models is on value *creation*, not just value *capture*. Following on from this is the heightened awareness of the roles played by customers, partners and users in creating value.

A popular framework is the Business Model Canvas, created by Alex Osterwalder and Yves Pigneur[219]. It helps managers bring together the various constituents of an existing business or new venture. In the two-dimensional version of the canvas, the value

7 Understanding impact

propositions are positioned at the centre, defined as the value delivered to customer segments. Components of the business model concerning customers appear on the right-hand side of the canvas: customer relationships (what kinds of relationships exist with customer segments), channels (ways to reach customers) and customer segments, although there is nothing here highlighting what capacities they themselves have. The left-hand side of the canvas focuses on organizational activities, resources and partners required to deliver the value propositions to each segment. Along the bottom of the canvas are two components relating to finance – cost structure and revenue streams. Such visualizations help managers organize the resources they're working with into a framework that can be shared, reviewed and refined.

A variant of this is the Social Business Model Canvas published by the Young Foundation, a social innovation intermediary[220]. This is a tool for managers and entrepreneurs creating ventures that aim to have a positive impact on society, which may be profit-making or non-profit. The Social Business Model Canvas borrows heavily from the Business Model Canvas, but has key differences. It puts the social value proposition at the centre of its canvas, inviting people using the canvas to ask what difference their project or venture will make and what impact measures will be used to assess this. Below this is a component labelled surplus, which is the difference between costs and revenues. A question located in this box on the canvas prompts people using this tool to consider where they want to reinvent any surplus; this is in contrast to the Business Model Canvas, which does not ask what happens to profits or surpluses. By including components for competitors and for the wider environment, this canvas prompts entrepreneurs creating new ventures

to pay attention to the shifting context in which they are operating. These small but significant differences emphasize how ventures aiming at social impact require dialogue about what impact actually means for the actors involved in a changing context.

A criticism that can easily be made of such frameworks is that they mix different levels of abstraction. For example, strategy can be understood as how an organization positions itself in relation to opportunities and issues in a changing context. A business model describes how it organizes itself to connect capacities and resources internally and in relation to other actors in the environment to achieve a purpose by co-creating and capturing value. Combining concepts from these two distinct areas into one framework, as the Social Business Model Canvas does, may not make sense. However, if strategy is understood as wayfinding on the ground in relation to turbulent contexts and to what users, competitors and partners are doing, then having such developments present on the canvas foregrounds the organizational capabilities required to set up fast learning cycles, and to launch clumsy solutions and learn.

A second criticism is the difficulty of representing on a single sheet of paper the dynamic and complex interactions between the various components of a business model. In particular, the perspective of service-dominant logic is difficult to represent in two dimensions, since it recognizes the mutual interdependencies between actors as value is co-created through their participation in an innovation ecosystem.[221]

On the other hand, having some of the fundamental concepts relating to value co-creation brought into relation with one another on a single page helps teams to develop a shared response to identifying

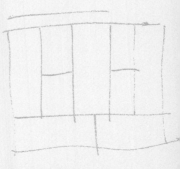

Business Model Canvas

and engaging with opportunities. Further, the argument embedded in the Business Model Canvas and other variants is that business models *can be designed*. Foregrounding this as a collective activity helps people designing innovative services bring into view the bounded entity they plan to introduce into the innovation ecosystem.

It is not clear, however, if the business model is the most important conceptual apparatus to use during the fuzzy front end of service innovation. For situations in which a novel service is being designed, which *may* be an opportunity but is not yet ready to be analyzed as a fully-fledged venture, then something else is required. This opens up more general questions of how to assess the potential value of a proposed new value proposition or design. One solution to this was developed by innovation consultancy IDEO, usually visualized as a Venn diagram. This has three areas of focus: desirability (do people want it?), viability (is it profitable?) and feasibility (can we build it?)[222]. The innovation sweet spot, argues IDEO, lies at the intersection of all three. What is appealing about this model is how it fits into existing managerial mindsets, since the three constituent elements map roughly on to marketing, finance and operations. But this is also its weakness. It replicates contemporary organizational divisions that have their origins in the goods-dominant logic based on meeting customers' needs within a value chain, rather than seeing value as co-created through the combining of capacities of actors within an innovation ecosystem.

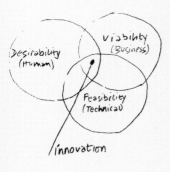

An alternative framework that is useful here has rather older origins. The Roman architect and engineer Vitruvius is known for his ten books of architecture, which were lost and then recovered in the European Renaissance, like many other Greek and Roman writings[223]. One of Vitruvius' formulations, dating back some 2000 years, remains powerful and in use today. He proposed that a successful building design exists at the intersection of three concepts: what in Latin he called *firmitas* (roughly translated as firmness, stability, or structural integrity), *utilitas* (commodity, usefulness, or meeting functional needs) and *venustas* (delight, style, proportion or beauty). A constituent element of a design can be analysed through more than one of these. For example, when designing a building, the amount and type of lighting can have a functional impact, such as providing a space that is bright enough to work in (*utilitas*), but it can also impact on the pleasure and wellbeing experienced by people using the building or their feeling of safety at night (*venustas*).

In the Business Model Canvas and in IDEO's trio of desirability, viability and feasibility, financial impact is as strongly weighted as the other components. In contrast, the concept of *firmitas* in Vitruvius' framework can be thought of as *resourcing*. It prompts a discussion as to whether a proposed design involves a good use of resources, is well put together, and is structurally sound. It focuses on the design as experienced by the people and organizations engaged with one another in a service, and the resources used to bring it into being, without being explicit about financial value or creating a financial surplus. Further, Vitruvius' trio of concepts departs from conventional ways of thinking about business and moves managers from different silos within an organization away from their domains of expertise. By not replicating the traditional functional divisions that exist in most organizations, the Vitruvian trio of performance (*utilitas*), experience (*venustas*) and resourcing (*firmitas*) compels people designing innovative services to consider the whole they wish to bring into being (see Figure 7).

These concepts have been used in healthcare innovation. For example, one study argued that conventional thinking about health services focused on safety, and effective use of resources, but excluded the experiential dimension of healthcare for patients and staff[224]. The researchers proposed assessing healthcare services through a Vitruvian trio of performance (is it safe and does it deliver health outcomes?), engineering (does it combine organizational resources and knowledge effectively?), and aesthetics (does it offer positive experiences for patients and stakeholders?). For a commercial service such as a telecommunications company with multiple customer service channels, *performance* could be assessed through establishing outcomes such as whether a customer's single call to a contact centre results in resolution. Outcomes associated with *experience* could include customer satisfaction or loyalty over a particular timeframe, not tied to the last service encounter or a specific contact channel. Outcomes linked to *resourcing* could include assessing whether customers and staff are involved in sharing their knowledge with others.

The framework based on Vitruvius does not offer a detailed analytical tool to help assess whether a service innovation is having the desired impact. However, it does provide a tool for thinking that helps bring into view different perspectives and knowledge during a process of defining outcomes for a new service. This is particularly important during the fuzzy front end of an innovation process, when different ways of framing a project are still being explored. Learning from researchers who developed a tool to assess design quality for building and construction based on

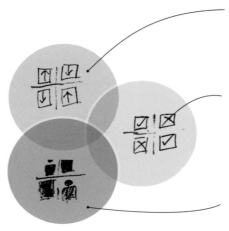

Performance (utilitas) What effects does the service have for the key actors over different timeframes? What does participation in the value constellation enable them to achieve?

Experiences (venustas) What behaviours, meanings and identities are created or changed? How do actors' behaviours embedded in socio-cultural routines and habits help constitute a service?

Resourcing (firmitas) What capacities, habits, knowledge, data, physical and digital assets, and skills are required to constitute the service?

Figure 7 Framework for assessing a service innovation concept, after Vitruvius

Vitruvius, such a framework can help:

> "articulate the subjective qualities felt by different stakeholders in the design process…Tools for thinking aim to elicit and represent knowledge about design in order to initiate conversations about client and user priorities, design possibilities and consequences. This is possible because results from different members of the project team and user groups can be compared and contrasted during design and subsequent evaluation processes."[225]

This emphasis on exploration and learning positions designing for outcomes as part of collective sense-making, rather than complying with the audit culture. Method 13 shows how to create a draft outcomes framework to help orient a team towards the impact it wants to achieve through a new project. The resulting sketch should be embedded in a more systematic attempt to work with specialists to explore, frame, understand, gather data about, and re-assess the impact a project is having. As a tool for thinking to be used at an early stage of an innovation project, a framework surfaces differences of perspective and understanding about outcomes. Further, it orients a team towards being explicit about what it is trying to achieve in ways that are meaningful for the actors involved.

Implications for service innovation

The chapter concludes by reviewing how the approaches discussed above help organizations understand the desired changes that the project wants to achieve that motivate team members, investors and funders and stakeholders. It has presented ways to challenge the audit culture embedded in contemporary life by shifting towards approaches to understanding impact based in collective discussion and learning. Through scenario planning, designing for outcomes, and creating frameworks to understand impact, teams can engage productively the irreducible uncertainties they face, and make this useful for sense-making and decision-making.

The capability of launching clumsy solutions to learn requires framing what intended changes the solutions are aiming at. Scenario planning highlights the multiple possible futures that could result from an initiative. Designing for outcomes enables teams to be attentive to how impact measures are framed, created, defined, operationalized and re-framed as new knowledge is created. This perspective highlights that participants such as organizational partners and staff members can self-organize to work towards desired outcomes, rather than being frozen within an audit culture.

Second, the capability of understanding value-in-use is supported by the perspectives discussed here.

Scenario planning involves constructing narratives about organizational futures in the immediate transactional and wider contextual environment. Constructing multiple versions of these narratives provides a broad set of possibilities for local, situated kinds of value-in-use realized by and with particular actors. Designing for outcomes focuses a team's attention on the effects a service has within someone's lived experiences, and how this is meaningful to them in their own terms. It also links this to the resources and capacities involved in constituting these outcomes. Creating outcomes frameworks as tools for thinking helps a team surface and contest its differing values, perspectives and knowledge.

Thirdly, the service innovation capability of increasing the variance of the actors involved is enhanced by the process of identifying and researching outcomes. Thinking of this as a collective, iterative process can bring into view unexpected effects and actors that are implicated from a service – effects and actors that were not originally considered to be relevant or part of the innovation ecosystem.

Finally, the service innovation capability that requires moving between concepts and knowledge, and inside and outside organizations, is enriched by the perspectives introduced in this chapter. Scenario planning explores the wider transactional and contextual environments within which a team or project exists, and helps bridge the boundaries between inside and outside an organization. Designing for outcomes helps a team identify and articulate the desired changes motivating its work. It translates abstract concepts into noticeable effects that are meaningful externally and internally within the worlds of targeted groups. The next chapter adds more detail on how teams can organize to work towards achieving the changes they want to happen.

7 Understanding impact

Case 13 Focusing on outcomes to design a B2B marketing solution

The expansion of consumer digital devices and software into people's day-to-day lives presents challenges to developers of B2B software. People familiar with social media and consumer web services who confidently access personal and shared data via smartphones and tablets can't understand why, when they are at work, the software they rely on as part of their job is hard to use and often gets in their way. In-house technology teams in large organizations often struggle to deal with the pace of change, as new releases of existing software and developments such as the cloud, social media and open data redefine expectations about what services should be able to do.

Many IT departments use the traditional waterfall approach to develop software. Having agreed a business case, analysts then elicit users' requirements, followed by building software, followed by testing prototypes, and finally launching software and training people in how to use it. IT departments and their suppliers typically measure success on metrics that capture quality in technical terms as well as cost and time to deliver. User satisfaction or acceptance is harder to define or establish.

An alternative approach is identifying outcomes that have meaning for the target end users and their organization, by focusing on the value-in-use the new software is intended to have for actors within the value constellation. This requires capabilities in understanding value-in-use – for example, researching people's work practices. It also involves working in small mixed teams, including users within fast learning cycles, to combine existing ways of doing things with the capabilities afforded by new software. A case that describes the design of software for a marketing team at a telecommunications firm brings this to life.

In 2010, a Dutch mobile operator contracted a Chinese original equipment manufacturer (OEM) · to replace its disparate operating and business systems with a single, unified, modular solution at one of its subsidiaries, here called Telco. Most of the operating and business systems were available as modules in the Chinese firm's solution. However, Telco concluded that the campaign management module – originally developed for a Chinese mobile operator – was not fit for purpose for its approach to marketing in Europe. A project was launched to jointly develop a new campaign management module to fit within the solution being implemented.

The goal of the redesign was to improve the usability of the software. This was measured by a combination of process output data (e.g. number of campaigns, time to develop a campaign) and proxy user effort score. User effort score is an approach to understanding customer loyalty that asks people to give a numerical rating to how much work they have to do to solve a problem[226]. This metric is based on research showing that customers who contacted an organization were more loyal if the provider got the basics of the service right, reducing the amount of work users had to invest themselves in accessing after-sales service. Variants of the user effort approach recognize the time, skills and work that customers put in to co-creating a service. In this project, the factors shaping user effort were: perceived time required to complete a task, its complexity, skill level, and the work required to complete key campaign activities.

The Dutch team was concerned that the waterfall approach to software development used by most current OEMs was slow, expensive and prone to over-engineered solutions that do not match users' ways of working. Instead, for this project they adopted an approach that combined the best of agile software development, lean start-up, and understanding the experiences of the end users in the marketing department.

A joint development team consisting of marketers from Telco and IT developers from the Chinese supplier was setup. The aim was for the developers to understand first-hand what the marketers wanted and for the marketers to appreciate what the proposed technology could and couldn't do cost effectively. All the design, development, testing and implementation work was done by the collaborative development team.

Developers observed how marketers went about their jobs, to develop a deeper understanding of their work. In place of the traditional but flawed use cases used in software development, the team created key jobs statements based on analysing what marketers did, the critical tasks involved, and the desired outcomes that were meaningful to them. Project manager Graham Hill explains:

> "This allowed the team to cut out the costly wishlist requirements that plague traditional software development. It also allowed them to prioritise their jobs so that the developers could focus on creating sub-systems for the priority jobs first."

Rather than develop the new campaign management module as a whole, the team broke it down into a set of functions. Based on the lean start-up idea of the Minimal Viable Product[227], they planned a minimum usable sub-system (MUS) for each function. Each MUS provided the minimum of functionality for a marketer to do one of their jobs significantly better than with current tools. A roadmap allowed additional functionality based on prioritized marketer jobs to be progressively added to each MUS as the module was developed.

Each of the prioritized sub-systems was developed by a small team of dedicated developers. When designing, the team created paper wireframes, which were signed-off by the marketers. These designs were then quickly turned into bare-bones software by the developers and reviewed remotely

7 Understanding impact

Case 13 (continued) Focusing on outcomes to design a B2B marketing solution

by the marketers. Feedback was rigorously documented and the final sub-system was then iterated prior to formal testing, handover and release. Hill explains: "This fast cycle of design-develop-test-decide was repeated as long as was necessary for users to sign-off the sub-systems". Having completed each MUS, the next iteration of development could be started.

As soon as each sub-system was released in beta, it was made available to the marketers to use in their day jobs. Even though each sub-system was only a minimum usable part of the full system, it was still more effective than the tools marketers were currently using. Each iteration improved the software and, by people using the components early on, Telco got the benefit of a deep exploration of value-in-use, as marketers used the software in their work. Training costs were reduced too, as the same marketers who had been closely involved in the design were able to act as ambassadors when the final system was released to the marketing department.

The new campaign management module went from early stage design to full implementation within 18 months. The modular approach taken meant the most highly prioritized sub-systems of the module were in use within 12 months, other sub-systems

being added as they were released. Hill describes the impact:

> "The users of the campaign management module found that it took less time to create a new marketing campaign than was the case before, was less complicated to use, required lower skill levels and created less re-work. The reduced user effort had the unintended benefit of freeing-up users to spend more time on the creative side of campaign development."

Others saw the benefits of the modular design approach too. Marketing staff at another European subsidiary of the telco were impressed with the software when it was shown to them. Hill comments: "It was almost as though it had been designed by fellow marketers".

Case 14 Using data to develop eco-driving behaviours at Fiat

Founded in 1899, Fiat is an industrial group employing more than 215,000 people worldwide. Its brands include Fiat, Alfa Romeo, Maserati and Ferrari. Its iconic Fiat 500, first sold in 1957, was relaunched in 2007 as an urban three-door hatchback with retro styling. Since then, more than one million new Cinquecentos have been sold around the world.

Each of these cars has a USB port on its dashboard or in the glove compartment, which presented Fiat with a huge opportunity to gather data about people's driving habits. According to Luis Cilimingras, Fiat advertising manager at the time, the car-maker's goal was to use this data to reduce CO2 emissions. He explained:

> "We spend hundreds of millions of euros redesigning engines and improving the aerodynamics and power trains, all for minimal improvements in emissions, maybe 2 or 3 percent. But…there is a margin of improvement in the way people drive of maybe 20 percent because people don't always drive in a perfect way. So it looked to us like we could take a holistic approach to the emissions by helping the customer to do a little bit more."[228]

Much of the debate around carbon emissions focuses on technological innovation. But Fiat saw an opportunity to use data from people's driving habits to encourage "eco-driving" – that is, driving with the intention of minimizing carbon emissions and fuel consumption. By harnessing and using data about driving habits from cars, Fiat turned the data into a potential resource for individual drivers, for businesses operating fleets of cars, and for society at large.

The way Fiat did this was to develop its eco:Drive[229] initiative, launched in 2008. eco:Drive is built on Blue&Me, a Bluetooth-based system developed jointly by Fiat and Microsoft that gives drivers hands-free control over in-car devices such as music players and mobile phones. eco:Drive aimed to make drivers an active part of a car's emissions-control system in a way that was enjoyable and easy to use[230]. Sensors record how a driver accelerates, brakes, changes gear and his or her steadiness of driving; these data are analyzed against the car's fuel economy and exhaust emissions[231].

To access the data, drivers remove a standard flash drive from their car's USB port, plug it into a computer and download information about their most recent trips. The eco:Drive software application then tells motorists how many kilograms of CO2 emissions the car produced during recent drives and gives projected financial savings from reduced fuel consumption[232]. The application gives drivers an "eco:Index" score out of 100, allows people to set their own targets to beat, and allows them to compare journeys they have made.

7 Understanding impact

Case 14 (continued) Using data to develop eco-driving behaviours at Fiat

As well as an online community for Cinquecento owners, Fiat developed a training tool to help drivers intentionally change their driving behaviours based on data from their cars. The eco:Drive Live system is a personal trainer, offering progressive tutorials to help drivers improve efficiency. The system also alerts the driver when conditions are affecting the efficiency of the vehicle[233].

In their 2010 report[234] on eco:Drive, based on data from more than 400,000 journeys uploaded by 5,700 drivers in five countries, Fiat concluded that driving with intent to reduce carbon emissions through behaviour change resulted in positive impacts. Drivers in the study made most changes during the first 30 days of the study, with the top 10% of drivers reducing their fuel consumption by 16%, and the average driver reducing consumption by 6%. The research showed that drivers using eco:Drive stopped and started less frequently and drove at a more consistent speed. However, other research suggests that early gains made from changes to the way people drive peter out[235]. Presenting data to drivers, as the eco:Drive system does, may help people understand the impact their driving has, but on its own does not necessarily lead to sustained changes in behaviour. Comments on the Fiat 500 drivers' forum help explain why.

Online discussion between drivers illustrates the associations some people have with driving, and in particular with driving this brand of car. This is valuable qualitative data that can be analysed through a socio-cultural lens to understand people's engagements with the eco:Drive initiative. For example, in one message posted on the forum, a driver announced:

> "Well I got my flash drive from Fiat tonight. Just down loaded the eco drive application to my Mac. Formatted the Fiat flash drive. Plug the flash drive into my USB slot in the car. Going to drive my car with the flash drive in for the next 5 days, to get data recorded on it. We see how my driving habits will be."[236]

Another contributor to the thread then commented:

> "Novelty that wears off after a few weeks at best, at least for me it did. These cars are way more fun when you drive them in a spirited manner rather than being overly careful and conservative"[237].

Another agreed that driving with the aim of keeping your eco:Index value down turns you into a different kind of driver. "Yeah, I've become disenchanted as well...drive it like a G-ma [grandma] and my index is only a freaking 60. Drive it like I want and it's a 54"[238]. These posts illustrate how driving with the aim of achieving specific value for the eco:Index to reduce carbon emissions and save fuel may be a driver's goal. But driving is also associated with enjoyment and freedom, including the freedom not to be bound by constraints.

Another contributor to the thread later commented: "In my opinion it is a neat little tool. I use it, but all I really need is the Avg. MPG [miles per gallon] on the dash and I'm good".[239] This driver did not understand the kinds of data that the eco:Drive system captures, which include acceleration and deceleration, which are fuel-hungry. This suggests that data-gathering, analysis, visualization and their integration into well-established cultural practices like driving is more complex than the design of the eco:Drive system allowed for.

On the one hand, by putting a USB port into more than a million cars, and making the eco:Drive software available to drivers, Fiat experimented with behaviour change beyond a manufacturer's traditional capability of technological innovation. This initiative captured, visualized and shared data and it tied driver behaviour to impacts – both environmental (CO2 emissions) and financial (fuel consumption). But on the other hand, it highlighted the difficulties of working towards sustained changes in driving behaviours, associated for many people with autonomy and pleasure.

7 Understanding impact

Method 13: Creating a future outcomes framework

Time involved	Preparation, five minutes
	Using the method, 60 minutes
Associated capabilities	Understand value as created in practice
	Launch clumsy solutions and learn
Methods to use before or after this one	Method 6 Segmenting by meaning
	Method 8 Problem/proposition definition

What you'll need
One table per group
Large sheets of paper, Post-it notes, Blue-Tack, marker pens
A facilitator to guide the teams
A documenter to photograph the resulting framework(s)

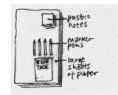

key question

'What are the desired changes that will result from the service?'

Purpose

The aim of this method is to help define and agree the target segments you want to focus on or work with, and the outcomes that the venture, service or product might have. Using this method starts a conversation about the changes your activities aim to produce, and how you will gather evidence to help you assess what is happening.

Outcomes

Using this method early on in a project prompts clarification of the changes you want the venture, service or product to introduce into people's lives. You'll end up with a better understanding of how you might evaluate changes, so you can share with others the proposed impact of your venture, service or product. It does not replace setting up assessment projects involving researchers who specialize in data-gathering and analysis, but helps orient a team to the changes they want to bring about.

How to do it

Review the concept of outcomes. Ask people to share their current perspectives on how change is understood. Discuss similarities and differences between their approaches. Invite them to explore examples of outcomes frameworks from their own specialisms or those of organizations and projects similar to what you are working on.

Identify the target segments. Ask people to reproduce the template by drawing it on a large sheet of paper. Then ask them to identify the key segments (of users, beneficiaries, customers or other key actors such as employers or volunteers) you aim to engage with and have an impact on.

Tip

Invite a diverse group of people to take part in the workshop, including people with backgrounds in operations, research methods, marketing, accountancy and finance, and/or people from different organizations or fields. Do involve service users or customers, and/or people who can share their perspectives. Ask people to bring examples of outcomes frameworks from other fields.

Your Method 6 framework will help you identify the groups you want to work with. Your Method 8 (problem/proposition definition) will help you articulate what outcomes people might want (or what outcomes others might want for them).

Create the outcomes. For each segment, describe the outcomes you hope to work towards and fill these in on the template, perhaps using Post-it notes. An outcome is a sustained change in someone's day-to-day behaviours or practices. Desired outcomes will be very domain specific. For example, a healthcare outcome might take the form of "reduced acute admissions to hospital", whereas for a call centre business an outcome might be "resolve customer issues at the first customer contact".

Using the Vitruvian framework, you can use the team's knowledge of a domain to consider outcomes within three areas and the time frames over which you expect these to take place. Some outcomes might fit in more than one category. Some examples that might be useful follow, but these will be shaped by the problem/solution definition and overall vision:

- *Performance (what is delivered/co-created with users and participants).* For example, access to services within a specific time frame; resolution on first contact via call centre, email, or social media channel; reports of incidents or complaints; numbers of resolved v unresolved issues; time to market; customer churn; service contract renewals.

- *Experience (meaning and associations for participants).* For example, quality of life; feeling connected to a place or community; perceived service quality; satisfaction with a customer experience; loyalty towards an organization; willingness to recommend an organization or service; users feeling empowered or enabled within a service; likelihood to leave a service contract.

- *Resourcing (use/renewal of resources).* For example, revenues; revenue growth; surplus or profits; surplus or profits growth; cost of operations; effective use of human resources; efficient use of financial capital; efficient use of space/IT resources; investment in staff; cost per transaction; customer acquisition; customer retention; customer effort; user-to-user support.

Explore the indicators. Next, define the indicators that you think will provide evidence that these outcomes have been achieved. There might be more than one indicator for each outcome.

Explore data-gathering. Consider how you might try to gather that evidence. What kind of data would be useful for each indicator? Is this data that you or others have access to already, or will you have to organize resources to capture and make sense of that data? Finally, identify the different audiences or stakeholders who will be interested in these outcomes.

Show and share. Compare outcomes frameworks created by different groups. Are their common themes and approaches? Are there important differences of perspective and knowledge that need to be reviewed and resolved?

Synthesize. Combine outcomes and indicators from different teams' work into a combined framework. Discuss implications from different organizational and actor perspectives. For example, what does the framework mean for the operations team, or for the accounts team? How might it shape relations with actors such as funders, investors, regulators and users or others to whom your project is accountable? Who should be involved in researching the intended and unintended consequences of your service, product or venture?

7 Understanding impact

Creating a future outcomes framework

Use this to define the desired outcomes for different segments and how you will know if they are achieved

Group	Insights about this group	Outcome 1	Indicators for outcome 1	Outcome 2	Indicators for outcome 2	Outcome 3	Indicators for outcome 3	Data-gathering required
First user segment								
Second user segment								
Third user segment								

Example

Outcomes framework	Insights	① Outcome	Indicators	② Outcome	Indicators	Data gathering
Committed Katys segment ③	Willing & able to contribute and wanting to build skills & networks	Increased skills & confidence	Interviews, job offers, qualifications	Broader network created	mentor, peer connections, visits	self-reporting, peer review, mentor feedback
Busy Brendas segment ②	Active & engaged but not given to recognising own needs	maintains health & well being	Participation in exercise or classes	Develops new skills or knowledge	mentor, training sessions completed	self-reporting, peer-review, mentor feedback
Segment Ⓐ older people in stable situations with few meaningful connections	Reducing loneliness & isolation will keep them in a stable situation	increased connections that are meaningful	Trips out, visits, conversations, joining or participating in clubs or societies	Able to contribute more to others	making a meal, helping with pets, or childcare or gardens	self-reporting, triangulated with carer/family/visitor accounts
Segment Ⓑ older people heading to less stable situation	poor health can reduce meaningful connections abruptly	connections maintained	visits received and made, regular conversations with close friends or family	Reduced use of acute health care services	attendance at out of house health services	self-reporting, health practitioner, or carer/family/visitor accounts

Method 14: Defining design principles

Time involved	Using the method, 60 minutes
Associated capabilities	Understand value as created in practice Move between concepts and knowledge, and inside and outside organizations
Methods to use before or after this one	Method 4 Mapping the user experience Method 8 Problem/proposition definition

What you'll need

Blank sheets of paper, marker pens

A facilitator to guide the teams

A documenter to photograph the results

A flipchart

key question

'What principles should guide the approach taken to designing a new service?'

Purpose

This method helps a team capture the things that they think matter to the main actors involved in creating a new service, venture or product. It involves a group in collectively articulating the principles that will underpin its future design work, addressing the perspectives not just of users but of organizations and the communities they engage with.

Outcomes

Using the method results in a simple but powerful list that captures a team's current understanding of what will shape how actors co-create value within a new or emerging service ecosystem. It helps align different organizational functions and perspectives by making explicit the values embedded in a new service.

How to do it

Discuss principles. Ask people to share knowledge of design principles from other areas of their life and work. Examples you might consult include the UK Government Digital Service's design principles or the Android user experience design principles. Effective design principles are those that help focus the work of people designing innovative services. They should be simple, but one word is usually not enough. They should be oriented towards action. Use verbs such as "do this" or "don't do that", and objects making clear who or what is having something done to them, such as "do this to me".

Identify principles relating to experiences. Get people to share views as to the meanings and associations that exist for actors in the future ecosystem around a new service, product or venture.

Tip

Don't just focus on people's experiences, but do start there.

A common term that often crops up is making experiences "delightful" – but resist this. Instead, aim to generate concepts that are more nuanced and specific to the situation the service is addressing.

Identify principles relating to performance. Discuss what is delivered or co-created with users and participants in a new ecosystem. A common term here is making services "useful". Define in more detail how, when and why they are useful and productive, and when they achieve something meaningful for the actors involved.

Identify principles relating to resourcing. Invite participants to suggest principles that relate to usage and renewal of resources. An example that is frequently used here is to make services "usable" or "accessible" – but again, try to explore in more depth what these terms could mean in the context of the service you are discussing.

Combine. Select a maximum of ten principles generated from discussion across the three different areas.

Discuss. Would these principles be recognizable to current service users or customers? Are they embedded in how things currently are arranged or organized? Are any of the principles particularly distinctive? Would competitors, partners or collaborators produce the same list? Who else should be involved in refining the principles? Should the design principles be made public? Should the staff and organizations involved in creating a new service be held accountable for working towards delivering the principles? How could that work? What review processes and tasks should be set up to ensure that, as designing proceeds, these principles do shape what emerges?

Synthesize. Refine the list of principles on a flipchart.

Example

Design principles

> Design for dialogue

> Make everyone's responsibilities clear

> Provide regular feed-back & reviews

> Support different levels of contribution, skill & availability

> Make support timely, relevant & respectful

> Everyone listens

7 Understanding impact

8 Organizing for service innovation

snapshot

— Agile approaches to service innovation enable collaboration and deliver results — that are meaningful to end users — more quickly than waterfall approaches.

— Teams that pay attention to what happens at the boundaries between inside and outside of an organization make better use of adjacent knowledge.

— Objects such as service blueprints enrol people in emergent service innovation teams and help people transform knowledge across the boundaries between them.

— Creating platforms within a service ecosystem requires balancing generativity and control.

THIS CHAPTER OFFERS CONCEPTUAL LENSES to help people designing innovative services develop capabilities in organizations so they can operate differently at the fuzzy front end of projects. There are many books that discuss how to develop organizational cultures and behaviours that help teams innovate. Distinctively, this book focuses on the early stages of projects when there may not yet be a clear direction, team or budget, and there may be yet significant changes in direction. At this risky stage, it can be hard to get colleagues and other stakeholders involved and to get things going when there are competing commitments.

The chapter begins with a summary of the main features of agile software development. Although service innovation is not solely about developing new software, and may not directly involve digital devices or networks at all, this approach offers some powerful concepts. An agile approach helps organizations speed things up, increase the likelihood of delivering something valuable to end users and customers, and create a positive working environment. Perspectives from organization studies deepen understanding of what goes on in agile approaches. The concept of *absorptive capacity* highlights the roles of "boundary spanners", who help organizations make use of external knowledge. The concept of the *boundary object* emphasizes the importance of objects and models in helping members of cross-functional teams learn about their differences and dependencies, and collaborate to transform their knowledge. Finally, research from organization studies highlights the importance of balancing generativity and control when designing innovative services. The chapter then summarizes what these lenses bring to the five dynamic capabilities required for service innovation.

Two cases studies from large organizations illustrate how these capabilities can be created and developed at the early stage of new initiatives. One describes a large commercial service provider, Capita, which built an internal innovation team as well as developing this capability for clients. The second case shares how a global financial institution, Barclays, developed an internal capability to innovate in services, not just in technology. Following this chapter, a set of recipes helps people designing innovative services respond to their particular challenges and opportunities and take action at an early stage of a new project.

8 Organizing for service innovation

Organizing for agility

The previous chapter introduced the Toyota Production System and showed how it had some unexpected ways of organizing manufacturing that reduced times from concept to market, and supported continuous improvement and employee and partner collaboration. This approach has had a significant impact on many aspects of organizational life and has been adapted for other contexts. One area that has built on aspects of this approach is software development. The authors of the Manifesto for Agile Software Development, published online in 2001, stated simply:

> "We are uncovering better ways of developing software by doing it and helping others do it. Through this work we have come to value:
> – Individuals and interactions over processes and tools.
> – Working software over comprehensive documentation.
> – Customer collaboration over contract negotiation.
> – Responding to change over following a plan.
>
> That is, while there is value in the items on the right, we value the items on the left more."[240]

The manifesto's 12 principles have influenced a generation of software developers and have now spread to other related fields such as project management. Table 7 summarizes the principles associated with agile software development, and then adapts them for the context of service innovation. Some do not need much adaptation. Others, such as the emphasis on working software, require rethinking the underlying

principle in the context of complex, multi-actor ecosystems.

Alongside these principles are some key roles, artefacts and events that together take shape as actions and behaviours that teams can adopt[242]. Since these are mostly tied to the specifics of software development, it is not useful to cover them all in depth here. However, there are some concepts embedded in this approach that can be adapted for the context of service innovation.

The roadmap. An overview that shows a timeline over which service offerings will be developed and delivered. Creating a roadmap involves an innovation team in estimating the resources they think will be required to set up cycles of exploring, developing, launching and learning about how actors participate in the creation and delivery of new service offerings. In agile software, roadmaps are seen as loose, as new requirements may result in changed priorities about what software is released when. Extending this principle to service innovation, the roadmap can be seen as a provisional collective statement of what the team aims to bring into being, which will change as teams launch services and learn from what unfolds.

The sprint. A short cycle of development in the innovation process, in which the team explores aspects of an emerging service ecosystem in depth. In software, sprints often last between one day and four weeks, and result in software that can be rolled out or shipped. In the context of service innovation, the output of a day-long sprint early on in a project could be a map of

Agile software development principles[241]	Principles for agile service innovation
Our highest priority is to satisfy the customer through early and continuous delivery of valuable software.	The highest priority is to support the co-creation of value by combining actors and capacities within new value constellations.
Welcome changing requirements, even late in development. Agile processes harness change for the customer's competitive advantage.	Embrace the changes that come from moving between concepts and knowledge and across organizational boundaries.
Deliver working software frequently, from a couple of weeks to a couple of months, with a preference to the shorter timescale.	Host regular workshops to create, review and discover the implications of artefacts such as analysis of user research, user journeys, service ecosystems, proposition statements, blueprints, prototypes, roadmaps, specifications, value maps and project plans.
Business people and developers must work together daily throughout the project.	Build collaborative mixed teams including specialists in customer experience, research, marketing, operations, technology, design, and finance. Support them in representing their knowledge, learning about differences and dependencies, and transforming their knowledge across the boundaries between them.
Build projects around motivated individuals. Give them the environment and the support they need, and trust them to get the job done.	Build projects around motivated people. Give them the environment and the support they need, and trust them to get the job done.
The most efficient and effective method of conveying information to and within a development team is face-to-face conversation.	Organize well-designed, well-resourced, and well-facilitated meetings and workshops. Create and nurture platforms to support distributed concept generation and peer review. Support co-located teams.
Working software is the primary measure of progress.	Launching services is the primary measure of progress.
Agile processes support sustainable development. The sponsors, developers and users should be able to maintain a constant pace indefinitely.	Agile processes support team and stakeholder involvement in sustained organizational learning.
Continuous attention to technical excellence and good design enhances agility.	Continuous attention to understanding value-in-use and value co-creation enhances agility.
Simplicity — the art of maximizing the amount of work not done — is essential.	Zooming out between the big picture and the detail and moving between simplicity and excess, helps focus resources on what matters.
The best architectures, requirements, and designs emerge from self-organizing teams.	Novel value constellations, that combine resources effectively resulting in value-in-use for actors in an ecosystem, emerge from self-organizing teams inside and outside of organizational boundaries.
At regular intervals, the team reflects on how to become more effective, then tunes and adjusts its behaviour accordingly.	At regular intervals, the team reflects on what shapes its culture, behaviour and learning, and then tunes and adjusts its behaviour accordingly.

Table 8 Agile principles adapted for service innovation

the service ecosystem and a set of blueprints created by team members that articulate the current vision for how combinations of resources will create value-in-use for key actors. A month-long sprint later on in a service innovation process might have a stronger operational focus, resulting in the launch of a platform within a service ecosystem.

The daily scrum. In agile software development, the scrum is a 15-minute meeting held each day during a sprint, where team members state what they completed the day before, what they will finish that day, and whether they have any roadblocks. In a service innovation sprint, the principle of scrum can be adapted for teams of people from different parts of the organization and the wider ecosystem, including key users, customers and partners, to check in with one another regularly.

Concept owner role. This role acts as the glue between users or customers, organizational or community stakeholders, and the development team. The concept owner is an expert on the ecosystem that is beginning to unfold, and on the value-in-use that will exist for key actors, including users and customers, through participating in it. The concept owner works regularly with the team to clarify and articulate the knowledge and concepts that emerge during the innovation process, and to make sense of and prioritize these. In agile software, the concept owner is sometimes called a customer representative. But in service innovation, in which there are potentially many different actors, it may not be possible to prioritize a single customer segment who the concept owner represents.

So, instead, the emphasis here is on balancing the requirements and capacities of the main actors in an innovation ecosystem.

Scrum master role. This role is about supporting the team, identifying and sorting out organizational roadblocks, and keeping the agile process consistent. At first glance, this might look like a traditional project management role. But often that role becomes about pushing the team to fit within a plan based on a waterfall model of development in which things happen sequentially. Instead, the agile approach recognizes the need for delivering meaningful impact and using resources effectively, but balances this with an understanding of the convergent and divergent phases of bringing something new into being, as new knowledge and concepts are created concurrently.

Agile approaches to service innovation are promising. They highlight the people, roles, artefacts, and combinations of skills and knowledge required to explore and generate new service concepts and new competences embedded within fast, cyclical processes. They are oriented to continuous learning, rather than continuous production. But accounts of agile development often rest on a simplified understanding of what goes on in self-organized teams comprised of people from different knowledge bases. They play down the difficulties faced by people working together at the boundaries of knowledge and what happens when, say, specialists from the culture of engineering collaborate with professionals embedded in the culture of customer experience. Research from organization studies provides the basis for a subtler understanding of what agile service innovation could look like.

Organizing for absorption

The first perspective explored here comes from research that showed how innovation capabilities are tied to organizational memory, influencing the ability to respond to new ideas. Researchers Wesley Cohen and Daniel Levinthal developed the concept of *absorptive capacity*, which they linked to learning and innovation[243]. They argued that the ability to exploit external knowledge is a critical component of innovative capabilities.

The researchers' argument was based on understanding how people learn. Memory development is self-reinforcing in that the more objects, patterns and concepts are stored in memory, the more readily is new information about these constructs acquired and the more able the individual is to use them in new settings. Learning is cumulative, and learning performance is greatest when the object of learning is related to what is already known. Adapting this for organizations, Cohen and Levinthal argued that prior learning experiences shape subsequent learning. They concluded that an organization's ability to evaluate and utilize outside knowledge is largely a function of the level of prior related knowledge. Such knowledge confers an ability to recognize the value of new information, assimilate it, and apply it to organizational ends. These abilities constitute what they called a firm's "absorptive capacity".

To understand the sources of a firm's absorptive capacity, Cohen and Levinthal focused on communications between the external environment and the organization, as well as among different parts of the organization, and on the character and distribution of expertise within the organization. They identified the following factors that determine an organization's absorptive capacity:

- The individual gate-keepers and boundary-spanners who are at the interfaces between the organization and its external environment.

- The individual gate-keepers and boundary-spanners who are at the interfaces between the organizational divisions and units.

- Whether gate-keeping and boundary-spanning is centralized or distributed across the organization.

- The background prior knowledge of individuals and of the organization's teams and units, and as a whole.

- Interconnections between teams and units, allowing for some degree of redundancy.

- An organization's investment in developing its own absorptive capacity.

Absorptive capacity is more likely to be developed and maintained as a byproduct of routine activity when the knowledge domain that the organization wishes to exploit is closely related to its current knowledge base. But if an organization wishes to acquire and use knowledge that is unrelated to its ongoing activities – for example, when creating new service ecosystems that involve actors about whom a development team does not have much knowledge and with whom there are few connections – then the firm must try to increase its absorptive capacity.

This analysis highlights the challenges of designing innovative services when the knowledge required is not closely related to existing knowledge bases. To address such situations, managers can enhance an organization's absorptive capacity by supporting and nurturing gate-keepers and boundary-spanners and clarifying the existing knowledge they and the teams have and do not have. By identifying and investing in boundary-spanners and gate-keepers at the interfaces of organizational teams and with the outside world, organizations increase their capacity to learn and absorb new knowledge. But another perspective within organization studies points to how it is not just people that are critical at the boundaries of teams and functions and between organizations and the outside world. This research shows how creating and using objects also supports learning and innovation.

Organizing for knowledge transformation

Being attentive to artefacts such as models, maps and sketches is influenced by social studies of science and technology. This orientation originated in research into how scientists and technologists go about their work, but the principles have also been applied to understanding how artefacts are embedded and situated in routine organizational practices.

To explore this I'll briefly return to the inventive habits associated with artists' and designers' studio inquiries, discussed in Chapter 5. Think about what you would expect to find in a studio. The emblematic objects associated with creative art and design include sketches, models, mock-ups, storyboards and material stuff relevant to the project to hand – whether these are plastics, fabrics or LEDs. These are the kinds of things that litter the walls, tables and floors of art and design studios. Now think about the kinds of objects that are typically created by organizations designing services. These might be written reports, presentations, business cases and spreadsheets, illustrations of conceptual frameworks and numerical models. Such artefacts can play an active role in organizational processes that go beyond capturing ideas.

In her ethnographic study of engineering designers, Kathryn Henderson noticed how sketches and other kinds of visual objects were central to the work they did. She described how:

> "sketching and drawing are the basic components of communication; words are built around them, but the drawings are so central that people assembled in meetings wait while individuals fetch visual representations left in their offices or sketch facsimiles on white boards. Coordination and conflict take place over, on, and through the drawings. These visual representations shape the structure of the work, who may participate in the work, and the final products of design engineering."[244]

Henderson used two sociological terms to help explain how objects like drawings come to have these capacities. The concept of the *boundary object*[245] helps explain how sketches and drawings facilitate various groups involved in a design process to negotiate their different kinds of expertise. A boundary object allows different groups to read different meanings particular to their needs from the same material. It is flexible enough to adapt to specific local needs and constraints, but robust enough to maintain a common identity. For example, if a team creates a service blueprint (Method 12), people from different parts of the organization can look at it from their particular perspectives. It allows marketers to see how their activities interact with people at different phases of their customer journeys, at the same time as enabling people from the accounts function to see how billing and payment processes and infrastructures fit into the intended user experience.

The second concept Henderson introduced is *enrollment*[246]. She used this to help explain how sketches and drawings enlist and organize group participation. These objects act as receptacles for concepts and knowledge created during a project. For people to take part in a design process, they must engage in the generation, editing, and correction of such drawings. Sketches invite people to engage with them, and regulate who is inside and outside the work. Henderson observed that engineering drawings are an output of design activity – but they are essential to work proceeding at all. This kind of sociological analysis highlights some of the hidden work that goes

on in organizations. It brings a focus on the visual and textual artefacts which Henderson argued constitute a kind of "social glue" to hold things together.

The concept of the boundary object brings attention to the objects, models, sketches, forms, lists, frameworks, specifications, reports, presentations, spreadsheets and maps that are part of designing innovative services. Researcher Paul Carlile deepened understanding of the importance of boundary objects in his research into new product development.[247] This is particularly relevant to designing innovative services in which mixed teams of specialists are involved in working together in an agile process. These specialists have different kinds of knowledge, and often work across the boundaries of the organization with people outside of it, and with other resources and capacities through the sorts of events and platforms discussed in Chapter 6.

Carlile identified three characteristics of objects that support effective collaboration at the boundaries between specialist knowledge practices. The first characteristic is that a boundary object establishes a shared syntax or language for individuals to represent their knowledge. In his study, for example, an engineering drawing helped design engineers and manufacturing engineers to see their specialist concerns represented in a single document.

The second characteristic is that a boundary object can provide "a concrete means for individuals to specify and learn about their differences and dependencies across a given boundary"[248]. Such an object allows specialists to clarify what they know and what matters to them in relation to the shared matter they are dealing with. By creating and using boundary objects, they begin to see the interrelationships and dependencies between their different ways of looking at the problem. They can identify differences of interpretation across their boundaries.

The third characteristic of effective boundary objects is to facilitate the process by which individuals can jointly transform their knowledge. By together looking at, discussing, annotating and drawing on sketches or frameworks, or by fiddling with physical models, specialists are able to alter their current approaches. Through these object-based practices they negotiate and find new solutions that address problems at the boundaries of their knowledge.

In summary, boundary objects have the capacity to *represent* knowledge across boundaries; they help specialists *learn* about what matters to each other by seeing how their knowledge is connected; and finally they support *transforming* knowledge and generating new knowledge, which is required for situations of creating novelty. This perspective illuminates what goes on in agile development approaches. The concept of the boundary object emphasizes how object-based practices enable cross-disciplinary teams to understand what matters to each other, identify dependencies and differences and collaborate to generate novel concepts at their knowledge boundaries that take things forward. To the concept of absorptive capacity introduced earlier, it adds a focus on how

knowledge can be transformed at boundaries, not just brought in from outside.

What this sociological lens surfaces is recognition that the documents and sketches produced during the early stages of an agile service innovation project are not simply representations of ideas, but that they do actual work. Objects such as maps of service ecosystems (Method 3), customer journey maps (Method 4) and blueprints (Method 12) enrol people into a project. They provide a way for people with different kinds of expertise to see what an emerging value constellation might mean for their own specialist concern and the interdependencies with other knowledge bases inside and outside the organization. At best, they can address shared challenges by transforming specialist knowledge to generate new knowledge and concepts.

Organizing to balance generativity and control

A final aspect of this discussion of organizing for service innovation requires turning to digital technologies. Digital networks and devices, and the data they capture, create and use, are resources that can be combined into new configurations to co-create value for and with participants. Youngjin Yoo and colleagues point to how digitization presents a tension between generativity and control in service innovation[249]. Generativity is the ability of a self-contained system to create, generate, or produce new content, structures, or behaviours without additional help or input from the original creators[250].

Services that include digital resources have the potential to be generative because of the ways that digital technologies are structured and configured in use. Firstly, digital devices are reprogrammable – for example, installing a new piece of software, such as downloading an app on to a smartphone, can change or add to what the hardware does. Secondly, digital devices are built on shared data formats (the 1s and 0s of code) and often on open standards too. This means that many different programmers can contribute to new developments. Thirdly, digitization means that there is loose coupling between data objects and the ways they are stored, processed and used[251]. This is in contrast to analogue objects – for example, a record can only be played on a record player, but a piece of software can run on many different kinds of device.

Yoo and colleagues showed how these characteristics of digital devices mean that a generative system or service is able to innovate beyond what was originally conceived of. Examples include digital platforms that enable organizations to innovate by mediating between the various actors in a service ecosystem. It is in the designing and usage of such platforms that the tension between generativity and control plays out. For example, when Apple initially introduced the iOS operating system, it maintained control over the applications (apps) that could be installed on Apple devices running the software. Later, Apple embraced the idea that third parties, over which it had little control, could develop applications for the platform. Yoo and colleagues comment: "Generativity became an essential element of Apple's product strategy".[252] In contrast, Google initially exercised much less control over its Android platform, and later limited what changes could be made to the core of the operating system and how it could be adapted by third parties.

Such platforms can be viewed as a kind of large-scale boundary object. They help mediate the concepts and knowledge inside and outside organizations, and between different specialist teams or functions and other actors in a service ecosystem. Like the boundary objects discussed above, they allow different groups or individuals to learn about what matters to each other. Platforms as boundary objects highlight differences and dependencies. At best, they can provide ways to transform knowledge at the boundaries between particular groups or teams. Depending on whether the actors involved embrace generativity or try to exercise control, platforms can result in novel concepts and knowledge unanticipated by the original creators of a platform.

Pulling things together

This book has argued that organizations need to develop specific capabilities to enable them to innovate in services in response to current developments. These developments include: turbulent operating environments with conflicting values and high stakes, in which it is not obvious which kinds of expertise are the right resources to move things forward; a move towards strategy as wayfinding on the ground, rather than a top-down process that happens in advance of taking action; a shift towards seeing value as created

8 Organizing for service innovation

through the mutual interaction of many actors in an ecosystem, rather than additively through linear value chains; a focus on value-in-use embedded in socio-cultural practices, rather than attending to the moments of transactions associated with value-in-exchange; and understanding that users and customers have capacities, not just needs. This concluding section shows how the concepts discussed in this chapter enrich understanding of how organizations can develop five service innovation capabilities.

Firstly, the capability of recombining resources into new ecosystems is illuminated by the concepts of absorptive capacity and boundary objects. Organizations that invest in and support boundary-spanners and gate-keepers to mediate between teams and between inside and beyond organizational boundaries can make better use of adjacent knowledge to combine into new configurations. Teams that create and use sketches, models and maps can support agile cross-disciplinary working by representing and sharing knowledge, revealing differences and dependencies, and transforming knowledge at boundaries. Such boundary objects constitute a social glue that holds a team together, as well as being receptacles for concepts and knowledge at particular points in time.

Secondly, the capability of increasing the variance of actors in a service ecosystem is opened up by the concepts of balancing generativity and control. Platforms and events can be set up to involve different kinds of actor and digital devices inside and outside of organizations in generating concepts and knowledge

within a service innovation process. The characteristics and usage of digital devices and networks lead to consequences that cannot be known or predicted in advance. Being attentive to generativity and control helps managers involved in designing innovative services to think through the consequences of increasing variance in a system.

Thirdly, the capability of launching new services and learning from how they unfold in practice is enhanced by the perspectives discussed in this chapter. The activities of creating, reviewing and adapting boundary objects enable actors in an emerging service ecosystem to move towards working more effectively together by recognizing shared knowledge and key differences and dependencies. Through their collective engagement with boundary objects, participants develop a shared culture and identity – they become enrolled in a project. Together, their agreements and disagreements about things like what constitutes value-in-use are where a team's creative work takes place. Their struggles bind them together as people trying to bring a new innovation ecosystem into being, by creating the concepts and knowledge that advance the project.

Fourthly, the capability of understanding value-in-use is illuminated by the concepts of absorptive capacity and boundary objects. Organizations that invest in boundary-spanners and set up routines to learn more about what goes on outside their boundaries are better able to absorb this adjacent knowledge. Agile approaches support ways for cross-functional teams to understand the dependencies and connections between knowledge about how value-in-use is co-created with actors and other kinds of knowledge such as operations or finance. The emphasis in agile approaches on regular service launches pushes development teams to getting new service propositions out into the world and seeing what happens in use.

Finally, the innovation capability of moving between inside and outside of organizations, and between generating new concepts and new knowledge, is enhanced by the perspectives offered in this chapter. The concept of absorptive capacity highlights the roles and processes by which gate-keepers and boundary-spanners mediate internal and external knowledge. This increases an organization's ability to make use of such knowledge. The concept of the boundary object draws attention to how drawings, maps, models and platforms help different specialists in agile teams learn, share, understand differences and dependencies and create new knowledge and concepts together inside and outside of organizations. Thinking about balancing generativity and control draws managerial attention to the processes and platforms that involve diverse actors in creating and sustaining service ecosystems.

Ending by starting

You're about to start a new project. How do you go about this? You draw a sketch of what could be a new configuration of resources that is an embryonic service ecosystem. You tape it to the wall. A colleague makes a comic strip that shows how things around a particular person happened differently, resulting in a desired change. At a workshop your colleagues summarize some of the drivers of change shaping the environment facing your end users, partners, competitors and suppliers over the next five years and the next decade. Someone sketches the user interface for an app, for some packaging, or a future advert for the service you can't yet fully describe. You wish you had more resources to do this.

Several people get together to create a service blueprint showing how resources can be combined to support a particular person's experience. Doing this starts a different conversation between colleagues who usually work separately. You host a sprint to define the outcomes the emerging project wants to achieve and, together, people discuss the challenges and opportunities the project presents for data-gathering and interpretation. You reflect on who you feel accountable to – not just the people who might invest resources in the emerging project, but the people now and in the future who might be affected as a result.

You re-draw the service ecosystem and spend time arguing with colleagues how to define the boundaries of what's in and what's out, and who the key actors are and the roles they play in holding the new value constellation together. With your colleagues you organize a two-day sprint that brings some key people together to explore the context and issue and the new proposition in more depth. You wish you had more time and more people resources. In a workshop you try out some role play that gets people play-acting what might happen differently as a result of the interventions you think need to happen. A member of the team starts talking frequently with someone from a partner organization who has a lot more knowledge, skills and data relating to aspects of the issue you are working on.

You decide to commission some research to better understand the day-to-day realities and worlds of the people you want to serve and to identify their capacities and emergent behaviours. You wish you had a bigger budget and more time. You organize a sprint that brings people together, including front line staff from a new partner organization, and this results in several different blueprints. You wonder if there is something important you are missing. You argue about what matters and sometimes this prompts you to reflect on why this emerging project matters to you and to the other people involved. The expanding team starts developing its own vocabulary to name the thing you are beginning to design. You discuss how to explore specific aspects of the emerging proposition and how best to do this.

Later, you and others will create a business case with an associated financial model. You will define the opportunity, the proposition and the impact you think it can have and the resources required to make it happen. You'll create a project plan, write a service specification and a value map, and do an assessment of the resources needed to move things on to the next stage. There will be presentations, workshops, documents to produce, and reports to review and update.

There will be meetings, water-cooler conversations, conference calls, more meetings and visits. The first sketch you did, which is still on the wall, looks wrong, but somehow right. Next to it is the comic strip. You don't take them down. What do you do at the beginning? You start doing things differently.

Case 15 Building service transformation capabilities at Capita

Capita[253] is a large UK-based company that specializes in outsourcing. For many years, outsourcing has been seen as a way for organizations to spend less on what they consider to be non-core functions, such as human resources, IT systems, web services, and other business processes. For some organizations, this has also included customer contact centres. Closely associated with offshoring – for example, setting up English-speaking call centres in India – outsourcing has a mixed reputation for many service businesses. On the one hand, hiring a company like Capita reduces costs to serve customers and to deliver back office processes. On the other, many organizations and their outsourcers find it hard to work together effectively to deliver high levels of customer service consistently over the channels and touchpoints that are usually involved – web services, social media, mobile, call centres, mail, and retail outlets.

The turbulent context in which organizations need to keep costs down, as well as find ways to innovate and engage customers differently, is the space in which Capita has been developing a capability in service innovation. Capita aims to get the basics of service encounters right for users, and also to help its clients create new kinds of business opportunity.

Using the example of one of Capita's clients, a consumer-facing telecommunications operator, brings the issues and opportunities into view.

Along with other companies in its sector, the telco faces a challenging future of reduced revenues and profitability. Telcos have become "dumb pipes" for the digital media that ends up on smartphones and tablets. So three key business drivers for Capita's client are: reducing the cost of serving customers; selling more to existing customers; and encouraging users to change their behaviours so that they self-serve using web channels, rather than phoning a call centre or visiting a retail store, which costs more to deliver. For the telco, outsourcing its customer service design and delivery to Capita shares the risks and gives a greater sense of control, since the long-term contract ties Capita to delivering particular levels of customer satisfaction and other outcomes.

As an outsourcer, Capita operates in two modes. The first is bidding for work, which requires the in-house bid team to use data the client provides and combine it with other research, to rapidly construct a robust financial and operating model of how the client's business could operate differently in the future. This is a process of a skilled team working under pressure with limited data to design and cost how to deliver and sustain a new service, and establish whether it is worth bidding for and how to price the bid. The second mode happens if the proposal is successful. This involves a complex change process, working closely with the client over many

such as voice calls, marketing communications, or web channels. The second capability was insights and analytics, that aimed to gather, structure and make use of qualitative and quantitative data about user behaviours and service operations. The third capability was using those insights and analytics to design the service encounters and supporting resources, based on defining design principles to prompt changes in the ways that different segments of users behave in their interactions with the telco.

Large organizations with customer service capabilities typically have lots of data, but struggle to understand value-in-use. "Their data is about the wrong things", says Joel Bailey, director of service design at Capita. "They can tell you what customers say about their last interaction, but they can't tell you the cumulative result of all those user experiences. They focus on transactions, rather than experience over time". The Capita team has developed skills in combining clients' data with other sources, and undertaking its own research in the form of focus groups or, less often, ethnography. Capita also triangulates data from different sources to produce models of customer segments that describe behaviours and propensity for particular service encounters.

years, usually across several sites, to bring a new innovation ecosystem into being. Capita does this by working with the client to research, design, build and deliver an integrated service combining people, processes and technologies.

Having won the bid to undertake a transformation process with the telco, Capita initiated the project by developing three capabilities, shared across their own team and the mobile operator's staff. The first was multi-channel customer experience management. This involved the telco and its partners working together to deliver particular experiences, combining different channel mixes and service encounters to particular user segments – instead of working in silos that own particular channels,

8 Organizing for service innovation

Case 15 (continued) Building service transformation capabilities at Capita

Having combined qualitative insights and data analytics to identify drivers of demand, Capita built a team to address one driver. This team focused on a user activity that leads to significant corporate spend – a common and frequent customer task that drove people to phone the call centre, or visit a store, to get help. This team included people from different parts of the business – engineers, operations managers, specialists in communications and branding, and service designers. Working together in an agile way allowed this group to generate concepts for service encounters that combined the telco and users' resources in new ways, and to support people in completing this task through self-service, without recourse to customer service channels, which were more expensive for the telco to provide.

On starting the project, Capita found several related initiatives within the telco, including systems thinking and customer insight teams. It set up a way of working that brought the strengths of these approaches together, centred on designing user experiences and service encounters for specific segments as a shared "boundary object". One example of this was a set of personas, that defined discrete segments of users, and that shifted the focus from data analytics to behavioural insights. The personas were seen as live rather than fixed, to be reviewed as data revealed changes in customer behaviours and activities.

When in bidding mode, and during the early phases of the transformation mode, Capita developed a capability that delivers what its clients seem to struggle to do. First, it used qualitative and quantitative data to identify and prioritize business and customer issues to address. Second, it created stories about end user experiences for specific segments of users. Mobilizing these helps mixed teams of people from both organizations (client and outsourcer) design, iterate and construct a new combination of resources linking the telco, its suppliers and its users, resulting in value-in-use.

Much of this work was about improving the basics of the customer experience, rather than innovation. New opportunities may come from strengthening the telco's capability to identify capacities among user segments and other actors to combine them into service concepts for new innovation ecosystems. Perhaps the more important innovation lies in developing and connecting the client's own capabilities and driving service design by helping it understand value-in-use.

Case 16 Developing agile innovation teams in financial services at Barclays

Barclays is an international financial services organization providing banking, credit cards, corporate and investment banking, and wealth and investment management to retail, small business and corporate customers. The bank operates in more than 50 countries and employed approximately 140,000 people in 2013. Barclays created the first ATM and introduced the first credit card in the UK and has strengths in technological innovation. Like other global financial organizations, Barclays faces challenges to innovate in a competitive and highly regulated marketplace. Other pressures include wary customers, regulators, shareholders and politicians keeping a close eye on the banking sector after the 2008 financial crisis and distrust about banks' decisions to pay some staff large bonuses at the same time as making many others redundant[254].

To improve its innovation capability, Barclays set up a design innovation function to work across the company, and appointed a chief design officer, Derek White[255]. This team included people from design, finance, operations and technology backgrounds with a shared focus on customer experiences driving new service development. The creation of this team represented a significant change in a firm with 300 years of history in a traditional industry, shifting it towards developing capabilities allowing it to innovate in services, not just in technology.

One of its first projects was Pingit[256], a mobile payment service that allows customers to send and receive money using just a mobile phone number and a UK bank account. The first such mobile payment service to be launched in Europe[257], Pingit was initially aimed at people wanting to make small and medium-sized financial transactions. Antony Jenkins, Barclays CEO, commented:

> "Pingit could revolutionize the way people send and receive money. For friends splitting the cost of dinner, repaying a borrowed £10 or people sending money to a son or daughter at university, it is free, quick, convenient, secure, and easy to use." [258]

Launched in 2012, the app had been downloaded more than 2.5 million times by early 2014[259]. By providing a payments service that was available to non-customers as well as customers, the app challenged traditional ways of doing things in the retail banking industry, both in the innovation ecosystem it created and in the way it went about organizing the team.

The capability of launching clumsy solutions to learn, starts with recognition that organizations will not get things right straight away, if ever. In a dynamic operating environment with imperfect data, organizations taking the approach of strategic wayfinding, rather than top-down strategic management, will benefit from fast cycles of organizational learning. However, this presents a particular

8 Organizing for service innovation

Case 16 (continued) Developing agile innovation teams in financial services at Barclays

challenge in financial services. Firms' operations are supervised by national and international regulators and are driven by regular reports to, and dialogue with, investors. Further, the culture of valuing a firm's activities almost exclusively through the lens of return on capital shapes how innovation and experimentation take place. One of the results of this has been the slow pace of development of new services.

In contrast, Barclays Global Design Office team was set up to learn at speed, and to work collaboratively with others within a wider ecosystem to learn from them. Derek White, chief design officer at Barclays, explains:

> "The learning cycle of entrepreneurs and start-ups is so much faster than it is in big business. And it's that speed, coupled with the approach to solution finding that these companies take, which will ensure that through partnering with them, and helping them grow, Barclays can stay at the forefront of innovation in the financial services sector."[260]

One of the reasons for the successful design and launch of Pingit, according to Barclays, was that there was a strong focus on users' experiences of using software in the context of their day-to-day lives. Customer research was used early on in its development[261]. Insights about user experience directly shaped Pingit's design, focusing on making it intuitive, engaging and secure[261].

The Barclays Design Office on the 22nd floor of the London headquarters building was designed to enable agile teamwork between people with different specialisms. Project teams work at tables Barclays call "hoppers" to bring together people assigned to a project – for example, a designer, a business analyst, an operations or a technology specialist, and a program manager[262]. This way of working allowed Barclays to bring its app Pingit to market much more quickly than anticipated when the concept first emerged. Instead of following a traditional product development cycle – from research to specifying requirements to prototyping, revisions, and then launch – for Pingit, Barclays wanted to work differently. White explains:

> "When we first outlined the plan for Pingit, we were delivered a plan that said it would take between two and two and a half years to implement. From concept to execution, Pingit took us seven months".[263]

One of the things Barclays built into Pingit was making it available for use by non-customers – an usual step for financial services firms, which tend to focus on serving existing customers or trying to acquire new ones. By including non-customers among the target user segments for Pingit, Barclays demonstrated the value of involving actors it would normally ignore in its ecosystem. For Pingit to be successful, it needed to reach beyond the conventional view of customers, to an expanded network of people and small businesses. Usage data suggested that Friday night was "Pingit night", with high numbers of transactions. This indicated to Barclays that people were using Pingit for social activities such as sharing restaurant bills[264].

To further develop the ecology around the bank, Barclays set up an accelerator for new financial technology ventures, launched in 2014. Along with more conventional benefits such as business advice and seed investment, this accelerator programme gave teams access to the Pingit application programming interface (API)[265]. By setting up an accelerator and working with non-customers, Barclays illustrates a capability in combining resources into new innovation ecosystems.

8 Organizing for service innovation

Recipes at the fuzzy front end of designing innovative services

Recipe 1: Quick wins to improve an existing service

Exploring issues	Analysis	Generating and exploring ideas	Synthesis
Dive into the issues relating to the current service from different perspectives	Clarify what's important, to who and why	Create and explore alternatives from different perspectives	Explore organizational implications

Start   **Eight weeks later**

Method 5
Creating six personas

Method 6 Segmenting by meaning

Method 9
Sketching 10+ touchpoints

Method 11 Planning
prototyping and design games

Method 4 Mapping three existing
user/customer experiences

Method 13 Creating an outcomes framework

Method 10
Telling stories

Method 12
Service blueprinting

Method 8
Problem/proposition definition

Method 4 Mapping changed user/cus-
tomer experiences for specific segments

Method 14
Defining design principles

Recipe 2: Innovation exploration for an existing service and team

Exploring issues	Analysis	Generating and exploring ideas	Synthesis
Dive into the issues from diverse perspectives against different time horizons	Clarify what's important, to who and why	Create and explore alternatives from different perspectives	Define how to explore implications of new concepts and build knowledge

Start　　　　　　　　　　　　　　　　　　　　　　　　　**12 weeks later**

Method 1
Self-reflection

Method 13 Creating an
outcomes framework

Method 10 Telling stories

Method 2
Visualizing drivers of change

Method 6
Segmenting by meaning

Method 9
Sketching 15+ touchpoints

Method 11 Planning prototyping
and design games

Method 5
Creating 10-12 personas

Method 7
Opportunity mapping

Method 3 Mapping three future innovation ecosystems around the issue

Method 12 Service blueprinting

Method 4
Mapping five experiences of the issue

Method 8
Problem/proposition definition

Method 4 Mapping future user
experiences for specific segments

Method 14
Defining design principles

Method 3 Mapping three innovation
ecosystems around the issue

8 Organizing for service innovation

Recipe 3: Innovation exploration for a new team working together on an issue

Exploring issues	Analysis	Generating and exploring ideas	Synthesis
Dive into the issues from diverse perspectives against different time horizons	Clarify what's important, to who and why	Create and explore alternatives from different perspectives	Define how to explore implications of new concepts and build knowledge

Start   **16 weeks later**

Method 1 Self-reflection

Method 10 Telling stories

Method 10 Telling stories

Method 11 Planning prototyping and design games

Method 2 Visualizing drivers of change

Method 6 Segmenting by meaning

Method 9 Sketching 20+ touchpoints

Method 13 Creating an outcomes framework

Method 3 Mapping three innovation ecosystems around the issue

Method 5 Creating 10-12 personas

Method 3 Mapping three future innovation ecosystems around the issue

Method 5 Revise personas

Method 4 Mapping five experiences of the issue

Method 7 Opportunity mapping

Method 12 Service blueprinting

Method 14 Defining design principles

Method 9 Sketching 15+ touchpoints

Method 8 Problem/proposition definition

Method 4 Mapping future user experiences

Method 1 Self-reflection

Afterword

The week I finished the manuscript for this book, I went to a talk at the *London Review of Books* book-shop. This involved a dialogue between curator Hans Ulrich Obrist and writer Tom McCarthy. Obrist and McCarthy were there to talk about a recent publication in which they were both involved that reproduced maps by artists and scientists. It ended up being a discussion about the making and using of maps. It also involved talking about the making of contemporary art in societies in which art is mostly a commodity, as well as – sometimes – a critical practice.

McCarthy noted how some of the methods associated with the avant-garde, such as the Situationists' *dérive* or psychogeographical wandering, have now been incorporated into global corporations. He also mentioned that his forthcoming novel was an account of a corporate anthropologist, suggesting – although since the book was not yet out I could not be sure of this – that such a creature is necessarily to be scorned.

Sitting there that warm evening, I found that listening to the talk allowed me to practice for a couple of hours a sort of *dérive*. In my case this perambulation was not through the city, but around the organizations, services, ventures and practices described in my own map – this book – remixed in real time with the artists and maps being described by Obrist and McCarthy. This wandering revealed to me that the manuscript I'd just finished made me an apologist for the incorporation of experimental art methods and ethnography into corporations, at the expense of the criticality and distance that both practices espouse and rely on.

Although I included some cases from policy and social innovation contexts, and the worked examples of the methods are based loosely on my consulting work in social entrepreneurship[266], this book is not overtly political or critical of the current state of affairs in the world. Re-reading it, I find myself caught up in replicating the power structures and drive for capital to reproduce itself. And yet my starting point for writing the book was that I, like most other people I work with or teach, want to live and work in a world that is quite different from the one I currently inhabit.

This afterword, then, is a kind of mirror reflection of the opening chapter and of the self-reflection proposed in Method 1. The book draws on the strong and weak ties I have with particular organizations and individuals that result from being associated with some privileged institutions where I have worked. It brings into view projects, approaches and methods that are important to make sense of and share more widely. But it neglects whole chunks of the world – in particular, Asia, Africa, the Middle East, Central and South America, the Global South, the extremely poor and those at severe risk of climate change. It prompts thinking about vision and values but offers few hints about what I want to work towards. The accountabilities that have guided me are to imagined future readers who resemble the MBA students who have taken my elective in designing better futures. But it does not engage with others who might be negatively affected by any resulting ventures or projects that commodify human experience in the service of making money.

But as the first chapter argues, starting off matters. So I end this book with the realization that finishing it does not mean closing things down. Rather, ending it here and sending it off into the world is a movement *towards*. It starts something off but recognizes the limitations and assumptions carried along with the accounts I have presented. It allows me to think about what comes next, and ask if not this, then what?

References

Chapter 1

1   Kao, J. (1996). Jamming: The art and discipline of business creativity. New York: Harper Collins.

2   Brown, T. (2009). Change by design: How design thinking transforms organizations and inspires innovation. New York: Harper Collins; and Martin, R. (2009). The design of business: Why design thinking is the next competitive advantage. Cambridge: Harvard Business Press.

3   Alexander, C. (1971). Notes on the synthesis of form. Cambridge: Harvard University Press.

4   Simon, Herbert. A. (1996). The sciences of the artificial. 3rd edition. Cambridge: MIT Press, p. 111.

5   Hatchuel, A. and Weil, B. (2009). C-K design theory: An advanced formulation. Research in Engineering Design, 19: 181–192.

6   Le Masson, P., Weil, B. and Hatchuel, A. (2010). Strategic management of innovation and design. Cambridge: Cambridge University Press.

7   Hatchuel, A. (2001). Towards design theory and expandable rationality: The unfinished programme of Herbert Simon. Journal of Management and Governance, 5 (3–4): 260–273.

8   Le Masson, P., Weil, B. and Hatchuel, A. (2010). Strategic management of innovation and design. Cambridge: Cambridge University Press.

9   See also Verganti, R. (2009). Design-driven innovation: Changing the rules of competition by radically innovating what things mean. Boston: Harvard Business Press.

10 Chesbrough, H. (2006). Open innovation: The new imperative for creating and profiting from technology. Cambridge: Harvard University Press.

11 Khurana, A. and Rosenthal, S. (1998). Towards holistic "front ends" in new product development. Journal of Product Innovation Management, 15 (1): 57–74.

12 Herstatt, C. and Verworn, B. (2001). The fuzzy front end of innovation. Working paper No.4. http://www.tuhh.de/tim/downloads/arbeitspapiere/Arbeitspapier_4.pdf

Case 1

13 http://www.fjordnet.com/workdetail/3/

14 Based on an interview with Daniel Freeman of Fjord.

Case 2

15 Based on an interview with Phillip Joe of Microsoft.

Chapter 2

16 https://www.fairphone.com/

17 https://www.casseroleclub.com/

18 McCarthy, I.P., Frizelle, G. and Rakotobe-Joel, T. (2000). Complex systems theory: Implications and promises for manufacturing organizations. International Journal of Technology Management, 2(1–7): 559–79.

19 Funtowicz, S. and Ravetz, J. (1993). Science for the post-normal age. Futures, 25(7): 739–755.

20 Rayner, S. (2006). Jack Beale memorial lecture on global environment. Wicked problems: Clumsy solutions – diagnoses and prescriptions for environmental ills." http://www.insis.ox.ac.uk/fileadmin/InSIS/Publications/Rayner_-_jackbealelecture.pdf

21 Mintzberg, H., Ahlstrand, B. and Lampel, J. (2009). Strategy safari: Your complete guide through the wilds of strategic management. 2nd edition. Harlow: Pearson.

22 Mintzberg et al (2009). p. 17.

23 Chia, R. and Holt, R. (2009). Strategy without design: The silent efficacy of indirect action. Cambridge: Cambridge University Press. p xi.

24 Chia and Holt (2009). p. 166.

25 Chia and Holt (2009). p. 5.

26 http://www.grameeninfo.org/index.php?option=com_content&task=view&id=26&Itemid=175

27 http://www.thetoasterproject.org/

28 http://www.thetoasterproject.org/page2.htm

29 Molotch, H. (2003). Where stuff comes from: How toasters, toilets, cars, computers and many other things come to be as they are. New York: Routledge.

30 Norman, R. and Ramírez, R. (1993): Designing interactive strategy: From value chain to value constellation. Harvard Business Review, 71 (4): 65–77.

31 For an overview see Erkko, A. and Thomas, L. (2014). Innovation ecosystems: Implications for Innovation Management? In Dodgson, M., Gann, D., Phillips, N. (eds) The Oxford handbook of innovation management. Oxford: Oxford University Press.

32 Vargo, S. and Lusch, R. (2004). Evolving to a new dominant logic in marketing. Journal of Marketing, 68 (1): 1–17. See also Ramírez, R. (1999). Value co-production: Intellectual origins and implications for practice and research. Strategic Management Journal. 20: 49–65; Payne, A., Storbacka, K. and Frow, P. (2008). Managing the co-creation of value. Journal of the Academy of Marketing Science, 36 (1): 83–96; and Ng, I. (2014). Creating new markets in the digital economy: Value and worth. Cambridge: Cambridge University Press.

33 As mentioned by a participant in an innovation workshop in Stockholm, 2014.

34 Kretzmann, J. and McKnight, J. (1993). Building communities from the inside out: A path toward finding and mobilizing a community's assets. Chicago: Center for Urban Affairs and Policy Research.

35 Ambrosini, V., Bowman, C. and Collier, N. (2009). Dynamic capabilities: An exploration of how firms renew their resource base. British Journal of Management, 20(1): S9–S24.

Case 3

36 Botsman, R. and Rogers, R. (2010). What's mine is yours: How collaborative consumption is changing the way we live. Harper Collins.

37 https://www.airbnb.co.uk/press/news/airbnb-celebrates-1-million-total-guests-from-the-united-kingdom

38 https://www.airbnb.co.uk/about/about-us

39 http://www.forbes.com/sites/tomiogeron/2013/01/23/airbnb-and-the-unstoppable-rise-of-the-share-economy/

40 Botsman, R. and Rogers, R. (2010). What's mine is yours: How collaborative consumption is changing the way we live. Harper Collins.

41 http://www.gq-magazine.co.uk/entertainment/articles/2013–07/04/airbnb-joe-gebbia-interview

42 http://www.fastcompany.com/3027107/punk-meet-rock-airbnb-brian-chesky-chip-conley

Case 4

43 https://turbovote.org/faq

44 Based on an interview with David Lipkin of Method.

45 http://pivotallabs.com/wordpress/wp-content/uploads/2013/09/NYC-Votes-Case-Study.pdf

46 https://turbovote.org

Chapter 3

47 Based on interviews with Joe Ferry and his lecture at Saïd Business School in 2009.

48 See http://www.wallpaper.com/travel/qa-with-joe-ferry-head-designer-virgin-atlantic/3391

49 http://webarchive.nationalarchives.gov.uk/20100113205514/designcouncil.org.uk/design-council/1/our-people/council-members/joe-ferry/

50 See for example Ong, A., and Collier, S. (2005). Global assemblages: Technology, politics, and ethics as anthropological problems. Malden, MA: Blackwell.

51 Shaw, C., Dibeehi, Q. and Walden, S. (2010). Customer experience: Future trends and insights. Basingstoke: Palgrave McMillan.

52 ibid.

53 Rowson, J. (2011). Transforming behaviour change: Beyond nudge and neuromania. London: Royal Society of Arts.

54 Suchman, L. (1987). Plans and situated actions: The problem of human-machine communication. New York: Cambridge University Press.

55 See for example Dolan, P., Hallsworth, M., Halpern, D., King, D., Metcalfe, R. and Vlaev, I. (2010). MINDSPACE: Influencing behaviour through public policy. London: Cabinet Office and The Institute for Government.

56 http://www.klm.com/travel/gb_en/prepare_for_travel/on_board/your_seat_on_board/meet_and_seat.htm

57 It also glosses over hugely important differences in underlying ontologies and epistemologies which are not directly relevant here.

58 Winograd, T. and Flores, F. (1986). Understanding computers and cognition: A new foundation for design. Norwood: Ablex.

59 Winograd and Flores (1986), p. 165.

60 Hand, M., Shove, E. and Southerton, D. (2005). Explaining showering: A discussion of the material, conventional, and temporal dimensions of practice. Sociological Research Online, 10(2).

61 Hand et al ibid.

62 http://www.lancaster.ac.uk/staff/shove/exhibits/transcript.pdf

63 Thanks to Simon Blyth for this memorable summary of Shove's ideas as stories, skills and stuff.

64 Shove, E. and Pantzar, M. (2005). Consumers, producers and practices: understanding the invention and reinvention of Nordic walking. Journal of Consumer Culture, 5(1): 43-64.

65 See http://palojono.blogspot.com.au/2007/07/recording-ethnographic-observations.html.

66 Wasson, C. (2000). Ethnography in the field of design. Human Organization, 59(4): 377-388.

67 New, S. and Kimbell, L. (2013). Chimps, designers, consultants and empathy: A "Theory of Mind" for service design. Cambridge Academic Design Conference.

Case 5

68 http://xnet.kp.org/innovationconsultancy/

69 Brown, T. (2009). Change by design: How design thinking transforms organizations and inspires innovation. New York: Harper Collins, p. 172-174.

70 Lin, M., Hughes, B., Katica, M., Dining-Zuber, C., and Plsek, P. (2011). Service design and change of systems: Human-centered approaches to implementing and spreading service design. International Journal of Design, 5(2): 73-86.

71 Lin et al ibid.

72 http://xnet.kp.org/innovationconsultancy/nkeplus.html

73 Lin et al ibid.

74 Lin et al ibid.

75 Lin et al ibid.

Case 6

76 Pascale, R., Sternin, J. and Sternin, M. (2010). The power of positive deviance: How unlikely innovators solve the world's toughest problems. Boston: Harvard University Press.

77 Sternin, J. and Choo, R. (2000). The power of positive deviance. Harvard Business Review, 78(1): 14-15.

78 Singhal, A. (n.d.) Positive deviance and social change.

79 Marsh, D., Schroeder, D., Dearden, K., Sternin, J. and Sternin, M. (2004). The power of positive deviance. British Medical Journal, 329: 1177-1179.

80 Pascale, R. and Sternin, J. (2005). Your company's secret change agents. Harvard Business Review, 83(5): 72-85.

81 Thuesen, L. (2010). Learning from the behaviour of inmates and guards helps solving wicked challenges in the Danish Prison and Probation Service. http://www.positivedeviance.org/pdf/vulnerablepopulationsprojects/PDandWickedProblemsinDPPS.pdf

82 Thuesen 2010 ibid.

83 Thuesen, L. and Munger, M. (n.d.). The quest for the "what and the "how" as a driver for sustainable social change in the prison system of Denmark. Unpublished manuscript.

84 Thuesen 2010 ibid.

85 Thuesen, L. and Munger, M. (n.d.). The quest for the "what and the "how" as a driver for sustainable social change in the prison system of Denmark. Unpublished manuscript, p. 3.

86 Pascale, R. and Sternin, J. (2005). Your company's secret change agents. Harvard Business Review, 83(5): 72-85.

Chapter 4

87 https://www.gov.uk/government/uploads/system/uploads/attachment_data/file/267100/Applying_Behavioural_Insights_to_Organ_Donation.pdf

88 Nickerson, J., Yen, C.J., and Mahoney, J. (2011). Exploring the problem-finding and problem-solving approach for designing organizations. Academy of Management Perspectives, 26(1): 52-72.

89 http://www.fastcompany.com/3018598/for-99-this-ceo-can-tell-you-what-might-kill-you-inside-23andme-founder-anne-wojcickis-dna-r

90 Chui, M., Löffler, M. and Roberts, R. (2010). The internet of things. McKinsey Quarterly.

91 Miles, M. and Huberman, M. (1994). Qualitative data analysis: An expanded sourcebook. Thousand Oaks: Sage.

92 boyd, d. and Crawford, K. (2011). Six provocations for big data. http://papers.ssrn.com/sol3/papers.cfm?abstract_id=1926431

93 http://anthrodesign.com/

94 McCracken, G. (2009). Chief culture officer: How to create a living, breathing corporation. New York: Basic Books.

95 Cefkin, M. (ed.) (2009). Ethnography and the corporate encounter. Reflections on research in and of organizations. New York: Berghahn Books.

96 Madsbjerg, C. and Rasmussen, M. (2014). The moment of clarity: Using the human sciences to solve some of the world's toughest problems. Cambridge: Harvard Business Press.

97 Wang, T. (2013). http://ethnographymatters.net/2013/05/13/big-data-needs-thick-data

98 Geertz, C. (1973). Thick description: Toward an interpretive theory of culture. In Geertz, C. The interpretation of cultures: Selected essays. New York: Basic Books, pp. 3-30.

99 Wang ibid.

100 For example, IDEO. (2008). Design for social impact. http://www.ideo.com/images/uploads/news/pdfs/IDEO_RF_Guide.pdf

101 http://www.nytimes.com/2014/02/16/technology/intels-sharp-eyed-social-scientist.html

102 http://www.pottyproject.in/

103 http://gotoreport.gotomobile.com/reports/interview-with-microsoft-ethnographer-tracey-lovejoy

104 http://gotoreport.gotomobile.com/reports/interview-with-microsoft-ethnographer-tracey-lovejoy

105 http://blog.okfn.org/2013/06/18/g8-highlights-open-data-as-crucial-for-governance-and-growth/

106 http://blog.okfn.org/2013/06/18/g8-highlights-open-data-as-crucial-for-governance-and-growth/

107 https://okfn.org/opendata/

108 Manyika, J., Chui, M., Farrell, D., Van Kuiken, S., Groves, P. and Almasi Doshi, E. (2013). Open data: Unlocking innovation and performance with liquid information. McKinsey Global Institute.

109 http://thewebindex.org/

110 http://data.gov.uk/apps

111 http://theodi.org/news/prescription-savings-worth-millions-identified-odi-incubated-company

112 http://www.economist.com/news/britain/21567980-how-scrutiny-freely-available-data-might-save-nhs-money-beggar-thy-neighbour

113 http://www.prescribinganalytics.com/

114 http://opengov.newschallenge.org/open/open-government/winners/

115 Manyika, J., Chui, M., Farrell, D., Van Kuiken, S., Groves, P. and Almasi Doshi, E. (2013). Open data: Unlocking innovation and performance with liquid information. McKinsey Global Institute.

116 http://www.opendata500.com/

117 https://twitter.com/HugoOC

118 http://ethnographymatters.net/2014/02/17/ethnography-in-communiti…tested-expectations-for-data-in-the-23andme-and-fda-controversy/

Case 7

119 http://www.euronews.com/2014/02/27/LEGO-outperforms-toy-market-in-2013-expects-to-build-on-that-success/

120 Madsbjerg, C. and Rasmussen, M. (2014). The moment of clarity: Using social sciences to solve your toughest business problems. Cambridge: Harvard Business Review Press, p. 108.

121 http://www.businessweek.com/articles/2014-02-20/innovation-firm-red-shows-clients-how-to-use-philosophy-to-sell-stuff#p1

122 http://www.euronews.com/2014/02/27/LEGO-outperforms-toy-market-in-2013-expects-to-build-on-that-success/

123 Madsbjerg, C. and Rasmussen, M. (2014). The moment of clarity: Using social sciences to solve your toughest business problems. Cambridge: Harvard Business Review Press.

124 Madsbjerg, C. and Rasmussen, M. (2014). The moment of clarity: Using social sciences to solve your toughest business problems. Cambridge: Harvard Business Review Press, p. 122.

125 Madsbjerg, C. and Rasmussen, M. (2014). The moment of clarity: Using social sciences to solve your toughest business problems. Cambridge: Harvard Business Review Press, p. 118.

126 Madsbjerg, C. and Rasmussen, M. (2014). The moment of clarity: Using social sciences to solve your toughest business problems. Cambridge: Harvard Business Review Press, p. 119.

Case 8

127 Holt, D. and Cameron, D. (2010). Cultural strategy: Using innovative ideologies to build breakthrough brands. Oxford: OUP.

128 Based on an interview with Simon Blyth of Actant.

129 Gaver, W., Dunne, T. and Pacenti, E. (1999). Design: Cultural probes. Interactions, 6(1): 21-29.

Chapter 5

130 https://twitter.com/johnthackara/status/445253892003991552

131 Not that Intel is particularly worse than other similar firms at articulating the opportunity.

132 Intel. (2012). The future of knowledge work. http://blogs.intel.com/intellabs/files/2012/11/Intel-White-Paper-The-Future-of-Knowledge-Work4.pdf

133 See Chapter 1.

134 Tonkinwise, C. (2012). A taste for practices: Unrepressing style in design thinking. Design Studies, 32(6): 533–545.

135 Elkins, J. (2001). Why art cannot be taught. Urbana: University of Chicago Press.

136 Ibid. p 30.

137 Stark, T. (1998). The dignity of the particular: Adorno on Kant's aesthetics. Philosophy and Social Criticism. 24(2/3): 61-83.

138 Lury, C. and Wakeford, N. (eds). Inventive methods: The happening of the social. London: Routledge.

139 https://www.vitsoe.com/gb/about/good-design

140 Hughes, T. (1987). The evolution of large technological systems. In: Bijker, W., Hughes, T., and Pinch, T. (eds). The social construction of technological systems. Cambridge: MIT Press.

141 http://red-dot.de/cd/en/jury/bewertungskriterien/

142 Tweening, or inbetweening, is the process used in animation to create the intermediate frames between one image and the next. Matt Jones speaking at the Design Research Conference, Chicago, 2013, https://vimeo.com/88445338

143 Kimbell, L. (2009). The turn to service design. In Julier, G. and Moor, L. (eds). Design and creativity: Policy, management and practice. Oxford: Berg, pp. 157-173.

144 Moss Kanter, R. (2011). Managing yourself: Zoom in, zoom out. Harvard Business Review. March: 112-116.

145 http://designfictionsf.nearfuturelaboratory.com/

146 http://nearfuturelaboratory.com/projects/corner-convenience/

147 http://emerge.asu.edu/

148 http://bergcloud.com/media/

149 http://littleprinter.com/

150 http://berglondon.com/blog/2009/09/15/nearness/

151 https://www.youtube.com/watch?v=VIkVTheRkGA

152 http://theodi.org/culture

153 http://bertrandclerc.com/products/metrography/

154 http://greyisgood.eu/texttrends/

155 http://shorttermmemoryloss.com/portfolio/project/watching-the-watchers/

156 http://www.translatingnature.org/the-lake/

157 https://www.bookworks.org.uk/node/89

Case 9

158 http://www.cnet.com/uk/products/google-glass/

159 http://www.theguardian.com/technology/2013/mar/06/google-glass-threat-to-our-privacy

160 Quoted by Matt Jones speaking at the Design Research Conference, Chicago, 2013 https://vimeo.com/88445338

161 Richard The speaking at the Design Research Conference, Chicago, 2013 https://vimeo.com/88445338

162 Richard The speaking at the Design Research Conference, Chicago, 2013 https://vimeo.com/88445338

163 Richard The speaking at the Design Research Conference, Chicago, 2013 https://vimeo.com/88445338

164 Richard The speaking at the Design Research Conference, Chicago, 2013 https://vimeo.com/88445338

165 http://www.google.co.uk/glass/start/explorer-stories/

166 http://www.newyorker.com/reporting/2013/08/05/130805fa_fact_shteyngart?currentPage=all

167 http://media.theage.com.au/national/selections/google-glasss-vision-5307360.html

168 http://www.google.co.uk/glass/start/explorer-stories/

Case 10

169 http://idnext.com

170 http://frugaldigital.org

171 Based on a Social Design Talk by Vinay Venkatraman in London in 2014 and an interview with him.

172 http://www.ted.com/talks/vinay_venkatraman_technology_crafts_for_the_digitally_underserved.html

Chapter 6

173 Described in Le Masson, P., Weil, B. and Hatchuel, A. (2010). Strategic management of innovation and design. Cambridge: Cambridge University Press. Chapter 11.

174 ibid. p. 266.

175 Ries, E. (2011). The lean startup: How today's entrepreneurs use continuous innovation to create radically successful businesses. Crown Business.

176 Kelly, T. and Littman, J. (2001). The art of innovation. London: Profile Books. p.112.

177 http://tynerblain.com/blog/2010/10/25/a-prototype-is-worth-a-kloc/

178 See Bill Buxton's distinction between sketching and prototyping user experiences in Buxton, B. (2007). Sketching user experiences: Getting the design right and the right design. San Francisco: Morgan

Kaufman; and Nesta's prototyping framework, which offers a simple description of how to move from stage 1 (exploratory) to stage 2 (hypothesis-driven) prototyping. http://www.nesta.org.uk/publications/prototyping-framework

179 Csikszentmihalyi, M. (2002). Flow. London: Random House.

180 Ehn, P. (1988). Work-oriented design of computer artifacts. Hillsdale, NJ: Lawrence Erlbaum Associates.

181 Ehn, P., Mölleryd, B. and Söjgren, D. (1991). Playing in reality. Scandinavian Journal of Information Systems. 2: 101-120.

182 http://www.govhack.org/

183 Boudreau, K. (2012). Let a thousand flowers bloom? An early look at large numbers of software app developers and patterns of innovation. Organization Science, 23(5): 1409-1427.

184 https://www.collaborationjam.com/

185 https://openideo.com/challenge/mayo-clinic/realisation

186 See Kimbell, L. (2011). Designing for service as one way of designing services. International Journal of Design, 5(2): 41-52.

187 See, for example, Polaine, A., Lovlie, L. and Reason, B. (2013). Service design: From insight to implementation. New York: Rosenfeld Media.

188 http://www.la27eregion.fr

189 http://www.slideshare.net/27region/flyer27eregion-engl-12266201

190 Interview with Laura Pandelle.

191 http://imagination.lancs.ac.uk/activities/IDEAS_Daresbury

192 Interview with Leon Cruikshank.

Case 11

193 http://www.mind-lab.dk/en/about_mindlab

194 Based on materials supplied by MindLab and on an interview with Laura Winge.

Case 12

195 http://enginegroup.co.uk/work/mercedes-benz-premium-after-sales-service

196 From an interview with Oliver King of Engine.

Chapter 7

197 http://svaconsultingquarterly.com/2013/09/05/stop-proving-start-improving/

198 Argyris, C. and Schön, D. (1978). Organizational learning: A theory of action perspective. Addison-Wesley.

199 Gann, D., Salter, A. and Whyte, J. (2003). Design Quality Indicator as a tool for thinking. Building Research & Information, 31(5): 318-333.

200 See discussions on the triple bottom line – e.g. Norman, W. and MacDonald, C. (2004). Getting to the bottom of triple bottom line. Business Ethics Quarterly, 14(2): 243-262.

201 Mulgan, G. (2007). Measuring social value. Stanford Social Innovation Review. http://www.ssireview.org/articles/entry/measuring_social_value

202 http://www.neweconomics.org/publications/entry/a-guide-to-social-return-on-investment

203 Puttnick, R. and Ludlow, J. (2013). Standards of evidence: An approach that balances the need for evidence with innovation. London: Nesta.

204 Puttnick, R. and Ludlow, J. (2012). Standards of evidence for impact investing. London: Nesta.

205 See Power, M. (1997). The audit society: Rituals of verification. Oxford: OUP; and Strathern, M. (2000). Audit cultures: Anthropological studies in accountability, ethics and the academy. London: Routledge.

206 http://svaconsultingquarterly.com/2013/09/05/stop-proving-start-improving/

207 Dunleavy, P., Margetts, H., Bastow, S. and Tinkler, J. (2005). New public management is dead: Long live digital era governance. London: London School of Economics and Political Science.

208 See van de Heijden, K. (2005). Scenarios: The art of strategic conversation. Hoboken: Wiley.

209 Ward, A., Liker, J., Cristiano, J. and Sobek, D. (1995). The second Toyota paradox. Sloan Management Review, 36, Spring: 43-61.

210 ibid.

211 Sobek, D., Ward, A. and Liker, J. (1999). Toyota's principles of set-based concurrent engineering. Sloan Management Review, 40(2): 67-83.

212 Neely, A. (2009). Exploring the financial consequences of the servitization of manufacturing. Operations Management Research, 2(1): 103-118.

213 Ng, I., Ding, D. and Yip, N. (2013). Outcome-based contracts as new business model: The role of partnership and value-driven relational assets. Industrial Marketing Management, 42(5): 730–743.

214 Ng, I., Ding, D. and Yip, N. (2013). Outcome-based contracts as new business model: The role of partnership and value-driven relational assets. Industrial Marketing Management, 42(5): 730–743.

215 Moss, I. (2010). The state of commissioning. London: Institute for Government.

216 ibid.

217 Teece, D. (2010). Business models, business strategy and innovation. Long Range Planning, 43(2-3): 172-194.

218 Zott, C., Amit, R., and Massa, L. (2011). The business model: Recent developments and future research. Journal of Management, 37(4): 1019–1042.

219 Osterwalder, A. and Pigneur, Y. (2009). Business model generation. Hoboken: Wiley.

220 I designed the Social Business Model Canvas with my then colleague at the Young Foundation, Stuart Thomason. http://www.growingsocialventures.org/en/course-content/social-business-model-canvas

221 Maglio, P. and Spohrer, J. (2013). A service science perspective on business model innovation. Industrial Marketing Management, 42(5): 665-670.

222 Brown, T. (2009). Change by design: How design thinking transforms organizations and inspires innovation. New York: Harper Collins.

223 Vitruvius, P. (1860). The ten books of architecture. http://books.google.co.uk/books?id=Blbg-kECerQC&printsec=frontcover&dq=vitruvius+1999&hl=en&sa=X&ei=SkUrU7msIeSd0AXj7YCoBg&ved=0CEEQ6AEwAzgK#v=onepage&q&f=false

224 Bate, P. and Robert, G. (2007). Bringing user experience to healthcare improvement: The concepts, methods and practices of experience based design. Oxford: Radcliffe.

225 Gann, D., Salter, A. and Whyte, J. (2003). Design Quality Indicator as a tool for thinking. Building Research & Information, 31(5): 318-333.

Case 13

226 Dixon, M., Freeman, K. and Toman, N. (2010). Stop trying to delight your customers. Harvard Business Review. July-August.

227 Ries, E. (2011). The lean startup: How today's entrepreneurs use continuous innovation to create radically successful businesses. New York: Crown Business.

Case 14

228 http://www.microsoft.com/eu/whats-next/multimedia/a-new-in-car-software-application-helps-drivers-reduce-co2-emissions.aspx

229 http://www.fiat.com/ecodrive/

230 http://www.microsoft.com/eu/whats-next/multimedia/a-new-in-car-software-application-helps-drivers-reduce-co2-emissions.aspx

231 http://www.microsoft.com/eu/whats-next/multimedia/a-new-in-car-software-application-helps-drivers-reduce-co2-emissions.aspx

232 http://www.microsoft.com/eu/whats-next/multimedia/a-new-in-car-software-application-helps-drivers-reduce-co2-emissions.aspx

233 http://www.uk-ecocars.co.uk/Fiat-EcoDrive.php

234 http://www.eco-drive.fiat.com/uploadedFiles/Fiatcouk/Stand_Alone_Sites/EcoDrive2010/en/ECO-DRIVING_UNCOVERED_full_report_2010_EN(1).pdf

235 Wengraf, Ivo. 2012. Easy on the gas: The effectiveness of eco-driving. London: RAC Foundation.

236 http://www.fiat500owners.com/forum/35-fiat-500-sound-systems-electronics/1885-eco-drive-application.html

237 http://www.fiat500owners.com/forum/35-fiat-500-sound-systems-electronics/1885-eco-drive-application.html

238 http://www.fiat500owners.com/forum/35-fiat-500-sound-systems-electronics/1885-eco-drive-application-2.html

239 http://www.fiat500owners.com/forum/35-fiat-500-sound-systems-electronics/1885-eco-drive-application.html

Chapter 8

240 Manifesto for agile software development. (2001). http://agilemanifesto.org/. This declaration may be freely copied in any form, but only in its entirety through this notice.

241 Agile software development principles. (2001). http://agilemanifesto.org/principles.html

242 See http://www.agilealliance.org/

243 Cohen, W. and Levinthal, D. (1990). Absorptive capacity: A new perspective on learning and innovation. Administrative Science Quarterly, 35(1): 128-152.

244 Henderson, K. (1991). Flexible sketches and inflexible databases: Visual communication, conscription devices, and boundary objects in design engineering. Science, Technology, and Human Values, 16(4): 448-473.

245 Star, S. L., and Griesemer, J. R. (1989). Institutional ecology, "translations," and coherence: Amateurs and professionals in Berkeley's Museum of Vertebrate Zoology, 1907-1939. Social Studies of Science, 19: 387-420.

246 Henderson, ibid.

247 Carlile, P. (2002). A pragmatic view of knowledge and boundaries: Boundary objects in new product development. Organization Science, 13(4): 442-455.

248 Carlile, ibid, p. 452.

249 Yoo, Y., Boland, R., Lyytinen, K. and Majchrzak, A. (2012). Organizing for innovation in the digitized world. Organization Science, 23(5): 1398-1408.

250 Tilson, D., Lyytinen, K., and Sørensen, C. (2010). Digital infrastructures: The missing IS research agenda. Information Systems Research, (21:4): 748-759.

251 Eaton, B., Elaluf-Calderwood, S., Sørensen, C. and Yoo, Y. (2011). Dynamic structures of control and generativity in digital ecosystem innovation: The case of the Apple and Google mobile app stores. Working paper. London School of Economics.

252 Yoo el al. 2010. p.1400.

Case 15

253 Based on an interview with Joel Bailey and Gordon Lee of Capita's service design team.

Case 16

254 http://www.bbc.co.uk/news/business-26131799

255 http://www.designcouncil.org.uk/sites/default/files/asset/document/dc_lbbd_report_08.11.13_FA_LORES.pdf

256 https://www.barclayscorporate.com/content/dam/corppublic/corporate/Documents/insight/evolving_%20payments_landscape.pdf

257 http://www.theguardian.com/money/2012/feb/16/barclays-pingit-money-sending-smartphone

258 http://www.theguardian.com/money/2012/feb/16/barclays-pingit-money-sending-smartphone

259 http://www.independent.co.uk/news/business/analysis-and-features/pingit-is-no-gimmick-can-pay-will-pay--with-a-money-transfer-app-9150471.html

260 http://group.barclays.com/mobile/about-barclays/news/1329930901190

261 http://www.designcouncil.org.uk/sites/default/files/asset/document/dc_lbbd_report_08.11.13_FA_LORES.pdf

262 http://www.designcouncil.org.uk/sites/default/files/asset/document/dc_lbbd_report_08.11.13_FA_LORES.pdf

263 http://www.designcouncil.org.uk/sites/default/files/asset/document/dc_lbbd_report_08.11.13_FA_LORES.pdf

264 http://www.theguardian.com/media-network/2012/jun/12/cloud-services-changing-workforce

265 http://www.the-logic-group.com/blog/2012/11/09/Payments TechnologyConference2012.aspx

Afterword

266 See Kimbell, L. (2014). Design ethnography, public policy and public services: Rendering collective issues doable & at human scale. In Denny, P. and Sunderland, R. (eds). Handbook of anthropology in business. Walnut Creek: Left Coast Press, 186-201.

Picture and illustration credits

Case 1 Courtesy Fjord LLC, part of Accenture Interactive.

Case 4 Courtesy NYC Campaign Finance Board.

Case 8 Photo by Dominic Oliver Cort. Courtesy Actant Consulting Ltd.

Case 10 Photo by Priya Mani. Courtesy Vinay Venkatraman.

Case 11 Photo by Laura Winge. Courtesy MindLab.

Case 12 Photo by James Samperi. Courtesy Engine Service Design.

Index